THE MEN AND THE BOYS

THE MEN AND THE BOYS

R.W. Connell

2000

UNIVERSITY OF CALIFORNIA PRESS
Berkeley   Los Angeles

University of California Press
Berkeley and Los Angeles, California

Published by arrangement with Allen & Unwin

ISBN 0-520-22868-5 (cloth)
ISBN 0-520-22869-3 (paper)

Printed in Australia by Australian Print Group, Maryborough, Vic.

9 8 7 6 5 4 3 2 1

To Kylie

Contents

PART 1

EXAMINING MASCULINITIES

1

Debates about men, new research on masculinities

ISSUES ABOUT MEN AND BOYS

In recent years, questions about men and boys have aroused remarkable media interest, public concern and controversy.

In the United States two 'men's movements' gained large, if temporary, followings in the 1990s, one based on new-age therapy, the other on right-wing evangelism. Both raised questions about men's identity and offered remedies for troubles in men's lives. In other English-speaking countries such as Australia and Canada, where identity movements have been weaker, there have been vigorous and sometimes bitter public debates about men's violence, men's health and boys' supposed 'disadvantage' in education.

There is no doubt about the historical source of these debates. The new feminism of the 1970s not only gave voice to women's concerns, it challenged all assumptions about the gender system and raised a series of problems about men. Over the decades since, the disturbance in the gender system caused by the women's movement has been felt by very large numbers of men. A growing minority of men has attempted to grapple with these issues in practice or in the realm of ideas.

Concern with questions about boys and men is now worldwide. Germany has seen pioneering feminist research on men, programs for male youth, and debates on strategies of change for men. There is an active network of researchers on men and masculinity in Scandinavian countries, where the post of Nordic coordinator for men's studies has recently been created. In 1998 Chile hosted a conference on masculinities in Latin America, which drew researchers and activists from as far apart as Brazil and Nicaragua.

In Japan there have been changes in media images of men, companionate marriages and shared child care, renegotiations of sexuality, and explicit critiques (by men as well as women) of traditional Japanese ideals of masculinity. A new 'men's centre' publishes papers and books exploring new patterns of masculinity and family life. In 1998 the South African feminist journal *Agenda* published an issue on new directions for men in the democratic transition after apartheid. In 1997 UNESCO sponsored a conference in Norway on the implications of male roles and masculinities for the creation of a culture of peace, which drew participants from all over Europe and some other parts of the world.

Concern with issues about masculinity has not only spread to many countries, but also into many fields. Health services are noticing the relevance of men's gender to problems such as road accidents, industrial injury, diet, heart disease and, of course, sexually transmitted diseases. Educators are discussing not just the idea of programs for boys, but also the practical details of how to run them. Criminologists have begun to explore why boys and men dominate the crime statistics, and violence prevention programs are taking increasing notice of gender issues.

Questions about men, boys and gender have thus ceased to be a specialist concern of a small group of intellectuals. They have moved into the public arena, and though media attention will wax and wane, there is no reversing that move.

So the intellectual debate on masculinity now has practical consequences. How we understand men and gender, what we believe about masculinity, what we know (or think we know) about the development of boys, may have large effects—for good or ill—in therapy, education, health services, violence prevention, policing, and social services.

It matters, therefore, to get our understanding of these issues straight. We need to know the facts, connect policy debates with the best available research, and use the most effective theories. That is the principle on which this book is written.

Issues about masculinity are important but not easy. They are made no easier by the recent influence of a school of pop psychologists who offer a highly simplified view of the problems of men. Their central idea is that modern men are suffering from a psychological wound, being cut off from the true or deep masculinity that is their heritage. A whole therapeutic movement offers to heal the wound by re-establishing bonds among men, with initiation rituals, retreats etc.

The popularity of books like *Iron John* by Robert Bly, *Fire in the Belly* by Sam Keen and *Manhood* by Bly's Australian follower Steve Biddulph, suggests that they have tapped into some real problems, at least among the middle-class white men who are their main audience. I think the key point they have realized is the importance of men's emotional lives—which strikes many in this audience as a revelation, precisely because conventional middle-class western masculinity tends to suppress emotion and deny vulnerability.

To emphasize that men do have emotional troubles, that masculine stereotypes can be damaging, that men suffer from isolation, and that men too can hold hands and cry—this is not a bad thing. Writers like Keen, especially, have eloquent things to say about the distortions of men's emotional lives, and how they are connected with violence, alienation, and environmental destruction.

But in pop psychology these understandings come at a considerable price. With the aid of the later and crazier works of Carl Jung, this school of thought has constructed a fantasy of the universal 'deep masculine', which is as stereotyped as anything in Hollywood (and which is contradicted by actual research, as will be seen throughout this book). Trying to find cross-cultural proof of the deep masculine, Bly and his followers raid non-western cultures for stories and symbols of masculinity which they rip out of context in a startling display of disrespect. The 'rituals' invented to fill the void in men's lives, though they can have an emotional impact, are as authentic as Disney World. Pop psychology itself rests on the authors' ability to tell persuasive and entertaining stories, not on their grasp of the facts. Some of the 'cases' in the American pop psychology literature about men are undoubtedly faked.

But the biggest problem of all in the pop-psychology approach to masculinity is its nostalgia, a persistent belief that solutions to the problems of men can be found by looking backwards. Pop psychology idealizes a pre-industrial past (a mythical one, in fact), when men knew how to be men, women knew how to be mothers, and there was no homosexuality or equal opportunity legislation to muddy the waters. Hence the weird result that pop psychologists' solution to the current problems of alienation and misunderstanding between men and women is often to argue for *more* gender segregation.

I was trained as a historian, I love studying the past, and I am confident that the human spirit is enriched by knowing the tumultuous path human society has travelled. But I also know that we cannot solve contemporary problems by nostalgia. We need new and more democratic patterns in gender relations, not re-runs of discredited patriarchies.

THE NEW SOCIAL RESEARCH ON MASCULINITY

To build a more civilized, more survivable, more just world is not a matter of wishful thinking. It is a difficult task, in which all the resources we can gather will be necessary. One of the more important of those resources is knowledge.

In grappling with problems about men, boys, and masculinity we have an important new resource, the social-scientific research on masculinities that has been building up over the past fifteen years or so.

This recent research has a pre-history, which goes back as far as Freud. From the beginning of the twentieth century, psychoanalytic research has shown how adult personality, including one's sexual orientation and sense of identity, is constructed via conflict-ridden processes of development in which the gender dynamics of families are central (Lewes 1988). Psychoanalytic case studies showed men's character structures to be internally divided, even contradictory; and showed both masculinity and femininity as the product of psychological compromises, often tense and unstable (Chodorow 1994).

Some researchers—most famously the Frankfurt School in its studies of the 'authoritarian personality'—grafted a social analysis onto the psychoanalytic base. This work began to trace alternative paths of masculine development and to debate their role as underpinnings of democracy and fascism (Holter 1996). In due course feminist psychoanalysis picked up this form of argument, though focussing on patriarchy rather than class as the structural background (Dinnerstein 1976).

Psychoanalysis, however, was regarded with suspicion by many in the social sciences. Around the mid-century a different framework became more influential. The concept of 'social role', which developed in anthropology in the 1930s, became immensely popular as a common language for the social sciences. A social-psychological version of role theory was applied to gender, producing the idea of 'sex roles'.

Sex roles were understood as patterns of social expectation, norms for the behaviour of men and women, which were transmitted to youth in a process of 'socialization'. In effect, social behaviour was explained as a massive display of conformity—which somehow seemed appropriate in the 1950s. A great amount of thin paper-and-pencil research was produced around this idea. Nevertheless the idea of a 'male role' also led to some intelligent studies of changing gender expectations for men, and difficulties faced by men and boys in conforming to the norms (Hacker 1957).

In the 1970s the 'sex role' idea was radicalized by feminism. The idea of gender-as-conformity became an object of dismay rather than celebration. Feminist analysis of how women's sex role oppressed women soon led to a discussion, among both feminist women and pro-feminist men, of the way men's sex role oppressed men.

This idea underpinned a burst of writing, even a small social movement, on the theme of men's liberation as a parallel endeavour to women's liberation (Pleck & Sawyer 1974). But it led to little new research beyond the existing conventions of paper-and-pencil masculinity/femininity scales. A vague concept of 'the male role' or 'men's role' persists in much recent talk and writing, but means little more than stereotypes or norms or even just sex differences.

In the 1980s a third approach to the gender of men matured, sometimes called social constructionism. Its main academic base is in sociology but there are vigorous branches in anthropology, history and media studies. Key intellectual underpinnings are the feminist analysis of gender as a structure of social relations, especially a structure of power relations; sociological concerns with subcultures and issues of marginalization and resistance; and post-structuralist analyses of the making of identities in discourse, and the interplay of gender with race, sexuality, class and nationality.

With ethnographic and life-history methods as key research techniques, in the last two decades there has been a cascade of studies of the social construction of masculinity in particular times and places. The locales include:

- a highland community in Papua New Guinea (Herdt 1981);
- a private school in inter-war England (Heward 1988);
- Hollywood films after the Vietnam war (Jeffords 1989);
- a high school in rural Texas (Foley 1990);
- a clergyman's family in nineteenth-century England (Tosh 1991);
- two body-building gyms in California (Klein 1993);
- a gold mine in South Africa under apartheid (Moodie 1994);
- an urban police force in the United States (McElhinny 1994);
- British industrial management (Roper 1994);
- official debates in colonial India (Sinha 1995);
- two gay communities in Australia (Dowsett 1996);
- the US Navy (Barrett 1996);

- drinking groups in Australian bars (Tomsen 1997);
- a US corporate office on the verge of a fatal decision (Messer-schmidt 1997);
- garages in an Australian working-class suburb (Walker 1998b).

We might think of this as the 'ethnographic moment' in masculinity research, in which the specific and the local is in focus. To say this is not to suggest the work lacks awareness of broader issues—Moodie's research on South African mining, for instance, is a classic study of the interplay of race, class and gender structures. Nor is ethnography, in the strict sense of anthropological field observation, its only method. Life-history studies are almost as common, and there are even some broad statistical surveys, especially in Europe (Holter 1989, Metz-Göckel & Müller 1985). The historical work of course uses archives, private letters, diaries and other documents as its sources.

There is, nevertheless, in most of this work a focus on the construction of masculinity in a specific setting, a concern to document and explain the particular patterns to be found in a definite locale.

The ethnographic moment brought a much-needed gust of realism to debates on men and masculinity, a corrective to the abstractions of role theory. This social research moved in a very different direction from the trend in popular culture at the same time, where vague discussions of men's sex roles were giving way to the mystical generalities of the 'mytho-poetic' movement and the extreme simplifications of religious revivalism.

KEY CONCLUSIONS OF RECENT RESEARCH

Though the rich detail of individual historical and field studies defies easy summary, certain empirical conclusions emerge from this body of research as a whole, which have more than local significance. I will present them here, as a general introduction to the field. These conclusions as a group are relevant to many practical problems, so I will refer back to this summary in a number of later chapters.

Multiple masculinities

It is clear from the new social research as a whole that there is no one pattern of masculinity that is found everywhere. We need to speak of 'masculinities', not masculinity. Different cultures, and different periods of history, construct gender differently.

There is now massive proof of this fact in comparative studies, especially ethnographies (e.g. Cornwall & Lindisfarne 1994). Striking differences exist, for instance, in the relationship of homosexual practice to dominant forms of masculinity. Some societies treat homosexual practices as a regular part of the making of masculinity (Herdt 1984); others regard homosexuality as incompatible with true masculinity.

We might therefore expect that in multicultural societies there will be multiple definitions and dynamics of masculinity. This proves to be true. The importance of ethnicity in the construction of masculinity is emerging strongly in recent work (e.g. Hondagneu-Sotelo & Messner 1994 [USA], Poynting et al. 1998 [Australia], Tillner 1997 [Austria]).

Diversity is not just a matter of difference between communities. Diversity also exists *within* a given setting. Within the one school, or workplace, or ethnic group, there will be different ways of enacting manhood, different ways of learning to be a man, different conceptions of the self and different ways of using a male body. This is particularly well documented in research on schools (Foley 1990), but can also be observed in workplaces (Messerschmidt 1997) and the military (Barrett 1996).

Hierarchy and hegemony

Different masculinities do not sit side-by-side like dishes on a smorgasbord. There are definite social relations between them. Especially, there are relations of hierarchy, for some masculinities are dominant while others are subordinated or marginalized.

In most of the situations that have been closely studied, there is some hegemonic form of masculinity—the most honoured or desired. For Western popular culture, this is extensively documented in research on media representations of masculinity (McKay & Huber 1992).

The hegemonic form need not be the most common form of masculinity, let alone the most comfortable. Indeed many men live in a state of some tension with, or distance from, the hegemonic masculinity of their culture or community. Other men, such as sporting heroes, are taken as exemplars of hegemonic masculinity and are required to live up to it strenuously—at what may be severe cost, in terms of injury, ill health, and other constraints on life (Messner 1992). The dominance of hegemonic masculinity over other forms may be quiet and implicit, but may also be vehement and violent, as in the case of homophobic violence (Herek & Berrill 1992).

Collective masculinities

The patterns of conduct our society defines as masculine may be seen in the lives of individuals, but they also have an existence beyond the individual. Masculinities are defined collectively in culture, and are sustained in institutions. This fact was visible in Cockburn's (1983) pioneering research on the informal workplace culture of printing workers, and has been confirmed over and over since.

Institutions may construct multiple masculinities and define relationships between them. Barrett's (1996) illuminating study of the 'organizational construction' of hegemonic masculinity in the US Navy shows different forms in the different sub-branches of the one military organization.

This collective process of constructing and enacting masculinities can be traced in an enormous range of settings, from the face-to-face interactions in the classrooms and playgrounds of an elementary school (Thorne 1993) to the august public institutions of imperial Britain at the height of world power (Hearn 1992). In different historical circumstances, of course, different institutions will be more or less prominent in the construction of masculinity. The institutions of competitive sport seem peculiarly important for contemporary western masculinities (Whitson 1990).

Bodies as arenas

Men's bodies do not determine the patterns of masculinity, as biological essentialism and pop psychology would have it. Men's bodies are addressed, defined and disciplined (as in sport: Theberge 1991), and given outlets and pleasures, by the gender order of society.

But men's bodies are not blank slates. The enactment of masculinity reaches certain limits, for instance in the destruction of the industrial worker's body (Donaldson 1991). Masculine conduct combined with a female body is felt to be anomalous or transgressive, like feminine conduct combined with a male body. Research on gender crossing (Bolin 1988) shows that a lot of work must be done to sustain an anomalous gender.

Gender is the way bodies are drawn into history; bodies are arenas for the making of gender patterns. This was a point underplayed by 'male role' discussions, and is underplayed even in some of the more recent research. It is important, then, to register the importance of such processes as violence (Tomsen 1997) and body culture (Klein 1993) in the construction and politics of masculinities.

Active construction

Masculinities are neither programmed in our genes, nor fixed by social structure, prior to social interaction. They come into existence as people act. They are actively produced, using the resources and strategies available in a given social setting.

Thus, the exemplary masculinities of sports professionals are not a product of passive disciplining. As Messner (1992) shows, they result from a sustained, active engagement with the demands of the institutional setting, even to the point of serious bodily damage from 'playing hurt' and accumulated stress. With boys learning masculinities, much of what was previously taken as 'socialization' appears, in detailed studies of schools (Thorne 1993, Walker 1988), as the outcome of intricate and intense manoeuvering in peer groups, classes and adult–child relationships.

Walker (1998a, 1998b), in a study of young working-class men and car culture, gives a striking example of the collective construction of masculinities in adult peer groups. The friendship groups not only draw lines to fend off women's intrusion into masculine social space, but draw in a whole technology as part of the definition of masculinity.

Internal complexity and contradiction

One of the key reasons why masculinities are not fixed is that they are not homogeneous, simple states of being. Close-focus research on masculinities commonly identifies contradictory desires and conduct. A striking example, in Klein's (1993) study of bodybuilders, is the conflict between the heterosexual definition of hegemonic masculinity and the homosexual practice through which some bodybuilders finance the making of an exemplary body.

Psychoanalytic research on men has long been aware of contradictory desires and conduct, though the emphasis on this point has fluctuated. Recent psychoanalytic writing (Chodorow 1994, Lewes 1988) has laid some emphasis on the conflicts and emotional compromises within both hegemonic and subordinated forms of masculinity. Life-history research influenced by existential psychoanalysis (Connell 1995) has similarly traced contradictory projects and commitments within particular forms of masculinity.

In Chapter 5, I document some contradictions within the exemplary masculinity of a professional sportsman. Tomsen (1998) points to another example, the ambivalence in anti-gay violence, which helps to make such violence a systemic feature of contemporary Western life, not just a matter of individual pathology. Poynting et al. (1998) describe, for an ethnic minority, the contradiction between young men's claim to authority and their experience of subordination under the pressure of racism. Masculinities are often in tension, within and without. It seems likely that such tensions are important sources of change.

Dynamics

There is abundant evidence that masculinities do change. Masculinities are created in specific historical circumstances and, as those circumstances change, the gender practices can be contested and reconstructed. Heward (1988) shows the changing gender regime of a boys' school responding to the changed economic and social strategies of the families in its clientele. Roper (1994) shows the displacement of a production-oriented masculinity among engineering managers by new financially oriented generic managers.

Since the 1970s the reconstruction of masculinities has been pursued as a conscious politics. Schwalbe's (1996) close examination of an American mythopoetic group shows the complexity of the practice and the limits of the reconstruction. In a very different context, a conscious reconstruction of gender practices is now on the agenda in southern Africa (Morrell 1998).

Yet the gender order does not blow away at a breath. Donaldson's (1998) study of ruling-class men shows a major reason why—the persistence of power and wealth, and the active defence of privilege. The eight 'men's movements' which Messner (1997) has traced in the United States have different, and sometimes sharply conflicting, agendas for the remaking of masculinity. The historical process around masculinities is a process of struggle in which, ultimately, large resources are at stake.

These emerging conclusions represent a major advance over earlier understandings of masculinity. They are, I think, the necessary starting point for all future work on problems about masculinity.

Nevertheless there are limits to what has been accomplished, and we still need to move forward. The descriptive work on masculinities must be thought through conceptually, and linked to a workable theory of gender. I will attempt this in Chapter 2, which discusses theories of masculinity and proposes a research agenda. A key argument is that the 'ethnographic moment' in masculinity research, just reviewed, needs to be supplemented by work on a larger scale. This problem is taken up in Chapters 3 and 4, which address issues about masculinities on the scale of world society.

2

New directions in theory and research

The studies summarized in Chapter 1 represent important gains over earlier, mostly speculative, discussions of men and gender. But to say this is not to suggest the new work is free of doubt or controversy.

Indeed several writers have recently emphasized the problems. Hearn (1996) has raised doubts about the usefulness of the concept of 'masculinities', and more recently (1998b) has spelt out the very diverse, and to some degree incompatible, positions that have been adopted in men's theorizing of men. Petersen (1998) has charged men's studies with epistemological naivety, narrow-mindedness and lack of concern with power. Clatterbaugh (1998), working through definitions of 'masculinity', has found them mostly vague, circular, inconsistent, or in other ways unsatisfactory.

While some degree of inconsistency is not a bad thing in a rapidly growing field—as this has been in the last ten years—it is also important to debate criticisms and try to improve the theoretical frameworks that we have. In this chapter I will look at some of the currently influential ways of thinking about men, gender and masculinities. I will develop the approach I think most helpful, and suggest the most promising directions for research and debate.

CURRENT DEBATE: CONCEPTS OF GENDER AND APPROACHES TO MASCULINITY

Hearn and Clatterbaugh are undoubtedly right: there are real difficulties in defining 'masculinity' or 'masculinities'. These terms are certainly used in inconsistent ways by different authors. They are often used in ways that imply a simplified and static notion of identity, or rest on a simplified and unrealistic notion of difference between men and women. Social science has put a lot of effort into mapping masculinities as actual patterns of conduct or representation. But in the language of the mythopoetic movement, 'masculinity' stood for an ideal existence of men, or a deep essence within men, set against the disappointing empirical reality—and this is a usage that seems to have had more resonance outside the academy.

Faced with difficulties in definition, we can abandon the field. Hearn and Clatterbaugh both, in a sense, wish to do this, because they both think the real object of concern is something else—'men'. If, as Clatterbaugh (1998, p. 41) puts it, 'talking about men seems to be what we want to do', why bother to introduce the muddy concept of 'masculinities' at all?

There is, I think, a good answer to this question. Why would we talk about 'men' in the first place? To talk at all about a group called 'men' presupposes a distinction from and relation with another group, 'women'. That is to say, it presupposes an account of gender. And whichever conceptual language we use, we need some way of talking about men's and women's involvement in that domain of gender. We need some way of naming conduct which is oriented to or shaped by that domain, as distinct from conduct related to other patterns in social life.

Unless we subside into defining masculinity as equivalent to men, we must acknowledge that sometimes masculine conduct or masculine identity goes together with a female body. It is actually very common for a (biological) man to have elements of 'feminine' identity, desire and patterns of conduct. This might be expected, if only from the fact that the upbringing of young children is, in our society's division of labour, mainly done by women. Without concepts such as 'masculinity' and 'femininity' we would be unable to talk about the questions of gender ambiguity that have been so important in recent cultural studies, or about the contradictions in personality that are so important in psychoanalysis. If we give up such terms, we merely create a need for other gender concepts that perform the same tasks.

And of course, we might want to talk about a lot more than 'men'. We might want to talk about democracy in gender relations, the many-layered resistances to equality, and how to form alliances to move towards it. We might want to talk about desire, its intractabilities, complexities and reversals. We might want to talk about work and its relation to consciousness, or about education and its vicissitudes. In all these cases we will need concepts that go beyond the categories of 'men' and 'women' to the many forms of practice through which they are involved in the world of gender.

There is, then, a need for concepts that name patterns of gender practice, not just groups of people. But the ambiguity of current concepts of 'masculinity' remains of interest. It is, surely, one marker of the current cultural flux in gender relations. To use the conceptual language I suggest below, the difficulty in formulating widely acceptable definitions of masculinity is one sign of the crisis tendencies in gender relations which have in a number of ways destabilized the situation of men.

To understand 'men' or 'masculinity' we must first have some idea of how to understand gender. There is, of course, a great deal of assistance available here. Stimulated by the new feminism, research on questions of gender has increased tremendously in volume over the last generation, and has become conceptually more profound. Gender research offers a critique of all existing fields of social science as well as exploring new subject matter. And it has reshaped the relation between social-scientific knowledge and social practice.

These changes have all depended on the recognition of the

profoundly social character of gender. Gender is far more than an individual trait somehow connected with bodily difference, like red hair or left-handedness. With gender, we are dealing with a complex, and powerfully effective, domain of social practice.

But how is this domain to be understood? In recent decades, the two most politically influential accounts of gender are accounts that we know to be wrong.

The first is the theory of 'sex roles'. Role theory explains gender patterns by appealing to the social expectations that define proper behaviour for women and for men. Exposing the irrationality of these norms, or their oppressive effects, has been a key to the popular success of feminism in fields like girls' education. In the school system this approach has underpinned an impressive growth of special programs to expand girls' options (Yates 1993).

Yet the intellectual weaknesses of sex-role theory are well understood. A theory based on 'expectations' or norms gives no grasp on issues of power, violence, or material inequality. It misses the complexities within femininity and masculinity, and it offers very limited strategies of change. Even in a field like education, role theory offered no protection against the backlash that emerged in the 1990s, which proposed an expansion of special programs for boys.

The second unsatisfactory account, which I call 'categorical theory', treats women and men as pre-formed categories. Biological essentialism is one version of this, but there are many writings about gender which are categorical without being biological-reductionist. The focus in this approach to gender is on some relationship between the categories which is external to their constitution as categories.

This is the concept of gender underlying most pop psychologies of masculinity, and also the huge literature of quantitative 'sex difference' research. It is not necessarily a conservative view. It is, for instance, the logical structure underlying most discussions of Equal Employment Opportunity (based on statistics contrasting men's employment with women's employment). It is also found in much of the discussion of sexual harassment and gender violence.

The categorical approach more readily addresses issues of power than sex-role theory did. But categorical theory too has difficulty grasping the complexities of gender, such as gendered violence within either of the two main categories (e.g. violence against gays). It has had little use for industrial politics and misses such issues as the importance of unionism for working-class women. And it readily leads to ethnocentric generalizations about women and men, which miss the importance of the global structures of exploitation and underdevelopment.

If role theory and categoricalism are unsatisfactory, what remains? Two significant alternatives can be found in recent debates: post-structuralist and materialist. By contrast to categoricalism, the issues of complexity, ambiguity and fluidity are central themes in post-structuralist and post-modernist theories of gender. Though these themes are not logically necessary consequences of a concern with discourse, in practice they have gone together. Perhaps writers who emphasized that gender was discursively constructed needed at the start to reject both biological categoricalism and concepts of fixed psychological identity (e.g. Hollway 1984).

Under the influence of Foucault, a school of gender researchers has studied how discourses ranging from medicine to fashion have classified, represented and helped to control human bodies, emphasizing how systems of knowledge function as part of an apparatus of power. The approach has been particularly fruitful in relation to sport, where the interweaving of cultural images of masculinity with the management and training of bodies has been powerfully effective (Rowe & McKay 1998).

Foucault's work on power/knowledge is employed by Petersen (1998) for a tilt at the whole basis of research and analysis on masculinity. Implausibly claiming that masculinity research neglects power (which is, in fact, a central theme in the field), Petersen more accurately argues that much of the discussion of masculinity smuggles in a kind of gender-essentialism, while conversely those arguments that are anti-essentialist have difficulty in conceptualizing the relationship between bodies and social processes. But what alternative can be found? What

Petersen commends as 'a recent shift in our theoretical understanding of the world' is actually a very specific school of cultural
theory with well-recognized weaknesses in gender analysis.
Foucault had no gender theory at all, though others have built
gender analyses using some of his ideas. Butler (1990), the
main proponent of a 'performative' account of gender, is strikingly unable to account for work, child care, institutional life,
violence, resistance (except as individual choice), and material
inequality. These are not trivial aspects of gender.

But a concern with the discursive construction of gender
can also point in directions other than the Foucauldian focus
on the subjection of bodies. In the innovative educational work
of Davies (1993), for instance, the way people are positioned
within discourses of gender is something that children in school
can learn about, and can learn to change. It is possible to teach
this skill, to develop classroom exercises where it becomes visible and discussable. Children can, in effect, be post-structuralists.
In quite practical ways Davies shows how both boys and
girls can move into and out of a masculine identity or subject
position.

Recognizing this possibility raises important questions
about when, and why, people hold on to a certain subject
position, adopt or reject the possibility of movement. This
issue has become important in recent discussion of boys'
education, especially around boys' involvement in humanities
(Martino 1994). Certain kinds of school subject matter are
liable to be rejected because the boys associate them with
femininity, wimpishness or being homosexual. We cannot get
far with such questions without asking questions about boys'
and men's interests in maintaining a particular status quo in
gender arrangements and a particular position within them.

The importance of material interests in accounting for men's
gender conduct is forcibly argued by McMahon (1999) in a
brilliant critique of journalistic, psychological and academic talk
about the 'new man' and the 'new father'. Indeed McMahon
suggests that the absence of any discussion of interests in
most of this literature is itself an ideological move favouring
men—and a move that has parallels in other structures of

inequality. To recognize the interests that men have in patriarchal society is not necessarily to fall back into categoricalism. McMahon avoids this trap by emphasizing how the social being of men is historically produced—in large measure, by the labour of women.

Though one could hardly speak of a 'school' comparable to post-structuralism, it is noticeable that the question of material interests and material practices has emerged in several recent contributions. Godenzi (2000), one of the few people to have offered a serious economic analysis of masculine practices, points to the diverse and sometimes indirect strategies by which men protect their interests in the face of challenges from women. Hearn (1996), like McMahon, emphasizes the material interests at play in gender practice, and raises the politically vital question of what mechanisms bind men together as a group. Hearn's (1998a) research on men's violence to women is an important example of how material practices—indeed, practices addressed to bodies—can be linked to the construction of meaning, the making of ideology.

But of all materialist analyses of men and masculinity, the most original and far-reaching is the work of Holter (1995, 1997), unfortunately still little known outside Scandinavia. Holter's full argument is much too complex to present here, but a key point is that masculinity and femininity are not simple opposites, are not even initially constituted as a *gender* opposition—as in role theory, categoricalism and most discursive accounts of gender. Rather, gender emerges as an

> expression of the whole relationship between the spheres of production and reproduction. Industrial capitalism itself 'engendered' its opposite, the world of domesticity as against the world of wage work, and women as the other of men. Modern gender is remarkable for its ability to absorb just about any social contradiction, shedding any concrete limitation and particularity. Thereby it emerges as a highly abstract system, a value system, yet posited as value's opposite . . .
>
> In this view, gender articulates a basic class relationship, inherent in the wage labour relationship itself. The 'one' of wage labour is *work*, and the one doing it is a *he*. The 'other'

is free time, freedom, not as universal freedom, but as posited by the first, relative to work. And the one making this free time possible, once more, is also positioned very specifically as against the first. Many traits of femininity may be interpreted on this background—woman as the larger ground, the larger ideal being, beyond work, related to pure consumption and a superior kind of freedom . . . (Holter 1995, p. 102).

Holter's 'social forms analysis' gives an account of gender, masculinity and femininity, as historically specific features of social life in modernity. They arise not from a timeless dichotomy of bodies but from the specific course of development of the large-scale structures of society. Holter is able to show that the association of men with wage labour and women with domesticity is neither biologically determined nor arbitrary. He is able to show how women come to be seen as bearers of gender, not just of femininity. We see how masculinity is in a certain sense an escape from gender, how men have a struggle to re-enter the gender institution of the family as full participants. Thus Holter can show why the political project of gender reform constantly strikes difficulties around the division of labour and institutional spheres.

Holter's argument is striking in its emphasis on institutions—the family and the workplace under industrial capitalism—as keys to the problems of gender. I am convinced he is right in this view, though I think his analysis suffers from being Eurocentric. The fact that capitalism is a global system, is not just industrialism but is also imperialism (see Chapter 3), has not yet become significant in Holter's analysis. But it is not hard to see how that connection could be made, and I think that will be an important basis of the next generation of theory.

Research on masculinities has sometimes been criticized for a focus on fixed identities, or for a presumption of stability in masculinity. I do not find this criticism a very compelling one. Research on the social construction of masculinities has placed a good deal of emphasis on the uncertainties, difficulties, and contradictions of the process (Messner 1992, Thorne 1993, and Chapters 5 and 6). Whether the outcomes are stable or unstable, mostly fluid or mostly fixed, is surely an empirical question, not one to be settled in advance by theory.

There are some cases, both in research and in practice (e.g. in anti-violence work), where patterns of masculinity are quite tough and resistant to change. There are other situations where they are unstable, or where commitment to a gender position is negotiable—which educators such as Davies and Martino make use of in their classroom work. Investigating the circumstances where gender patterns are less or more open to change seems an important task for research. It is the point of the theoretical discussion of crisis tendencies in gender relations.

A more convincing criticism has been directed at the concept of 'hegemonic masculinity', at least in some of its uses. Critics have pointed out a tendency to reify this term, so that it becomes effectively a fixed character type, something like the once-famous 'Type A personality'. Given this tendency, all the objectionable things men do—rape, assault, environmental degradation, dog-eat-dog business practices, etc.—can be loaded into the bag of 'hegemonic masculinity'. And the more extreme this image becomes, the less it has to be owned by the majority of men.

To put it more formally, there is a tendency in many discussions towards a psychologization of problems arising from gender relations, and a drift away from concern with institutions, power relations, and social inequalities. It may be helpful to recall that the concept of hegemony was introduced into discussions of masculinity to deal with *relational* issues—most importantly, the connections between the differences and hierarchies among men, and the relations between men and women (e.g. Connell 1983, Kimmel 1987).

THE GENDER RELATIONS APPROACH

The problems of role theory, categoricalism and more recently post-structuralism have led a number of theorists towards a relational account of gender. This gives us a way of understanding the different dimensions or structures of gender, the relation between bodies and society, and the patterning or configuration of gender.

Structures

In relational approaches, gender is seen as a way in which social practice is organized, whether in personal life, interpersonal interaction, or on the larger scale. It is common to refer to the patterning in social relations as 'structure', so the relational approach is sometimes summarized by describing gender as a social structure.

But as soon as one looks at the detail of interactions and institutions, it is clear that gender is not just one structure. For instance, different patterns emerge in emotional relationships from those that can be seen in economic relationships. Accordingly it has become familiar to identify multiple structures. In a previous book (Connell 1987) I suggested that the analysis of gender had to recognize at least three structures: the division of labour, power relations, and relations of emotional attachment or cathexis. Walby's (1990) analysis of modern patriarchy identifies six structures: the patriarchal mode of production, patriarchal relations in paid work, patriarchal relations in the state, male violence, patriarchal relations in sexuality, and patriarchal relations in cultural institutions.

Walby's distinctions seem uneven. It is difficult to deny that household production and paid employment are closely linked, and it seems more reasonable to treat them as part of the one structure of economic relations. Similarly, power in the state is continuous with power expressed as 'male violence', not least in war. But there seems a better case for recognizing the structure of relations in communication and culture as irreducible to the others.

Accordingly, I suggest a four-fold model of the structure of gender relations, which is used throughout this book:

Power relations The main axis of power in the contemporary European/US gender order is the overall subordination of women and dominance of men—the structure that women's liberation named 'patriarchy'. This general structure exists despite many local reversals (e.g. woman-headed households, female teachers with male students). It persists despite resistance of many kinds, now articulated in feminism and in gay and lesbian movements. These reversals and resistances mean a continuing problem of legitimacy for patriarchy, a problem which has been very effectively used by liberal feminism in rights-based campaigns (e.g. for equal employment opportunity).

(2) *Production relations (division of labour)* Gender divisions of labour are familiar in the form of task allocations, sometimes reaching extraordinarily fine detail. In the English village studied by Hunt (1980), it was customary for women to wash the inside of windows, men to wash the outside.

Equal attention should be paid to the economic consequences of gender divisions of labour, specifically the benefits accruing to men from unequal shares of the products of social labour. This may be called the *patriarchal dividend.*

This dividend is most often discussed in terms of unequal wage rates, but attention should also be paid to the gendered character of capital. A capitalist economy that operates through a gender division of labour is, necessarily, a gendered accumulation process. So it is not a statistical accident, but a part of the social construction of masculinity, that men and not women control the major corporations and the great private fortunes. Implausible as it sounds, the accumulation of wealth has become firmly linked to the reproductive arena, through the social relations of gender.

(3) *Cathexis (emotional relations)* Desire is so often seen as natural that it is commonly excluded from social theory. Emotion is, however, increasingly seen as an important topic for social theory (Barbalet 1998). When we consider desire in Freudian terms, as emotional energy being attached to an object, its gendered character is clear. This is true both for heterosexual and homosexual desire. The practices that shape and realize desire are thus an aspect of the gender order.

Accordingly we can ask political questions about the relationships involved: whether they are consensual or coercive, whether pleasure is equally given and received. In feminist analyses of

sexuality these have become sharp questions about the connection of heterosexuality to men's position of social dominance
(e.g. Buchbinder et al. 1987).

Symbolism The process of communication is increasingly recognized as a vital element of social processes. The symbolic
structures called into play in communication—grammatical and
syntactic rules, visual and sound vocabularies etc.—are important sites of gender practice. For instance, we often understand
gender differences through symbolic oppositions rather than
through images of gradation, and this reinforces belief in
gender dichotomy.

Gender subordination may be reproduced through subtle
and not-so-subtle linguistic practices, such as addressing women
by titles that define them through their marital relationships
to men. The symbolic presentation of gender through dress,
makeup, body culture, gesture, tone of voice etc. is an important part of the everyday experience of gender. As feminist
dress reformers knew (Wilson 1985), this presentation can be
a locus of political struggle and social change.

Bodies and gender

How do we know that these structures are all part of the same
thing, 'gender'? They are all linked by a specific involvement
with bodies. In gender processes, the everyday conduct of life
is organized in relation to a reproductive arena, defined by the
bodily structures and processes of human reproduction. This
arena includes sexual arousal and intercourse, childbirth and
infant care, bodily sex difference and similarity.

The relationship of bodies to social processes is difficult
to analyze, constantly a sore point for theory. I think this
is because a logically complex pattern of practice is involved,
where bodies are both agents and objects of practice.

Such body-reflexive practices are not internal to the individual. They involve social relations and symbolism; they may
well involve large-scale social institutions. Through body-reflexive
practices, more than individual lives are formed: a social world is
formed.

Through body-reflexive practices, bodies are addressed by social process and drawn into history, without ceasing to be bodies. They do not turn into symbols, signs, or positions in discourse. Their materiality (including material capacities to engender, to give birth, to give milk, to menstruate, to open, to penetrate, to ejaculate) is not erased, it continues to matter. The *social* process of gender includes childbirth and child care, youth and aging, the pleasures of sport and sex, labour, injury, death from AIDS and the struggle to live with AIDS.

I call the bodily point of reference a 'reproductive arena' not a 'biological base' to emphasize that we are talking about a historical process involving the body. Gender is social practice that constantly refers to bodies and what bodies do, it is not social practice reduced to the body.

Biological reproduction does not cause, or even provide a template for, gender as practice. For instance, lesbian and gay sexualities are gendered practices as much as heterosexuality is—they are sexualities organized with reference to female bodies and male bodies, respectively, as partners. It is also familiar that gender differentiations occur which have not the slightest logical connection with reproduction—for instance the crude gender coding in computer games. The connection with the reproductive arena is always social, a matter of the organization of social relations.

Biological-reductionist accounts of gender, which are still popular (see the critique by Fausto-Sterling 1992), present the exact reverse of the real situation. Gender exists precisely to the extent that biology does *not* determine the social. It marks one of those points of transition where historical processes supersede biological evolution as the form of change. Gender is a scandal, an outrage, from the point of view of essentialism.

Gender configurations

Social practice is creative and inventive, but not inchoate. Practice that relates to the structure of gender, generated as people and groups grapple with their historical situations, does not consist of isolated acts. Actions are configured in larger units, and when we speak of masculinity and femininity we are naming configurations of gender practice.

'Configuration' is perhaps too static a term. The important thing is the *process* of configuring practice. Masculinity and femininity must be understood as *gender projects*. These are dynamic processes of configuring practice through time, which transform their starting points in gender structures.

We find gender-configurations of practice however we slice the social world, whatever unit of analysis we choose. The most familiar is the individual life course, the basis of the common-sense notions of masculinity and femininity. The configuration of practice here is what psychologists have traditionally called 'personality' or 'character'. Later chapters of this book offer a number of examples.

Gender configurations emerge also in collective processes to do with ideology or culture. Here gender is organized in symbolic practices that have been made familiar by feminist critiques of sexist images of women in mass media, in school textbooks, in language etc. A similar critique of patriarchal images of masculinity has now emerged (e.g. Easthope 1986).

Social science has increasingly recognized another collective site of the gender configuration of practice: institutions such as the state, the workplace and the school. Many find it difficult to accept that institutions are substantively, not just metaphorically, gendered. This is, nevertheless, a key point.

To take the example of education, we cannot understand gender in schools without 'thinking institutionally', as Hansot and Tyack (1988) pithily put it. Educational institutions are gendered in multiple ways. Male staff predominate in higher education and in school administration, women staff predominate in kindergarten and elementary teaching. The knowledge conveyed to children is legitimated by patriarchal institutions, and some parts of it (technical education for instance) virtually segregate youth on gender lines. Most educational authority is masculinized, and so are parts of the non-academic curriculum, such as competitive team sports. Gender relations among the children are a constant preoccupation of peer group life, ranging from terms of casual playground abuse ('fag', 'wimp')

to elaborate dating rituals. These relations are constantly re-negotiated in the changing arenas provided by the school, as Thorne's (1993) ethnography brilliantly shows.

The patterning of all these relations within an institution (such as a school or a corporation) may be called its *gender regime*. The overall patterning of gender regimes, together with the gender patterning of culture and personal life, may be called the *gender order* of a society. It is implicit in these concepts that gender regimes and gender orders are historical products and subject to change in history.

Because gender is a way of structuring social practice in general, not a special type of practice, it is unavoidably involved with other social structures. It is now common to say that gender 'intersects'—better, 'interacts'—with race and class. We might add that it constantly interacts with nationality or position in the world order, as argued in Chapters 3 and 4.

CONCEPTUALIZING MASCULINITIES

Masculinity, understood as a configuration of gender practice in the terms just discussed, is necessarily a social construction. Masculinity *refers to* male bodies (sometimes directly, sometimes symbolically and indirectly), but is not *determined* by male biology. It is, thus, perfectly logical to talk about masculine women or masculinity in women's lives, as well as masculinity in men's lives.

Masculinities are configurations of practice within gender relations, a structure that includes large-scale institutions and economic relations as well as face-to-face relationships and sexuality. Masculinity is institutionalized in this structure, as well as being an aspect of individual character or personality.

Thus we can speak of a specific kind of masculinity being embedded in the gender regime of an institution such as an army, a corporation or a school. A small-scale but closely analyzed example is Walker's (1988) examination of the institutional role of football in maintaining order in an Australian inner-city boys' school. On the larger scale, the state itself institutionalizes particular masculinities and regulates relations between masculinities in the gender order of society.

This activity not only regulates existing gender relations. The state's activity also helps to constitute gender relations and the social categories they define. The best-analyzed example is the role of repressive laws and state-backed medicine in constituting the category of 'the homosexual' in the late nineteenth century (Greenberg 1988). The categories of husband and wife are also partly constituted by state action (e.g. through marriage law). Their meanings and relationships are shaped by a very wide range of state policies—labour market policy, welfare policy, child care and education policy, population policy—as comparative studies of welfare states have shown (O'Connor, Orloff & Shaver 1999).

Further, masculinity exists impersonally in culture as a subject position in the process of representation, in the structures of language and other symbol systems. Individual practice may accept and reproduce this positioning, but may also confront and contest it.

The relationship between personal life and structure constantly emerges as a key issue about masculinity. A striking example is the relationship between boys' engagement in sports and the hierarchical organization of sporting institutions, analyzed in Messner's (1992) research on professional athletes.

I have emphasized (Chapter 1) the empirical evidence that in any given social setting there is rarely just one masculinity. What used to be called 'the male role' is best understood as the culturally authoritative or hegemonic pattern of masculinity. But there are generally others. We need ways of understanding the differences, and the relations between different patterns.

Hegemonic masculinity need not be the most common pattern of masculinity. Other masculinities co-exist, or more precisely, are produced at the same time. These include subordinated masculinities, the most important example of which in contemporary European/American culture is gay masculinity. There are also marginalized masculinities, gender forms produced in exploited or oppressed groups such as ethnic minorities, which may share many features with hegemonic masculinity but are socially de-authorized. There are also masculinities which are organized around acceptance of the patriarchal dividend, but are not militant in defence of patriarchy. These might be termed complicit masculinities.

The principal axis around which the varieties of masculinity are organized is the overall social relation between men and women, that is, the structure of gender relations as a whole. A strong cultural opposition between masculine and feminine is characteristic of patriarchal gender orders, commonly expressed in culture as dichotomies and negations. Hegemonic masculinity is thus often defined negatively, as the opposite of femininity. Subordinated masculinities are symbolically assimilated to femininity (e.g. abuse of 'sissies', 'nancy-boys').

Adult masculinities are produced through a complex process of growth and development involving active negotiation in multiple social relationships. Earlier conceptions of 'sex role socialization' oversimplified the social relations and pictured children as much more passive than they are. The process is not so simple. It often involves reversals and dialectics of confrontation and denial, where masculinities are formed in opposition to institutional pressure, as well as through conformity.

For instance, Messerschmidt's (1993) analysis of both corporate crime and street gangs shows how breaking norms in the form of laws can be a resource in the construction of hegemonic and marginalized masculinities. As the cases in Chapters 6 and 8 of this book show, engagement with hegemonic patterns is widespread, but not final. An initial commitment towards hegemonic masculinity may be followed by distancing or even outright rejection.

The result in adulthood is generally a complex personality structure, not a homogeneous one, in which contradictory emotions and commitments co-exist. For instance in adult sexuality, a predatory heterosexuality may co-exist with desire to be nurtured, a pattern that Bishop and Robinson (1998) identify even among the 'clients' of international sex tourism in Thailand. A public heterosexuality may co-exist with a homoerotic desire which is nevertheless feared and denied.

The enactment of masculinity in adult life is partly an outcome of this process of development, which defines a person's capacities for practice, and partly a matter of the social situations in which the person acts. Men whose masculinities are formed around the continuing social subordination of women are likely to act in ways that sustain the patriarchal dividend.

Yet men's interests are divided. This is partly a result of the subordination of some masculinities within the pattern of hegemony, and partly a result of the interplay between gender relations and structures of class, race and nationality. In certain situations men's relationships with particular women or children, or groups including women and children, define interests that are stronger than their shared interest as men. In all these ways men's general interest in patriarchy becomes incoherent or contestable.

Precisely such a contest has been created by the growth of contemporary feminism, presenting a challenge of which virtually all men in Western countries are aware. The result is the growth of new forms of politics addressing masculinity as an object of social action, producing the spectrum of masculinity politics noted in Chapter 1. This issue will be explored further in the final section of the book.

AGENDA FOR RESEARCH

What directions should the study of masculinities now take? No one can legislate for a field of study, but one may argue that some issues are strategic. I suggest the following are now among the most important, and I have attempted to explore them in the chapters of this book.

1. In Chapter 1, I outlined the results of the 'ethnographic moment' in masculinity research. Productive as this has been, we now need to move beyond it, to think about gender relations on the scale of world society. Feminist researchers have been discussing the global position of women, and the gender dimension in international politics and trade, for a

considerable time (e.g. Bulbeck 1988, Enloe 1990). There is also a discussion by gay theorists of the globalization and hybridization of gay identities (e.g. Altman 1996).

If we can recognize the global dimension of gender relations and sexuality, we must think about how masculinities are constructed by global forces and how men, in all their diversity, are positioned in global society. An international dimension keeps cropping up in local studies, from Walker's (1998b) study of 'car culture' in the Australian working class to Tillner's (1997) work on masculinities and racism in Austria. We need to consider how particular masculinities were produced by globalizing forces, throughout the history of imperialism and neocolonialism; and we need to study the constitution of masculinities and the gender politics of men under contemporary globalization. These issues are addressed in Chapters 3 and 4.

2. Understanding bodies and body issues is another important task. Body issues (sport, violence, health, sexuality) were important to women's liberation and men's liberation debates in the early 1970s, and it is not surprising that they have come back into focus.

In Chapters 5, 6 and 7, I present some research evidence about men's embodiment, sexualities and desires. These fieldwork studies were completed before the agenda about globalization came into focus and, accordingly, these chapters are still in the ethnographic moment. Issues about bodies can, however, be analyzed on a global scale, and this is the focus of Chapter 4. Issues about bodies are not only research questions, they include very important practical problems. AIDS prevention is discussed in Chapter 7. Other health issues are considered in Chapter 10. The question of men's violence is now the subject of sophisticated research and debate; in Chapter 12, I try to connect this with the problems of international peacemaking.

3. Public interest in questions about masculinity is often driven by practical concerns. It is very important that social-scientific research should be connected with these practical issues. In the last decade there have been significant public debates about

such issues as boys' education, men's health, and men's violence. In Chapter 8, I present some research evidence of my own on the interplay of masculinity and education, and in Chapter 9, I review the wider research literature on schooling and develop a framework for understanding issues about boys' education. In Chapter 10, I survey the debate about men's health and suggest ways in which social-science research on masculinities can be linked to biomedical literature on men's health.

4. Developing a more explicit understanding of the process of change in masculinities is a task of both theoretical and practical importance. Research has firmly established the possibility of change. Historians have gone a considerable distance in mapping the fact of change, at least in representations and discourses of masculinity (e.g. Phillips 1987).

But we have not got very far beyond the sex-role reformers of the 1970s in the practical capacity to achieve change or in the techniques with which we attempt it. Developing models of change which bring together collective processes with individual experience, and use the full range of our understanding of gender processes, could be an important contribution not just to gender studies but also to the solution of pressing social problems. Chapter 11 considers a more general model of change and current issues of political strategy, and Chapter 12 explores change in relation to violence and peacemaking.

5. There is clearly a need to consolidate the analysis of masculinity in relation to class, race and ethnicity, and other issues of power. Poynting et al. (1998) rightly argue that ethnicity is not an add-on. Practices of ethnicity are present all the time in constructions of masculinity. This applies to the masculinities of the dominant ethnic group as much as to the masculinities of subordinate groups—though there are different problems in understanding 'whiteness', only now emerging as an important topic in ethnic studies.

A similar situation applies to class. Donaldson's (1998) exploration of the making of masculinities in settings of great wealth should not be seen as a study of an exotic minority, but as a key move in understanding social dynamics as a whole.

In this book I have attempted to bring these issues out at each level, from a discussion of globalization to specific polity problems. Class, for instance, is explored in some depth in Chapter 7, and ethnicity is considered in relation to health in Chapter 10.

6. The patriarchal dividend, I have argued in this chapter, is a key to the politics of masculinity. There is a need to make the question of interests more concrete. The initial women's liberation conceptualization of patriarchy assumed advantages for men. But so far as feminism in the last twenty years has pursued the issue, it has mainly been through studies of the disadvantages of women. We need to explore the places men occupy in the system of production and exchange.

Some of the needed facts are hard to come by. There is, for instance, little evidence about gender patterns in wealth— though it is usually the case that disparities in wealth are even greater than in income. Beyond questions of distribution are questions of process. It is clear that contemporary world capitalism involves a gendered accumulation process; but the mechanisms of this accumulation are still obscure.

The issue of the patriarchal dividend cannot be separated from the issue of globalization. The collapse of Stalinism in Russia and Eastern Europe, and the shift of China towards capitalist industrialization, has created for the first time the conditions for a genuinely global capitalist economy. This makes it urgent to study the gender dimension in market relations, and in the state forms associated with markets.

The market is often seen as the antithesis of gender (marked by achieved versus ascribed status etc.). But the market operates through forms of rationality that are historically mascu-line and involve a sharp split between instrumental reason on the one hand, emotion and human responsibility on the other (Seidler 1989). Holter, as noted above, has argued that modern masculinity is deeply connected with industrial capitalism. It is not a cosmic accident that multinational corporations are run by men. So the emerging masculinities of the international corporate economy, discussed in Chapter 3, are of immense importance for the future of gender relations at large.

There are, of course, other possible agendas for research on gender issues, on men and masculinity. It is quite conceivable that gender research will become simply another academic specialism, retreating into self-reference and obscurity. I hope not. If scholars of gender are to say something of importance to the rest of the human community, these six issues are questions we must address.

PART 2

GLOBALIZATION

3

Masculinities and globalization

Chapter 1 outlined some major findings of the new social research on the construction of masculinities. If we compare this picture with earlier accounts of the 'male sex role', it is clear that the ethnographic moment in research has already had important intellectual fruits.

Nevertheless, it has always been recognized that some issues go beyond the local. For instance, any study of the mytho-poetic movement must recognize it is only part of a spectrum of masculinity politics (Messner 1997, Schwalbe 1996). Historical studies such as Phillips (1987) on New Zealand and Kimmel (1996) on the United States have traced the changing public constructions of masculinity for whole countries over long periods. Ultimately, the large historical context, the big picture, is essential for understanding the small picture, the ethnographic detail.

This logic must now be taken a step further. What happens in localities is affected by the history of whole countries, but what happens in countries is affected by the history of the world. Locally situated lives are now (indeed have long been) powerfully influenced by geopolitical struggles, global markets, multinational corporations, labour migration, and transnational media.

To understand local masculinities, then, we must think in global terms. But how? That is the problem pursued in this chapter. I will offer a framework for thinking about masculinities as a feature of world society, and for thinking about men's gender practices in terms of the global structure and dynamics of gender.

THE WORLD GENDER ORDER

Masculinities do not first exist and then come into contact with femininities; they are produced together, in the process that makes a gender order. Accordingly, to understand the masculinities on a world scale we must first have a concept of the globalization of gender.

This is one of the most difficult points in current gender analysis because the very conception is counterintuitive. We are so accustomed to thinking of gender as the attribute of an individual, even as a particularly intimate matter, that it requires a considerable wrench to think of gender on the vast scale of global society. There are now about 6000 million people in the world.

Some relevant discussions, such as the literature on 'women and development', blur the issue of gender. They treat the institutions or processes that cross national boundaries (markets, corporations, intergovernmental programs etc.) as being gender-neutral in principle, but impacting on men and women unequally because of bad attitudes or bad policies. Such conceptions reproduce the familiar liberal-feminist view of the state as being in principle gender-neutral even though it is empirically dominated by men.

But the picture changes if we recognize that very large-scale institutions such as the state are themselves gendered, in quite precise ways (Connell 1990). The picture changes if we recognize that international relations, international trade and global markets are inherently, not accidentally, arenas of gender formation and gender politics (Enloe 1990). Then we can recognize the existence of a world gender order. This can be defined as the structure of relationships that connect the gender regimes of institutions, and the gender orders of local society, on a world scale.

A definition, however, is only a beginning. The substantial questions remain: what is the shape of that structure, how tightly are its elements linked, how has it arisen in history, what is its trajectory into the future?

Current business and media talk about 'globalization' pictures a tide sweeping across the world, driven by new technologies, producing vast unfettered global markets in which all participate on equal terms. This is certainly a misleading image. As Hirst and Thompson (1996) show, the global economy in fact is highly unequal and the degree to which it has become homogenized is wildly overestimated in business rhetoric. Multinational corporations based in the three great economic powers (the United States, the European Union, and Japan) are the major economic actors worldwide.

The structure bears the marks of its history. Modern global society was historically produced, as Wallerstein (1974) argued, by the economic and political expansion of European states from the fifteenth century on, leading to the creation of colonial empires. It is in this process that we find the roots of the modern world gender order.

Imperialism was, from the start, a gendered process. Its first phase, colonial conquest and settlement, was carried out by gender-segregated forces and resulted in massive disruption of indigenous gender orders. In its second phase, the stabilization of colonial societies, new gender divisions of labour were produced in plantation economies and colonial cities, while gender ideologies were linked with racial hierarchies and the cultural defence of empire. The third phase, marked by political decolonization, economic neo-colonialism, and the current growth of world markets and systems of financial control, has seen gender divisions of labour remade on a massive scale in the 'global factory' (Fuentes & Ehrenreich 1983), as well as the spread of gendered violence alongside Western military technology.

The result of this history is a partially integrated, highly unequal, and turbulent world society, in which gender relations are unevenly linked on a global scale. The unevenness becomes clear when the different substructures of gender defined in Chapter 2 are examined separately.

Power relations

The colonial and post-colonial world has tended to break down purdah systems of patriarchy in the name of modernization, if not of women's emancipation (Kandiyoti 1994). At the same time, large-scale organizations have appeared, notably the state and corporations, which, with few exceptions, are culturally masculinized and controlled by men. As Enloe (1990) has vividly shown, the world of international politics is heavily gendered, with women marginalized in diplomacy, military aid, and trade negotiations. In post-colonial capitalism the power of local elites depends on their relations with the metropolitan powers. So the hegemonic masculinities of neocolonial societies are uneasily poised between local and global cultures.

Production relations (division of labour)

A characteristic feature of colonial and neo-colonial economies was the restructuring of local production systems to produce a male wage-worker/female domestic-worker couple (Mies 1986). This need not produce a 'housewife' in the Western suburban sense. For instance where the wage work required male migration to plantations or mines (Moodie 1994) the result might be more economic responsibility for women, not less. But it has generally produced the same identification of masculinity with the public realm and the money economy, and femininity with the domestic realm, which is a core feature of the modern European gender system (Holter 1997).

Cathexis (emotional relations)

Missionary activity, both religious and cultural, has attacked indigenous homosexual and cross-gender practices, such as the native American 'berdache' and the Chinese 'passion of the cut sleeve' (Hinsch 1990). Recently created Western models of romantic heterosexual love as the basis for marriage, and of gay identity as the main alternative, have now circulated globally. Yet as Altman (1996) observed, they do not simply displace indigenous models, but interact with them in extremely complex ways.

Symbolism

Mass media, especially electronic media, in most parts of the world follow North American and European models and relay a great deal of metropolitan content, including its gender imagery. A striking example is the reproduction of a North American imagery of femininity by Xuxa, the blonde television superstar in Brazil (Simpson 1993). In counterpoint, 'exotic' gender imagery has been used in the marketing strategies of newly industrializing countries (e.g. airline advertising from South-East Asia)—a tactic based on the longstanding combination of the exotic and the erotic in the colonial imagination (Jolly 1997). Major powers also may use gender symbolism to renegotiate their position in the world system. Jeffords (1989) shows this in the 'remasculinization of America' after defeat in the Vietnam War, through the symbolic media of films and novels.

Clearly the world gender order is not simply a blown-up copy of a European–American gender order. The European–American gender order was changed by colonialism; and elements from other cultures now circulate globally. Yet in no sense do they mix on equal terms to produce a United Colors of Benetton gender order. The culture and institutions of the North Atlantic countries are hegemonic within the emergent world system. This is crucial for understanding the kinds of masculinities produced in globalization.

THE REPOSITIONING OF MEN AND THE REMAKING OF MASCULINITIES

The positioning of men and the making of masculinities may be analyzed at any of the levels at which gender practice is configured, including the body, personal life or collective social practice. At each level we need to consider how globalization influences configurations of gender. Here I will discuss the process at the levels of personal life and collective practice. Issues about bodies will be discussed in greater detail in Chapter 4.

The impact of global forces on personal life can be seen in individual life histories. Sometimes the link is indirect. An example is young working-class men on the fringe of the regular labour market (Connell 1995, Chapter 4). The fact of chronic unemployment, which makes it impossible for them to construct a masculinity organized around being a 'bread-winner', arises from the local economy's changing position in the global economy.

In other cases, such as executives of multinational corporations and the financial sector servicing international trade, the link is obvious. The requirements of a career in international business set up strong pressures on domestic life. Almost all multinational executives are men, and the assumption in their trade magazines and advertising is that they will have dependent wives running their homes and bringing up their children.

At the level of collective practice, masculinities are involved in the cultural remaking of gender meanings under globalization; they are also affected by a rather different process, the reshaping of the institutional contexts of practice.

The growth of global mass media, especially electronic media, is an obvious vector for the globalization of gender. Popular entertainment circulates stereotyped gender images, deliberately made attractive for marketing purposes. The example of Xuxa in Brazil has already been mentioned. International news media are also controlled or strongly influenced from the metropole, and circulate Western definitions of authoritative masculinity, criminality, desirable femininity etc. At places and times where local cultures are in flux, such as Eastern Europe after the collapse of communism, these imported definitions can have tremendous impact.

But there are limits to the power of global mass communications. Some local centres of mass entertainment differ from the Hollywood model; for example, the Indian popular film industry centred in Mumbai. Further, media research shows that audiences are highly selective in their reception of media messages. Audiences do know there is an element of fantasy in mass entertainment. Just as economic globalization can be exaggerated, so can cultural homogenization. The creation of a 'global culture' is a more turbulent and uneven process than is often assumed (Featherstone 1995).

More important than cultural standardization, I would argue, is a process that began long before electronic media existed—the export of institutions. Gendered institutions not only circulate definitions of masculinity and femininity. Gendered institutions, creating specific conditions for social practice, call into existence specific patterns of practice.

Thus, certain patterns of collective violence are embedded in the organization and culture of a Western-style army, which are different from the patterns of pre-colonial violence. Certain patterns of calculative egocentrism are embedded in the working of a stock market; certain patterns of rule following and domination are embedded in a bureaucracy.

The colonial and post-colonial world saw the installation, on a very large scale, of institutions on the North Atlantic model: armies, states, bureaucracies, corporations, capital markets, labour markets, schools, law courts, transport systems. These are gendered institutions, and their functioning has directly reconstituted masculinities in the periphery. This is not necessarily by direct modelling or copying of the gender patterns themselves; it can also occur indirectly, as a result of pressures for change which are inherent in the institutional form.

To the extent particular institutions become dominant in world society, the patterns of masculinity embedded in them may become global standards. Masculine dress is an interesting indicator. Almost every political leader in the world now wears the uniform of the Western business executive.

The more common pattern, however, is not the complete displacement of local patterns but an articulation between the local gender order and the gender regime of the new institutions. Case studies such as Hollway's (1994) account of bureaucracy in Tanzania illustrate the point. There, domestic patriarchy linked up with masculine authority in the state, in ways that subverted the government's formal commitment to equal opportunity for women.

The world gender order is patriarchal, in the sense that it privileges men over women. There is a 'patriarchal dividend' for men arising from unequal wages, unequal labour-force participation, and a highly unequal structure of ownership, as well as cultural and sexual privileging. This has been extensively documented by feminist work on women's situation globally (e.g. Taylor 1985), though its implications for masculinity have mostly been ignored.

The conditions thus exist for the production of a hegemonic masculinity on a world scale, that is to say, a dominant form of masculinity which embodies, organizes and legitimates men's domination in the gender order as a whole.

The conditions of globalization, which involve the interaction of many local gender orders, multiply the forms of masculinity in the global gender order. At the same time, the specific shape of globalization, concentrating economic and cultural power on an unprecedented scale, provide new resources for dominance by particular groups of men.

This dominance may become institutionalized in a pattern of masculinity which becomes, to some degree, standardized across localities. I will call such patterns 'globalizing masculinities'. It is among globalizing masculinities, rather than narrowly within the metropole, that we are likely to find candidates for hegemony in the world gender order.

GLOBALIZING MASCULINITIES

In this section I will offer a sketch of major forms of globalizing masculinity, in three historical phases of the making of a world gender order.

Masculinities of conquest and settlement

The creation of the world-spanning empires and their social order involved peculiar conditions for the gender practices of men. Colonial conquest itself was mainly carried out by groups of men—soldiers, sailors, traders, administrators, and a good many who were all these by turn (such as the 'Rum Corps' in the early days of the colony of New South Wales).

These men were drawn from the more segregated occupations and milieux in the metropole, and it is likely that the men drawn into colonization tended to be the more rootless. Certainly the process of conquest could produce frontier masculinities which combined the occupational culture of these groups with an unusual level of violence and egocentric individualism. The vehement debate among their contemporaries about the genocidal violence of the Spanish conquistadors—who in 50 years completely exterminated the population of Hispaniola in the West Indies—suggests that the pattern was recognized at the time (Las Casas 1971).

The political history of empire is full of evidence of the tenuous control over the frontier exercised by the state. The Spanish monarchs were unable to rein in the conquistadors, the governors in Sydney were unable to hold back the squatters and the governors in Capetown were unable to hold back the Boers. Gold rushes broke boundaries everywhere. At one stage what was virtually an independent republic was set up by escaped slaves in Brazil.

This lack of control probably extended to other forms of social control too, such as customary controls on men's sexuality. Extensive sexual exploitation of indigenous women was a common feature of conquest. In certain circumstances frontier masculinities might be reproduced as a local cultural tradition long after the frontier had passed, such as the gauchos of southern South America and the cowboys of the western United States.

In other circumstances, however, the frontier of conquest and exploitation was replaced by a frontier of settlement. Sex ratios in the colonizing population changed, as women arrived and locally born generations succeeded. A shift back towards the family patterns of the metropole was likely.

As Cain and Hopkins (1993) have shown for the British empire, the ruling group in the colonial world as a whole was an extension of the dominant class in the metropole—the landed gentry—and tended to reproduce its social customs and ideology. The creation of a certain pattern of masculinity among settlers might be the goal of state policy, as it seems to have been in late nineteenth-century New Zealand, part of a general process of pacification and the creation of an agricultural social order (Phillips 1987). Or it might be undertaken through institutions created by settler groups, such as the elite schools in Natal studied by Morrell (1994).

The impact of colonialism on the construction of masculinity among the colonized is much less documented, but there is every reason to think it was severe. Conquest and settlement disrupted all the structures of indigenous society, whether or not this was intended by the colonizing powers (Bitterli 1989). Indigenous gender orders were no exception. Their disruption could result from the pulverization of indigenous communities (as in the seizure of land in eastern North America and southeastern Australia), gendered labour migration (as in gold mining with black labour in South Africa: Moodie 1994), or ideological attacks on local gender arrangements (as in the missionary assault on the transgender 'berdache' tradition in North America: Williams 1986).

The varied course of resistance to colonization is also likely to have affected the making of masculinities. This is clear in the region of Natal in South Africa, where sustained resistance to colonization by the Zulu kingdom was a key to the mobilization of ethnic-national masculine identities in the twentieth century (Morrell 1996).

Masculinities of empire

The imperial social order created a hierarchy of masculinities, as it created a hierarchy of communities and races. The colonizers distinguished 'more manly' from 'less manly' groups among their subjects. In British India, for instance, Bengali men were supposed effeminate while Pathans and Sikhs were regarded as strong and warlike. Similar distinctions were made in South Africa between 'Hottentots' and Zulus, in North

America between Iroquois, Sioux and Cheyenne on one side and southern and southwestern tribes on the other.

At the same time, the growing emphasis on gender difference in European culture in the eighteenth and nineteenth centuries provided symbols of overall superiority and inferiority. Within the imperial 'poetics of war' (MacDonald 1994), the conqueror was virile, while the colonized were dirty, sexualized and effeminate or childlike. In many colonial situations indigenous men were called 'boys' by the colonizers (e.g. Zimbabwe: Shire 1994).

Sinha's (1995) interesting study of the language of political controversy in India in the 1880s and 1890s shows how the images of 'manly Englishman' and 'effeminate Bengali' were deployed to uphold colonial privilege and restrain movements for change. In the late nineteenth century, it was generally true that racial barriers in colonial societies were hardening rather than weakening. Gender ideology began to fuse with racism in forms that the twentieth century never untangled.

The power relations of empire meant that indigenous gender orders were generally under pressure from the colonizers, rather than the other way around. But the colonizers too might change. The barriers of late colonial racism were not only to prevent pollution from below. They were also to forestall 'going native', a well-recognized possibility—the starting-point, for instance, of Kipling's famous novel *Kim* (1901).

The pressures and profits of empire might also work changes in gender arrangements among the colonizers. In the colonies, a large supply of indigenous domestic servants made wives more leisured and managerial, as shown in Bulbeck's (1992) study of Australian women in Papua New Guinea, and entrenched a division of spheres between men and women. In the metropole, empire also had effects on the gender order, most spectacularly in symbolic definitions of masculinity. Frontier heroes such as Lawrence of Arabia (Dawson 1991) became exemplars of masculinity. A whole social movement, the Boy Scouts, drew imagery and rituals from empire for its program for the training of boys.

The world of empire created two very different settings for the modernization of masculinities. In the periphery, the forcible restructuring of economies and workforces tended to individualize, on the one hand, and rationalize on the other. A widespread result was masculinities in which the rational calculation of self-interest was the key to action, emphasizing the European gender contrast of rational man/irrational woman. The specific form might be local—for instance the Japanese 'salaryman', a type first named in the 1910s, was specific to the Japanese context of large, stable industrial conglomerates (Kinmonth 1981). But the result generally was masculinities defined around economic action, with both workers and entrepreneurs increasingly adapted to emerging market economies.

In the metropole, the accumulation of wealth made possible a specialization of leadership in the dominant classes. Struggles for hegemony occurred in which masculinities organized around domination or violence were split from masculinities organized around expertise. The class compromises that allowed the development of the welfare state in Europe and North America were paralleled by gender compromises. Gender reform movements, most notably the women's suffrage movement, contested the legal privileges of men and forced concessions from the state.

In this context, agendas of reform in masculinity emerged in the metropole from the late nineteenth century: the temperance movement, companionate marriage, homosexual rights movements. Eventually this led to the pursuit of androgyny in 'men's liberation' in the 1970s (Kimmel & Mosmiller 1992).

Not all reconstructions of masculinity, however, emphasized tolerance or moved towards androgyny. The vehement masculinity politics of fascism, for instance, emphasized dominance and difference, and glorified violence, a pattern still found in contemporary racist movements (Tillner 1997).

Masculinities of post-colonialism and neo-liberalism

The process of decolonization naturally disrupted the gender hierarchies of the colonial order. Where armed struggle was involved, there might be a deliberate cultivation of masculine hardness and violence (as in South Africa: Xaba 1997). Some activists and theorists of liberation struggles celebrated this as a necessary response to colonial violence and emasculation. Women in liberation struggles were perhaps less impressed. However one evaluates the process, one of the consequences of decolonization was another round of disruptions of community-based gender orders, and another step in the reorientation of masculinities towards national and international contexts.

Nearly half a century after the main wave of decolonization, gender hierarchies persist in new shapes. With the collapse of Soviet communism, the decline of post-colonial socialism, and the ascendancy of the new right in Europe and North America, world politics is more and more organized around the needs of transnational capital and the creation of global markets.

Neo-liberal politics has little to say, explicitly, about gender. It speaks a gender-neutral language of 'markets', 'individuals' and 'choice'. New-right politicians and journalists denounce 'political correctness' and 'feminazis', and new-right governments have abolished or downgraded equal opportunity programs and women's policy units.

But the world in which neo-liberalism rules is still a gendered world, and neo-liberalism has an implicit gender politics. The 'individual' of neo-liberal theory has the attributes and interests of a male entrepreneur. The attack on the welfare state generally weakens the position of women, while the increasingly unregulated power of transnational corporations places strategic power in the hands of particular groups of men.

It is not surprising that the installation of market capitalism in Eastern Europe and the former Soviet Union has been accompanied by a reassertion of dominating masculinities and, in some situations, a sharp worsening in the social position of women (Novikova 2000).

In these circumstances it is reasonable to conclude that the hegemonic form of masculinity in the current world gender order is the masculinity associated with those who control its dominant institutions: the business executives who operate in global markets, and the political executives who interact (and in many contexts merge) with them. I will call this pattern 'transnational business masculinity'.

This form of masculinity is not readily available for ethnographic study, but we can get some clues to its character from its reflections in management literature, business journalism, corporate self-promotion, and from studies of local business elites (e.g. Donaldson 1998).

Transnational business masculinity appears to be marked by increasing egocentrism, very conditional loyalties (even to the corporation), and a declining sense of responsibility for others (except for purposes of image-making). Gee et al. (1996), studying recent management textbooks, noted the peculiar construction of the executive in 'fast capitalism' as a person with no permanent commitments, except to the idea of accumulation itself. The occupational world here is characterized by a limited technical rationality ('management theory') which is increasingly separate from science.

Transnational business masculinity differs from traditional bourgeois masculinity by its increasingly libertarian sexuality, with a growing tendency to commodify relations with women. Hotels catering for businessmen in most parts of the world now routinely offer pornographic videos. In many parts of the world there is a well-developed prostitution industry catering for international businessmen.

Businessmen themselves do not require bodily force, since the patriarchal dividend they benefit from is accumulated by impersonal, institutional means. But corporations increasingly use the exemplary bodies of elite sportsmen as a marketing tool (note the phenomenal growth of corporate 'sponsorship' of sport in the last generation), and indirectly as a means of legitimation for the whole gender order.

MASCULINITY POLITICS ON A WORLD SCALE

Recognizing global society as an arena where masculinities are formed allows us to pose new questions about the politics of masculinity. What social dynamics in the global arena give rise to masculinity politics, and what shape does global masculinity politics take?

As I have noted, the gradual creation of a world gender order has meant many local instabilities of gender. These range from the disruption of men's local cultural dominance as women move into the public realm and higher education, through the disruption of sexual identities that produced 'queer' politics in the metropole, to the shifts in the urban intelligentsia that produced 'the new sensitive man' and other images of gender change.

One response to such instabilities, on the part of groups whose power is challenged but still dominant, is to reaffirm local gender hierarchies. A masculine fundamentalism is, accordingly, a common response in gender politics at present.

A soft version, searching for an essential masculinity among myths and symbols, is offered by the 'mythopoetic' men's movement in the United States, and by the religious revivalists of the Promise Keepers (Messner 1997). A much harder version is found, in the United States, in the right-wing militia movement (Gibson 1994). An equally hard version is found in contemporary Afghanistan, if we can trust Western media reports, in the militant misogyny of the Taliban. It is no coincidence that in these two cases, hardline masculine fundamentalism goes together with a marked anti-internationalism. The world system—rightly enough—is seen as the source of pollution and disruption.

Not that the emerging global order is a hotbed of gender progressivism. Indeed, the neo-liberal agenda for the reform of national and international economies involves closing down historic possibilities for gender reform. I have noted how neo-liberalism subverts the gender compromise embodied in the metropolitan welfare state. It has also undermined the progressive liberal agendas of sex-role reform represented by affirmative action programs, anti-discrimination provisions, child-care services, and the like. Right-wing governments have persistently cut such programs in the name either of individual liberties or global competitiveness. Through these means the patriarchal dividend to men is defended or restored, without an explicit masculinity politics in the form of a mobilization of men.

In the arenas of international relations, the international state, multinational corporations and global markets, masculinities are deployed and a reasonably clear hegemony exists. The transnational business masculinity described above has had only one major competitor for hegemony in recent decades: the rigid, control-oriented masculinity of military command, a variant of which is the military-style bureaucratic dictatorships of Stalinism. With the collapse of Stalinism and the end of the cold war, Big Brother (Orwell's famous parody of this form of masculinity) is a fading threat. The more flexible, calculative, egocentric masculinity of the 'fast capitalist' entrepreneur holds the world stage.

We must, however, recall two important conclusions of the ethnographic moment in masculinity research described in Chapter 1. Different forms of masculinity exist together, and the hegemony of any given form is constantly subject to challenge. These are possibilities in the global arena too.

Transnational business masculinity is not completely homogeneous. Variations are embedded in different parts of the world system, which may not be completely compatible. We may distinguish a Confucian variant, based in East Asia, with a stronger commitment to hierarchy and social consensus, from a secularized Christian variant, based in North America, which shows more hedonism and individualism, and greater tolerance for social conflict. In certain arenas there is already conflict between the business and political leaderships embodying these forms of masculinity. Such conflict is found in debates over 'human rights' versus 'Asian values', and over the extent of trade and investment liberalization.

If these are contenders for hegemony, there is also opposition to hegemony. The global circulation of 'gay' identity (Altman 1996) is an important indication that non-hegemonic masculinities may operate in global arenas, and may even find a certain political articulation, in the case of gay masculinities, around human rights and AIDS prevention.

Critiques of dominant forms of masculinity have also been circulating internationally, among heterosexual men or among groups which are predominantly heterosexual. Three examples in the English-speaking world are the 'anti-sexist' or 'pro-feminist' men's groups in the United States, with their umbrella group NOMAS (National Organization of Men Against Sexism), which has been running since the early 1980s (Cohen 1991); the British new left men's groups, which produced the remarkable magazine *Achilles Heel* (Seidler 1991); and the Canadian White Ribbon campaign, the most successful mass mobilization of men opposing men's violence against women (Kaufman 1999).

There are parallel developments in other language communities. In Germany, for instance, feminists launched a discussion of the gender of men in the 1980s (Hagemann-White & Rerrich 1988, Metz-Göckel & Müller 1985). This has been followed by an educational (Kindler 1993), a popular psychology (Hollstein 1992), a critical (*Widersprüche* 1995, BauSteineMänner 1996), and a religious (Zulehner & Volz 1998) debate about masculinities and how to change them.

In Scandinavia, gender reform has led to the 'father's quota' of parental leave in Norway (Gender Equality Ombudsman 1997) and to a particularly active network of masculinity researchers. In Japan, a media debate about 'men's liberation' and some pioneering books about changing masculinities (Ito 1993, Nakamura 1994) have been followed by the foundation of a men's centre and diversifying debates on change.

These developments at national or regional level have, very recently, begun to link internationally. An International Association for Studies of Men has begun to link men involved in critical studies of masculinity. Certain international agencies, including UNESCO, have sponsored conferences to discuss the policy implications of new perspectives on masculinity (Breines et al. 2000).

Compared with the concentration of institutional power in multinational businesses, these initiatives remain small-scale and dispersed. They are, nevertheless, important in potential. The global gender order contains, necessarily, a greater diversity of forms than any local gender order. This must reinforce the consciousness that masculinity is not one fixed form. The plurality of masculinities at least symbolically prefigures the variety and creativity of a democratic gender order.

4

Globalization and men's bodies

UNDERSTANDING MEN'S BODIES

In popular ideology (at least in the English-speaking world) masculinity is often believed to be a natural consequence of male biology. Men behave the way they do because of testosterone, or big muscles, or a male brain. Accordingly, masculinity is fixed.

But we know from the recent historical and cross-cultural research discussed in Chapter 1 that masculinities do change; that what counts as 'masculine' behaviour differs from one culture to another; even that the relationship between homosexuality and heterosexuality differs greatly from one culture to another. Are men's bodies, then, *irrelevant* to masculinity?

The answer is 'no'. But to understand how men's bodies are actually involved in masculinities we must abandon the conventional dichotomy between changing culture and unchanging bodies.

Here, the findings of another field of research become important. The new sociology of the body (Connell 2000), influenced by Foucault as well as by feminism, has developed a sophisticated account of the way bodies are drawn into social and historical processes. Through social institutions and discourses, bodies are given social meaning. Society has a range of 'body practices' (Turner 1984) which address, sort and modify bodies. These practices range from deportment and dress to sexuality, surgery and sport.

Taking as an example Theberge's impressive essay 'Reflections on the body in the sociology of sport' (1991), the new sociology of the body describes disciplinary practices that regulate the body (e.g. exercise regimes, the rules of sports), studies their interplay with power structures and social differences (notably gender, in the case of sport), and considers the structural basis of disciplinary power (such as the role of media corporations). In Theberge's essay, this approach allows a sophisticated account of the formation of gendered bodies and their hierarchies, in the material practices of sport.

The new sociology of the body thus gives us *social* explanations of facts and experiences which, in conservative ideology, have been taken as proof of the *natural* hierarchy of male and female bodies.

Some of the most illuminating recent studies of masculinity have taken exactly this approach to men's bodies. They include Klein's (1993) study of the bodybuilding subculture in the United States; Henriksson's (1995) study of the social context of gay men's sex life in Sweden; and Gerschick and Miller's (1994) study of the turbulence in masculinity associated with physical disability.

There is, however, a persistent difficulty in the new sociology of the body. Partly because of the influence of Foucault, researchers have tended to see bodies as the passive bearers of cultural imprints. Bodies are the blank pages on which meanings and stories are 'inscribed'.

Very recently, this tendency has been criticized by researchers in a variety of fields, including sexuality (Dowsett 1996) and disability (Shakespeare 1998). Their arguments emphasize the body's agency in social practice, and the importance of the material diversity of bodies.

This point is nowhere more important than in relation to gender. Gender is, fundamentally, a way in which social practice is ordered. In gender processes, the everyday conduct of life is ordered in relation to a reproductive arena, as discussed in Chapter 2. This arena includes sexual arousal and intercourse, childbirth and infant care, bodily sex difference and similarity. It is thus constituted by the materiality of bodies. The crucial point, however, is that this arena is an arena of social practice; it is not a 'biological base' prior to the social. As we learn from the sociology of the body, bodies are in history, not outside. Human life does not occur on any other terms. The embodiment of gender is from the start a social embodiment.

Body-reflexive practices (defined in Chapter 2), like all practices, are governed by, and constitute, social structures. They are not necessarily homogeneous and may indeed be internally contradictory.

Each of the large-scale structures of the gender order—the structures of power relations, production relations, relations of cathexis, and symbolism—is thus linked to the reproductive arena via body-reflexive practices such as labour, violence, sexuality and self-interpretation. These practices enter chains of interaction which are not only face-to-face local interactions, but may (and often do) involve large-scale institutions and long-distance communications.

For instance, the body-reflexive practices of the professional athlete Steve, discussed in Chapter 5, ramify through volunteer lifesaving clubs, sports institutions, corporate advertisers, and mass media. There is a complex history, unique to his life though its components are familiar in many others, in which these institutions were woven together.

This approach gives us a framework for understanding the social embodiment of masculinities. The materiality of male bodies matters, not as a template for social masculinities, but as a *referent* for the configuration of social practices defined as masculinity. Male bodies are what these practices refer to, imply or address.

The body-reflexive practices that construct particular masculinities can be analyzed in relation to each of the four structures of gender, as I will do below. And because these practices link into sequences of social interaction which involve institutions and structures, they give us a way of thinking about the links between bodies and gender on the largest scale, the scale of global society.

IMPERIALISM AND MEN'S BODIES

Many accounts of the history of gender and sexuality are unilinear and strikingly Eurocentric, telling a single tale of transition from 'traditional' to 'modern'. This is no longer intellectually credible. The history of gender is plural, given the different gender orders of diverse cultures. A degree of unity was imposed on the world, not by an abstract evolution towards modernity, but by the very concrete global discontinuity of imperialism.

Chapter 3 outlined the historical process by which a world gender order was created and new forms of masculinity brought into being. Decisive events in the creation of the modern gender order were the economic and political expansion of European states from the fifteenth century on; the creation of colonial empires based on the North Atlantic metropole; the creation of neo-colonial systems of economic, political and cultural dependency; and the contemporary system of global markets dominated by the trilateral powers of the 'North'. In the course of these events some historic forms of masculinity were swept away (such as the Mandarin patriarchy of Confucian China and the aristocratic masculinity of Polynesia), others were disrupted and transformed (such as the masculine ceremonial authority of Aboriginal Australia), others brought into being (such as the frontier masculinities of the colonizers).

The creation of colonial economies involved men's bodies in the most straightforward of ways. Men provided the main labour force and their bodies were deployed by large-scale labour migration. With slavery this meant forced migration from one colonized region to another. With settler colonies it meant 'free' migration from the metropole. There were also many arrangements in between, such as indentured labour in colonial mining and plantation agriculture.

Labour migration was, and is, a strongly gendered process

with powerful effects on the making of masculinities—effects which change with the changing economic circumstances.

Moodie and Ndatshe's (1994) study of black labour in South African gold mining provides a classic demonstration. The Witwatersrand gold mines employed a large black labour force supervised by whites. Initially most of these workers were peasant proprietors who migrated temporarily to the mining district and used their wages to build up the resources to establish a peasant household. A particular pattern of masculinity was associated with this adjustment to the colonial economy. The migrant workers shared authority with their wives back in the homeland as economic partners, and custom allowed 'mine wives', with older and younger mineworkers in temporary homosexual and domestic relationships.

By the 1970s the old moral economy of the mines was breaking down, peasant agriculture was becoming unviable, mining wages were rising, and a more urban workforce was recruited. The old pattern of masculinity was now displaced by one associated with the process of proletarianization. The gender practice of the younger miners was more vehemently heterosexual, more inclined to violence, more inclined to treat women as economic dependents, and more insistent on the meaning of masculinity as bodily superiority. It is not accidental that this pattern more closely resembles the hegemonic masculinity of the European-North American metropole.

The formation of masculinities and the meaning of men's bodies is persistently connected with the racialization of global society. 'Race' was—and to a large extent still is—understood as a hierarchy of bodies, and this has became inextricably mixed with the hierarchy of masculinities.

In some circumstances this meant a 'feminization' of colonized men. As mentioned in Chapter 3, in many parts of the colonized world indigenous men were called 'boys', and in other parts they were defined as unmasculine because they were thought weak or untrustworthy. But other groups of colonized men could be seen as hypermasculine, especially when involved in violence—e.g. the Sikhs in India, the Zulu in South Africa, the Sioux in North America. In the contemporary

United States the African-American population has become a recruiting ground for exemplars of heroic masculinity in sports, especially as boxers, footballers, and basketballers.

The perception could, of course, change. In the early European settlement of Australia, indigenous men were sometimes seen as fine specimens of manhood. The first British governor actually named a beach 'Manly' (a term of praise) because of the Aboriginal men he saw there, and a suburb of Sydney still bears this name. But as the settlers took Aboriginal land, and conflict intensified, the colonizers redefined indigenous men as treacherous and animalistic.

Empire, then, marks a decisive historical change in the social embodiment of masculinities. Under imperialism men's bodies are shifted around the world, trained and controlled in new ways, sorted and symbolized on different principles. Furthermore the global society created by imperialism becomes an arena of gender formation and gender politics, in which new patterns of masculine embodiment appear. Let us focus on this process in the most recent of the periods identified in Chapter 3, the period of post-colonialism and global market society.

CONTEMPORARY GLOBALIZATION AND MEN'S BODIES

The social embodiment of masculinity can be analyzed in relation to each of the four structures of gender defined in Chapter 2. The following notes are far from a complete analysis, but I hope will provide starting points for understanding.

Power

Power impacts on bodies most directly in the form of violence. As European-style armies were created in almost every former colony, it was men who were recruited into them. It is still overwhelmingly men who staff and command them, and military prowess in many parts of the world is part of the definition of hegemonic masculinity.

The violence of the police and prison systems is mostly

directed on men's bodies. In countries like the United States and Australia, men are incarcerated at about ten times the rate of women. Private violence is also masculinized; in Australia, for instance, men are 90 per cent of those charged with homicide. I will explore this issue in more detail in Chapter 12.

If certain theories of globalization are correct, institutionalized power over men's bodies should be declining, as the state withers away and the peaceful commerce of markets takes over. The size of super-power military forces has indeed fallen since the end of the cold war, and some other military forces have shrunk with 'decompression' after the collapse of authoritarian regimes. Yet the level of social violence does not necessarily fall, as the South African case shows. Right-wing elected governments in various countries revive military spending and confrontations, as well as nuclear testing. The number of men incarcerated has grown spectacularly in the United States, with the 'war on drugs' and harsher sentencing policies. Other governments are beginning to follow this fine example. State welfare has indeed declined under globalization, but state violence, in some respects, has increased.

What is unquestionable is the growth in power of large-scale businesses operating internationally, and the power of the men who control them. The embodiment of transnational business masculinity has yet to be studied in detail. However, two points leap to the eye. The first is the immense augmentation of bodily powers by technology (air transport, computers, telecommunications), making this, to a certain extent, a 'cyborg' masculinity. The second is the extent to which international business men's bodily pleasures escape the social controls of local gender orders, as their business operations tend to escape the control of the national state.

Production and the division of labour

Capitalism as a social system separates a masculinized sphere of production and circulation from a feminized sphere of consumption and domestic labour (Holter 1997). Most men are defined in this system as 'breadwinners', and one of the most important dynamics in the creation of a global market society is the transformation of growing numbers of men around the world into wage labourers.

The unskilled labourer has essentially one commodity to put on the market: his bodily capacity to labour. Under the imperative of profit, wage labour consumes the body through cumulative fatigue, industrial illness and injury etc. In a common pattern in working-class life, the physical capacity to endure these effects becomes a test of manliness (Donaldson 1991). In the semi-proletarianized world of the 'informal economy' now found on a huge scale in third-world cities, the protections are less, the physical effects stronger, the health outcomes worse.

Many potential wage workers, of course, cannot find jobs. In the political economy of neo-liberalism, 'restructuring' pursued through corporate downsizing, and retrenchment as prescribed by the International Monetary Fund, systematically produces unemployment. There is evidence, from health surveys in countries like Australia (Mathers 1994), that unemployed men have particularly bad health compared with other groups of men—a consequence of poverty, stress, loss of health insurance and social support (see Chapter 10).

Cathexis
Globalization both sustains massive differences in income, and provides the technology for rapid movement around the world. Thus it creates the conditions for sex tourism. Studies of sex tourism emphasize the racialized character of the encounter. The client, typically a first-world man, purchases an 'exotic' experience which reinforces his sense of superiority, as is clearly seen in the international sex trade in Bangkok (Bishop & Robinson 1998). Thus sexuality reproduces the general structure of tourism as a faked cultural encounter, resting on the racialization of world society accomplished by imperialism.

Research inspired by the HIV/AIDS pandemic has documented the global circulation of Western gender forms, such as the urban 'gay' identity and associated sexual practices. But it is also clear (Altman 1996) that Western gay identity has not simply obliterated indigenous forms of homoeroticism. A very complex hybridization with local gender regimes and sexual cultures has occurred, with some new gender configurations springing from the encounter.

Symbolization

With the global circulation of gender images in US-dominated mass communications, a similar effect appears. These images are increasingly reproduced in other parts of the world. Thus boys in Australia start wearing baggy shorts, wear baseball caps backwards, and call each other 'homies'.

At a more profound level, the use of commercial competitive sport as the dominant symbol of hegemonic masculinity appears to be on the rise globally, helped by media overkill on the World Cup and the Olympic Games. At the same time the image of the thrusting, competitive, individualist businessman is being reproduced globally in business media.

However, hybridization occurs as well as displacement. In Australia it is still the cricket hero or the rugby or Australian Rules footballer who is the best known model, not the baseballer or basketballer. But these sports have recently been restructured on the model of American commercial leagues. Local narratives of military heroism, or civil endurance, remain as exemplars of masculinity alongside the global media images. So at the symbolic level there is not a simple homogenization of masculine embodiment. Rather there is a patchwork of increasing complexity, as more and more forms of masculinity are brought into contact, and some of them interact.

IMPLICATIONS FOR GENDER REFORM

Conservative, essentialist ideologies see masculine embodiment as the limit of politics. Masculinity, being 'natural', can never be changed. The research discussed above shows that the opposite is true: masculine embodiment is an arena of politics, open to change and constantly affected by social power. It is, therefore, possible to conceive of a *democratic* politics of masculine embodiment, a politics directed towards social justice and peace.

Many people think that activism around issues of masculinity must follow the model of feminism; that it requires a 'men's movement' mobilizing for gender reform. There are reasons why this model might not be appropriate, which I will explore in Chapter 11. Yet there are many arenas where reform of men's gender practices can be undertaken with some chances of success, some of which directly concern men's bodies.

Health is an important case. It is possible to pursue men's health programs as part of a 'backlash' anti-feminist politics, competing for funding with women's health initiatives. It is also possible to pursue health issues for men in cooperation with women's health initiatives, creating coalitions around shared interests in reducing alcoholism, road trauma, and other toxic consequences of contemporary masculinities (Connell et al. 1999).

Similarly with violence. As the recent UNESCO conference showed, a wide spectrum of anti-violence activism already exists, and some of that directly addresses masculinity (see Chapter 12). The de-militarization of masculinities is a project that will face great opposition, but will also find diverse and widespread support.

The training of boys' bodies in schools is another important arena. Ethnographic studies of schools show that certain areas of school life serve as 'hot spots' or vortices in the construction of masculinities: the discipline system, sports, and some aspects of the gender-divided curriculum (see Chapter 9). Here, too, coalitions around reform agendas are possible.

Reform agendas have tended to underplay issues about bodies. I would emphasise that, given the importance of body-reflexive practice in the construction of gender, the remaking of masculinities is necessarily a re-embodiment.

Change in masculinity requires the invention and the circulation of different body practices. Democratic change requires more caring and egalitarian interactions between bodies, and the exploration of a greater diversity of bodily pleasures. In the next section of the book, moving to a closer focus, I will examine some of those pleasures and practices as they appear in individual lives.

PART 3

BODIES AND DESIRES

5

An iron man

It is a basic proposition of the current research and political work that masculine character is socially constructed, not inherited with the Y chromosome. But it is now clear that the old understanding of how this construction occurred, a more or less smooth and consensual socialization into a unitary male role, is not adequate.

As the research discussed in Chapter 1 shows, there are different kinds of masculine character within society that stand in complex relations of dominance over and subordination to each other. What in earlier views of the problem passed for the 'male sex role' is best seen as hegemonic masculinity, the culturally idealized form of masculine character (in a given historical setting), which may not be the usual form of masculinity at all. It is also clear that masculinities are constructed through processes that are often discontinuous or contradictory (and often experienced as such), for which the model of a 'socializing agency' will not work. This has been most clearly seen in psychoanalytic thinking about the formation of masculinity (Connell 1994).

In this chapter I hope to add to the understanding of hegemonic masculinity and its construction in personal life, by a case study of a champion sportsman. The case raises interesting questions about the interplay between the body and social process, and suggests some lines of thought about sport and its commercialization as a phenomenon of gender and class relations.

I hope also to illustrate the usefulness of the life-history method for studying these social processes. There has been a revival of interest in life-history research, but it tends to be presented as merely the subjective side of social science (e.g. Plummer 1983). I would argue that life-history research gives us a great deal more than this. Properly handled, the theorized life history can be a powerful tool for the study of social structures and their dynamics as they impinge on personal life and are reconstituted by personal action.

BEING A CHAMPION

Steve Donoghue is an 'iron man'. This deliberately pretentious phrase is a technical term in surf sports. The iron-man race at surf carnivals is an event involving a combination of swimming, running and surf-craft riding. Both short and long forms of the race exist; the long races may take four and a half hours to complete. In surf sports, this event occupies a position analogous to a combination of the marathon and the pentathlon in track and field. A champion of the iron-man event holds a great deal of prestige. Steve is one of a very small group of athletes who trade the Australian national championships among themselves.

Steve, in his twenties at the time he was interviewed, lives in a beachfront flat with his girlfriend. He gets up at 4.30 every morning to start his training, which takes four to five hours a day. When it is done he has the rest of the day to himself because he has no job. More exactly, his job is to be an iron man and to market himself as a sports personality.

The training schedule is rigorous and, at his level of performance, essential—as Steve explains in a fascinating passage of the interview:

The main thing . . . is the discipline and motivation side of it. [If] you can't put the five hours in every day, it doesn't matter how old you are—you're not going to win. You've got to have the talent, you've got to have the technique and the ability and everything—and the training is what counts really. Your natural ability only takes you so far, about 60 to 70 per cent of the way, and the rest is where the training comes in, and you've got to be able to. If you are 28 or 30 you have still got to have the time to train. [If you] haven't got business problems, or kids through marriage, or whatever, well, then you'll be right . . . Just as long as you keep loving it, you can keep backing up and wanting to train and really feeling keen the whole time, you've got no troubles.

Where does the love come from?

I don't know. I love the beach. And I love the sun and everything to do with the water. The waves, the water. I love the idea—I've always loved this, even when I was at school—of being able to make a living out of sport. I have loved the idea of not having to work, like a strict nine to five set job, you know, like other people, being indoors . . . Five hours a day is still a lot but it is something which I enjoy that people are not telling me what to do. And there's not a set wage, if I go well I can really make a lot of money out of it. I just like that. I like everything to do with it really. I like the people I get involved with.

This lyrical picture of pleasure and success in the sun and water is characteristic of Steve's self-presentation in the interview. Though there is ideology here, much of the feeling and tone is genuine enough; Steve has realized a schoolboy dream. It comes as something of a shock, then, to find that he also talks of his regime this way:

You're up at 4.30 to go training and that goes most of the day. And you are too tired to go out anyway and you've got to get your rest. It is a pretty disciplined sort of life. It's like being in jail.

This sudden douche of cold water comes in the middle of a discussion about girlfriends. Steve notes that 'a lot of the guys don't have girlfriends'. It is just too hard to combine with training: 'The girl wants to go out with you all the time and, you know, party here and there.' This affects the athlete's performance. So Steve's coach 'doesn't like it, tries to put it down, tries to stop anything serious'. (The coach has a financial interest in his athlete's performance, although Steve does not mention this.)

Steve has a girlfriend, who drifts in and out during the interview. And that seems to be her status in Steve's life, too. She is given a clear message about what really counts for him:

Yes, I've got a girlfriend. I think there is no problem as long as you don't have to go out all the time, [as long as] they understand that, and you've got to take training first, and competition first. That's your living, that's your life. That's what I enjoy the most. It is hard, though . . .

It's good if you have a girlfriend that is involved with sport, involved with the same sort of interest that you've got. Not iron man or like that! But the same sort of, doing the training here and there so it can work out. Well, when you're doing some training, well, they'll do something else. And if you have someone who is completely different, which I have had girlfriends in the past like that, it doesn't seem to work. You might start off all right, but you end up splitting up, because you fight all the time. It gets on their nerves when you are training all the time, you won't go out here and here. It's just rat shit.

What would be the attraction for the 'girls' in Steve's life (the slightly childish language is also characteristic) in having a lifestyle not far removed from that of an armchair? In the first place, this is par for the course in the Australian surfing sub-culture, which is male supremacist to a marked degree (Pearson 1982). If a 'girl' stands up for her own interests, Steve disposes of her and acquires another. As he notes complacently else-where in the interview, he has 'never had trouble' with sexual relationships. And in conventional terms, he is a real catch.

He is handsome, healthy, easygoing, sexually experienced, famous, and on the verge of becoming rich.

Steve's 'job' of being an iron man nets him prizes, sponsorships, and endorsements which add up to a phenomenal income for a young man recently out of high school. Asked where he would see himself in five years' time, he replies simply, 'A millionaire'. His aim is to be this by the time he retires, at about 30. At present he is expanding his sponsorship deals with several large companies, is buying into surf businesses, and has just signed up with a multinational marketing company:

> I just want to keep winning, keep winning, and keep rolling
> the money. So when I do get off I've got something to show
> for what I've done.

Fame is accepted with the same combination of pleasure and complacency as the cash and the sex. He wanted fame, and now he enjoys it. But there is a problem:

> Well, you can go out at night and you've got to set an example
> for yourself. You can't go stupid like other people can. Like
> Joe Blow can get away with drunk-driving charges and no one
> will know. If it was me it would be on the front page. Things
> may be not even that serious. Because if I was just mucking
> around down the street—it's hard really, people think, 'He's
> got to do this', and they set you in a certain way . . . behave
> in your own limits, you can't go wild or anything. If I go
> out at night I can't get in a fight. That can happen because
> people think they can . . . say smart comments, and you
> can hear them, and they try and big-note themselves with
> friends. And I've had fights before where people have, I have
> just snapped. But that's only happened once or twice, that's
> not bad really, considering some of the situations I've had.

This is very much a problem about masculinity. Steve, the exemplar of masculine toughness, finds that his own exemplary status prevents him from doing exactly what his peer group defines as thoroughly masculine behaviour: going wild, showing off, drunk driving, getting into fights, defending his own prestige.

It is also clear in this passage how social the whole business is—the smart-aleck banter among friends, the social pressure that 'sets you in a certain way'. Here we have a vivid glimpse of the production of an exemplary masculinity as a collective practice. It is an accomplishment not of Steve as an individual (throughout this passage he is kicking against the pricks), but of the whole social network in which Steve finds himself enmeshed.

SOFT PATH, HARD GOAL

How did he get to be an exemplar of masculinity? Steve's own account of his childhood and adolescence portrays a simple progression from active child to schoolboy hero to adult champion. He seems to swim endlessly through a warm bath of admiration from family, teachers and friends. His grandfather was a sporting hero and Steve pictures himself as growing up effortlessly in the same mould.

Without denying the reality of this picture, we may question what it means. Steve's childhood was not a conventional idyll. His parents separated when he was young, and he has few memories of the family together. His clearest childhood memory of his father is in a game of hide-and-seek on the day of the weekly visit, when his father vanished and could not be found for 45 minutes. At the least, this is a memory of anxiety. It is hardly over-interpreting to suggest that this remains a haunting memory because the 'lost father' remained a major emotional issue for Steve.

His mother figures as the main adult in Steve's narrative of growing up. She certainly encouraged and organized his swimming, and paid for his travel to championship meetings. He sees her as having the same qualities as him—'intelligent and strong like I am'—and unwilling to be pushed around. There is some identification here, and she remains an emotional presence for him. Asked near the end of the interview his views on violence, he says the only scene he can imagine that would provoke him to murder would be 'if someone killed my mother'.

Yet Steve also records that she moved to another city after her children had left the nest, and the loss does not seem troubling to him. Indeed, he is now pleased to be re-establishing contact with his father, who is taking an interest in his son's career and helping him negotiate sponsorship deals. Steve has not lacked figures to model himself on.

Thus Steve has been inserted into his career by a close network of family, friends and school. He remembers anxiety about moving up to high school—fear of being physically beaten up by the big boys—but soon formed a group of friends and stuck with them right through school. Physically big as a child, he did well in school sporting events and particularly well in swimming. By age 13 he was far enough advanced in formal competition that he gave up football in order to specialize in swimming—a decision that signals the shift from sport as pleasure to sport as a kind of career.

Sport was a career path that elicited a lot of communal support. Steve was the school swimming champion, and his prowess won the district competition for his school. He was 'a bit of a hero' and a leader among his peers, and was treated with indulgence by his teachers. His mother strongly supported his swimming career, which must have shaped household routine from an early stage. Steve's regime as a teenager involved swimming in the morning, school in the day, then more swimming at night. He didn't much want to study, and he completed high school mainly because his friends were still there. When he left school, the study part simply dropped out of his day and the swimming part went on.

At this point Steve was handed over to a new network, and the transition has been complete. Steve hardly sees the once close-knit group of high-school friends any more. Asked what makes someone decide to take up the iron-man event, Steve describes a social practice rather than a choice:

> There is no decision really. It's just that you've got to be round the beach for starters. And you have got to be involved with the surf club, so that narrows it right down. You've got to have a love of the water. You've got to have a swimming

background, pretty well. And you've got to be disciplined and dedicated enough to put the time and work in.

The surf club is a key part of the new network. Steve joined it as a teenager and was thus absorbed into a slightly older peer group, a group of young adult men absorbed in a cult of physical masculinity.

The surf club in Australia is a high-profile voluntary organization with a public-service rationale—it organizes beach lifesaving services—but also with a strong sporting and social flavour. Its networks merge into competitive sport on one side and consumer capitalism (especially advertising and sporting-goods retailing) on the other. In both directions, Steve was brought into contact with 'older guys' and absorbed some of their sexual, commercial, and technical know-how. His first coital experience was organized at the surf club and witnessed by his friends there, when he was about 17:

> *I remember the first time I had sex with a girl; I was at a toga party down at S Surf Club and I was round the rocks and that—pretty funny, yes—all the guys came round and watched . . . I ran back and I was the hero.*

As his career became focussed and he began to earn big money, Steve's peer group once again narrowed and stabilized. 'My friends are the guys I train with.' The replay is almost conscious: 'All the training you do, and all the time you put in, you are around them nearly as much as you are at school.' With his authoritarian trainer in the role of a schoolmaster, the continuity is striking, though the setting is now different. The peer group travels around the country to the big events, and the classroom furnishings are black leather-upholstered couches, expensive video systems, and live-in girlfriends.

THE BODY AND THE SELF

Masculinity is not inherent in the male body; it is a definition given socially, which refers to characteristics of male bodies. If the body is very much at odds with the social definition,

there is trouble, as in the situations of transvestites and trans-
sexuals. If the body complies with the social definition it is
easier for the meanings to take hold; and sometimes the body
cues the social definition. In Steve's case the cue was being
tall and strong as a child.

He remembers this with pleasure. The key to the memory
is the social meaning of being big. Steve's bodily attributes
were appropriated in quite specific social practices. One was
the rough-and-tumble atmosphere of an all-boys school, where
Steve's group depended on him. The element of nurturance
is very interesting: 'We all stuck together; it was really good.
I was sort of—I was always bigger than the rest of the guys, I
sort of looked after them.'

The other practice was competitive sport organized by
adults. Steve's size meant that he won competitive events early
on, consistently enough to define him as a champion in the
making. His body was certainly given this definition before
adolescence, because at 13 he was making the career decision
to specialize in swimming.

In Steve's pseudotechnical discussion of the components of
success, quoted above, he acknowledges both elements. He
calls the bodily cueing 'natural ability', and he theorizes it as
inherited from his grandfather. He also acknowledges the
highly specific social practice that appropriates the body (training, feeling keen, not having business problems) and turns it
into an engine of competitive success.

To call this discussion pseudotechnical is to say that Steve's
representation of this process is highly ideological. (I would
guess he is quoting his coach, whose relation to sporting
ideology is discussed in the next section.) This is not to deny
Steve's precise knowledge of his body and its capacities. All
top-level sports performers do have this knowledge. Indeed, it
is common among adolescent boys engaged in sport, whatever
their level of skill. Teenage football players, for instance,
develop a detailed knowledge of their own bodies' capacities,
and their exact suitability for different positions in the team.

Steve Donoghue is quite eloquent about the particular kind

of skill that is involved in top-level performance in his sport. It is far from being pure brawn:

> *I can spread my energy over a four-hour race to not die, to not have to start up slowly. I can start at a pace and finish at a pace every time. When I swam, I used to do 200 metres, which is four 50-metre laps. I can start off, and any 50 is pretty well to the tenth of a second the same time each lap, and I wouldn't even be looking at a watch . . . It's mental. You've got to be fit to do it, but there are so many guys that are fit and not many are able to do that . . . I'm just lucky naturally. But also distance-wise I can measure the distance out without having to think about it and say, 'Right this pace you are going, you will be able to keep going to the end and you will have no energy left at the end—you will have done the best race you can do over that distance.' And I've just done that all the time.*

What Steve calls 'being lucky naturally' is in fact a skill developed by ten years of hard practising.

There is more to this than a technical knowledge of skills and capacities. Steve's whole person has become caught up in practices that centre on his body and its performances. Asked 'Where would you like to be as Steve? Nothing to do with business or money, just you?', he fumbles and then starts to grapple with this nexus:

> *I haven't even thought about it. I might be just the way I am, but I don't, I never look to the future. Everything is—not day to day—but season to season. I am more interested in winning and racing than anything, and that takes up my whole time, all the preparation and the time I put in. Last winter I was up at T [surf resort]; we were training five hours a day, and the only thing I was thinking about was getting through that day and getting to the next day. Having to make my body, too much energy and not enough rest, to be functional at as good a rate for the next day's training session. That is all I would be thinking about.*

In effect, the body becomes the focus of the self in quite a radical way. Social life is drastically curtailed to suit the logic of peak bodily performance. As Steve remarked, 'It's like being in jail.' Even more strikingly for a fit young heterosexual, sexual life is monitored and constricted because of its effect on performance. The kind of regime Steve sustained at school, and sustains now, leaves little room or energy for interests outside his sport. Even his casual peer group life is centred on others in the sport. Despite coming from a bourgeois background, he had little interest in schoolwork, seems to have no cultural interests beyond popular music, and cannot sustain a relationship with a woman who has interests outside of sport.

The picture, then, is of a psychological focus on the body together with a severely constricted social world and an impoverished cultural world. This is confirmed by a series of questions, asked at the end of the interview, about Steve's views on current issues:

Feminists?

I don't like the ones that dress up in men's clothes and that sort of stuff, but I just think I don't mind women doing that sort of stuff. I'm the sort of guy that opens the car door for a girl all the time.

Gay men?

I've got no gay friends—I don't think I have. I'm not into television and hairdressing and anything like that . . . As long as they keep to themselves and away from me I'm happy. I'm against them really. I can't see the reason why they are—I can't understand it—but a lot of people say they are born that way so I don't know. I'm [with a laugh] not into bashing them or anything like that.

Politics?

Nothing to do with it whatsoever. The last vote they had here I didn't even know it was on that day. I was down the beach in the surf.

In this bleached, featureless world centred on the care and maintenance of his body, punctuated by races, it is not surprising that Steve's only tangible goal is to collect dollars: 'Keep winning, keep winning, and keep rolling the money.' He has in view no use for the money except being able to live in comfort, so his only way of defining a purpose is to pick an arbitrary figure. Becoming a millionaire is 'just a goal, just something that I might aim for'; he is almost apologetic about its arbitrariness. The business of winning has consumed his life. With everything subordinated to bodily performance as the means of success, there is nothing very tangible that the success is for. So a goal has to be invented within the mechanism of races and dollars to give Steve the impression that his effort is leading to something worthwhile.

This cycle could, of course, be disrupted. The most likely disruptions are an injury (Steve has had some); a pregnancy (Steve could easily afford an abortion but the girlfriend of the day might insist on marriage and in that case would have a lot of social pressure behind her); or the emergence of a new champion who overshadows Steve and thus undermines his worth to sponsors. The last will certainly happen in time, but Steve has specialized in an event in which champions are good for a relatively long period. He has researched this point and has concluded that an iron man does not peak until 'around 30 or close to . . . so in that way I've got at least five years left'.

WANTING TO WIN: THE IDEOLOGY OF COMPETITIVE SPORT

Steve's attempts to make sense of his experience—his daily life is a highly unusual one for a young man—draw heavily on the ideological complex that has developed around the combination of competitive sport and commercial mass media.

The transformation of traditional recreations into commercial spectacles got under way in the nineteenth century and in the twentieth century became a powerful process, first in the rich countries and then globally. Gruneau and Whitson's (1993) study of the Canadian national sport, ice hockey, provides the classic analysis of the political and economic networks that have come to be enmeshed in sport. In this respect, surf sports are now like stadium sports. This commercial nexus gives Steve Donoghue his livelihood, so it is, not surprisingly, his first port of call for interpretations.

Very much in the foreground is the business of winning. The classic Olympic ethic of valuing the participation rather than the victory—always contradictory in competitive sports—is ignored and with it amateurism. Steve has always seen sport as a way of earning a living. To do that he has to win, keep winning, and be focussed on winning all the time.

The basis for this is 'natural talent' and being 'lucky' in one's capacities. This is media talk: it is the language in which a champion projects modesty in a television or newspaper interview after a big victory. The talent has to be developed, and Steve claims to have added to what nature gave him. It is again characteristic of media constructions of championship that this claim is a moral one. Steve acquires ideological virtue by his rigorous training regime; this is what he insists makes a champion.

Steve does not talk much about his coach in the interview, but the coach's presence is clear. Leading coaches often function as organic intellectuals of commercial sport, articulating a meaning for, and a public defence of, the practices in which the whole industry is engaged. Coaches are likely to be a good deal older than the youthful champions. To a considerable extent their success as coaches depends more on their skills as ideologists, persuading their charges to stick to the training regime and psyching them up for big events, than on their technical knowledge.

Steve gives an interesting glimpse of his coach's ideological tactics:

When I compete for a big race I get myself worked up. My coach has always said he used tactics like hating people—well, not hate—but, I suppose hate the opposition through things they have said about me. And he uses that to get me riled

up to win, thinks I always get better when I am angry. And
he has used that, he has even put that in [media] articles
and stuff.

Clearly Steve's coach is trying to articulate masculinity and
sporting performance through aggression. It is a common tactic
in body-contact sports like football.

I have the impression that this is not a very appropriate
device for Steve. He is not an aggressive character. The tone
in which he discusses his sport is euphoric, not mean; he talks
more about loving the water than wanting to do down enem-
ies. He is certainly competitive, but that is a settled practice,
a feature of the organization of his life, rather than an out-
growth of hostility. When Steve talks about the psychological
side of competition, he inflects it in a rather different way. He
talks of 'mental toughness' and his ability to 'control the pain'
and to 'make my body believe that I am not hurting as much
as I am'.

Again this is borrowed language. Steve got these terms
from sport psychologists who tested him and explained to him
their ideas about why he won. But it is probably closer to the
particular version of masculinity that Steve has constructed
for himself around the lonely business of long-distance sporting performance. This is an inward-turned competitiveness,
focussed on the self.

The commercialization of sport gives Steve one other way
of seeing himself:

The thing with sponsors is that they are after an individual.
The people I am sponsored with, except the beer company,
it's just me. It's no one else to do with the surf, or anything
like that. So obviously they were after what I had done, and
also my personality, my looks.

You haven't ever felt like a body being marketed?

No not really. I'm an individual. It's funny, like even with
board-riding there might be a bloke who is not as good as
the other guy but his personality, and just the way his

*charisma—he'll get a bigger amount of sponsorship than the
other guy. It's just an individuality.*

The irony of this, given what we have already seen of the
impoverished social and cultural life Steve leads, hardly needs
underlining. A 'personality', in media terms, is simply someone
who has publicity; it is a question of recognizability, not of
content. So even Steve's claim to individuality is a standard
package constructed for him by his employers.

REFLECTIONS

Steve lives an exemplary version of hegemonic masculinity. To
live it does not mean to understand it. Steve has great trouble
giving an account of masculinity when directly asked to explain
a remark that 'men should be men':

> *I don't know, I really don't know. I just meant that as—
> I think just being strong and not—I was talking about gays,
> I think. I don't know. I don't even know why I said it
> really, just came out.*

What do you think it means to be a man, for you?

> *Not be a gay; I don't know. I've done interviews on that sort
> of stuff before, people said, 'You're scared of spiders and all
> that sort of stuff?' Yes I am; I have got fears like any
> other people. I am scared of heights. So I don't think any of
> that has got anything to do with being a man.*

The best definition he can think of is 'be strong' and 'not be
a gay'. Other respondents in our study, less exemplary than
Steve, have much more complex and fluent answers to this
question.

The exclusion of homosexual desire from the definition of
masculinity is, of course, a key feature of modern hegemonic
masculinity. It makes sense for Steve to grasp at this straw,
especially because his life has long been substantially homo-
social (i.e. an all-boys' school, a masculinized surf club and peer
group, and a masculinized sport). His consciousness of this

pattern is tellingly shown by his specific (and quite unnecessary) exclusion of iron-man events as possible sports for his girlfriends. It is a familiar point that there is a lot of homosexual affect floating around in such milieux. Steve simply blanks this out as we saw in his response to the subject of gay men.

To say that a particular form of masculinity is hegemonic means that it is culturally exalted and that its exaltation stabilizes the gender order as a whole. To be culturally exalted, the pattern of masculinity must have exemplars who are celebrated as heroes. Steve certainly enacts in his own life some of the main patterns of contemporary hegemonic masculinity: the subordination of women, the marginalization of gay men, and the connecting of masculinity to toughness and competitiveness. He has also been celebrated as a hero for much of his life, in school and in adult sport. He is being deliberately constructed now as a media exemplar of masculinity by the advertisers who are sponsoring him.

It is here that the contradictions poke out. Being an exemplar of masculinity actually forbids Steve to do many things that his peer group and culture define as masculine: 'it's like being in jail'. Steve experiences this prohibition as a very tangible pressure. Similarly, sustaining the training regime that yields the bodily supremacy, giving him his status as a champion, is incompatible with the kind of sexual and social life that is expected by affluent young men: 'you end up splitting up'. In this case Steve's coach articulates the prohibition, and Steve manoeuvres around it as best he can.

At a deeper level, the body-reflexive practice (see Chapter 4) that sustains Steve's performance is contradictory. Consider the focussing of both his social and his psychological life on the body, and the inward-turned competitiveness that seems related to his particular sport. There is a definite narcissism here, something often observed about athletes. This is a problem given the dominant cultural construction of masculinity as outward turned and denying the subjective.

Even more of a problem, the narcissism is necessarily unstable, unable to rest in self-admiration or indulgence (which would destroy the performance). In Steve's construction of competition (for instance his remarks about controlling pain), the decisive triumph is over oneself and specifically over one's body. The magnificent machine of Steve's physique has meaning only when subordinated to the will to win. And the will to win, as we have already seen, is a curiously hollow construction in Steve's psychological makeup. The will to win does not arise from personal 'drive' (a familiar word in sport talk that Steve, tellingly, does not use at all). It is given to him by the social structure of sporting competition. It is his meaning, as a champion.

So we are returned to the social structures in which masculinities are produced. Indeed, we are led to see masculinity as an aspect of social structure, not just a form of personal character. As a configuration of gender relations, here meshed with consumer capitalism, hegemonic masculinity appropriates Steve's body and gives it a social definition. But it does this in ways that are full of contradiction, visible even behind the euphoria of Steve's tale of pleasure and success.

The long-term effect is hard to judge, but the short-term effect is clear. Steve gets his pleasure and success at the cost of his adulthood. I have remarked on oddly childish turns of phrase and thought and on the psychological continuity of Steve's life since the beginning of high school. He is, of course, young. But most other men his age are facing the problems of earning a livelihood, constructing long-term relationships, building households, making hard choices, and facing social issues.

Steve has been taken in hand by the institutions of competitive sport and commerce and protected from common issues and problems. Though Steve cannot see it, for he has little experience of the world, his employers genuinely do not want an individual. They want someone to occupy a spot constructed by gender symbolism and the needs of commerce: a handsome, happy, nicely spoken, beach-sport hero who will make no difficulties about advertising their products. (Steve is, for example, sponsored by a beer company, which not everyone would see as a responsible move by a sporting champion.) At the moment he neatly fits the spot, and as long as he keeps up his winning status and his image, the money will keep rolling in and Steve will be preserved in his extended adolescence.

6

'I threw it like a girl': Some difficulties with male bodies

Exemplary masculinities in Western societies are typically defined by a specific body-reflexive practice: sport, violence, heterosexual performance, bodybuilding. The commercial promotion of these exemplars is a striking feature of how hegemony is maintained in gender relations. Yet closer examination shows bodies repeatedly breaking the bounds or failing the uses proposed for them. The hitters in football become too violent, the bodybuilders become too narcissistic, the studs grow tired, the filmed hunk grows so unbelievable that self-parody is the only way out.

So, as well as studying the social construction of masculinity, we need to study the reverse—the disassembling, unmaking or disruption of those configurations of practice we call masculinities. This is not just intellectual deconstruction, it is something that happens in practice. And in this process, bodies are centrally involved. In this chapter I will explore these issues through episodes in the lives of two Australian men who in different ways found themselves in tension with hegemonic masculinity, after having at least partially engaged with it.

LOOKING AT JELLY: ADAM SINGER

Adam Singer, in his early thirties at the time he was interviewed, is a professionally qualified technical specialist working
in the city office of a large organization. He entered this
organization directly from his training and has been promoted
uneventfully inside it. In economists' language, he is firmly
located in an internal labour market. As a university-trained
specialist he is one of the professional elite in his industry, in
contrast to his father who worked his way up to a supervisory
position by long hours of work from a starting point in a
manual trade.

To this extent Adam is a paradigm of the technically skilled,
highly educated employee, and his interview helps understand
the gender order in the modernized sectors of the economy.
In some of his comments on social issues Adam takes the
character of modernity on himself. He holds clearly defined
progressive views on sexual politics, for instance expressing
support for feminism—without making the exception of
'extremists' that men commonly do. He ignores the consol-
ations of religion, and works on his relation to the world in
the context of growth-movement 'workshops'.

More post-modern than modern, perhaps, is his cool
relationship to the job. There is no 'calling' here. He went
into his profession because his parents wanted him in a technical job, and other options looked worse. He is annoyed by
the supervision and control that working for a large organization entails, and has agreeable but not close relationships with
workmates.

The emotional engagement lacking from work is found in
full measure in sexuality. Adam is one of those people invoked
by Sartre (1943) when he criticizes Freud's assumption that
sexual motives govern all lives, but acknowledges that some
people can shape their lives around libido. 'I was very sexual
from as young as I can remember,' Adam says. He offers plenty
of corroborating detail: 'explorations' with other children,
sexual games with peers in primary and secondary school, a
number of relationships with women and men in adulthood,
an active though changing masturbatory life.

The early stages seem very conventional. Adam's parents were not exactly progressive; Adam recalls his mother as denying his sexuality, his father beating him for exposing his bottom. The only unusual thing is how much detail of childhood sexuality Adam recalls: from his curiosity about a baby girl to the 'nudist colony' set up by the boys at primary school in the bush beyond the school fence. The boys also seem to have been a conventional lot, jeering at the girls—'you've got a slot there, you could put a penny in it!'—and exposing their penises to the girls in class. The picture of the collective construction of masculinity, and the sexualization of this process, is familiar.

Puberty was not a big deal. 'We were sexual in primary school . . . so in high school nothing really changed.' But there was an institutional change, the secondary school was a different social setting. In another part of the interview Adam used a striking phrase for this: going to high school 'I felt powerful'.

The school was segregated, so Adam's explorations here were more likely to be with boys. He describes regular sessions with his close school friends, locking themselves in a room and exploring emotions and bodies—though not to orgasm. The age structure of the high school (a six-year institution in Australia, Year 7 to Year 12) introduced him to 'men', that is, post-pubescent students who became emotionally important to him in more ways than one. He also acquired a few girlfriends, going as far as kissing them but not beyond.

Going to university broke Adam's connection with his youthful peer group. He discovered orgasm, by masturbation, and that became an active part of his sexuality. He built a platonic relationship with 'a girl', a fellow student. Equally deliberately he began a relationship with a man, to find out if he was gay. Then he travelled with a woman and 'lost his virginity' to her. Back home, now in employment, he had an intermittent sexual relationship with another woman; then fell in love with an artist and had a red-hot relationship for a month before being dropped. Next came a long on-again off-again relationship with a man who was more in love with Adam than Adam was with him. Then some shorter relationships.

The picture Adam paints—warts and all, he does not spare himself—is of a struggle to build sexual relationships with people he cares about but who, with one brief and brilliant exception, do not give him the combination of sexual excitement and cultural recognition that he really wants. As an adult, Adam wants sexuality in the context of a relationship; he is not interested in 'fast-lane' sex. But somehow the elements of sexual fulfilment and secure human relationship keep falling apart.

By the time he was a student Adam had in mind that he might be gay, and I now want to turn to the experiences that lay behind this. It is easy to find pointers in his childhood to why he might develop a sense of difference. They include an early willingness to be 'eccentric', a history of pre-pubescent and adolescent erotic play with boys, being warned off 'exploring' with a little girl by an angry parent, and feeling 'smothered' when he kissed a bigger girl. But it is interesting that Adam does not himself present this as a pre-history of gayness, and he is surely right. There is nothing here outside the experience of many boys who become exclusively heterosexual.

Conventional psychiatric explanations locate origins of homosexuality in damaged relationships with the father and over-identification with the mother. Contrary to this picture, Adam's story suggests an unusually successful ego-development that allows separation from both parents, and allows resistance to the cultural pressures towards compulsory heterosexuality. Adam explored sexuality, and made his commitments, and has had to live out the consequences.

But we should not too much individualize this choosing. It was vital for Adam that 'being gay' was an identity that was ready and waiting for him. It was already defined by the cultural dynamics and sexual politics of the previous twenty years.

Part of the cultural dynamic impinging on Adam was a social definition of the body that is the object of cathexis.

Adam describes his ideal lover facetiously: a 'big muscly man who I feel I can cuddle up to, and I love being nurtured'.

There is more than a joke here. It is clear that this image is emotionally effective, that the combination of affect and body-image has autobiographical depth. In high school he admired the older adolescent 'men'. In one of his unsuccessful adult relationships he was turned off by a lover's 'emaciated' body. He wishes for a 'really strong, healthy body' for himself. He dislikes 'real queens'.

The physical imagery here is gendered, and the gender is inherently embodied. Adam does not cathect a category abstracted from its bodily presence. The embodiment is even a conventional one. We see a lot of 'big muscly men' and 'strong, healthy bodies' in beer advertisements, though there the images are coded heterosexual. What is different here is the relationship entered (or imagined). This is so disruptive in gender terms as to pose questions about how Adam constructed gender or had gender constructed for him.

Adam's childhood was spent in a conventional suburban nuclear family: mother close and omnipresent, father more distant and admired. Adam recalls 'running out and waving goodbye when he went to work. I used to love him coming home and love watching him go to work'. There was a lot of jealousy with an older brother, and this seems to have been part of a generally tense household with a lot of bickering between family members.

Right at the end of the interview Adam lets out that his father battered his mother, and that scared him. He tells a vivid story of his father losing his temper, when Adam had put weeds in the coalpit, and rubbing dirt in Adam's mouth. The anger rather than the physical violence is the point of the story.

This is the kind of relationship envisaged in the classical psychoanalytic theory of the oedipus complex, the core of Freudian theories of the formation of masculinity. Fear of the father drives a repression of desire and a process of identification. Oedipal emotions were certainly present. Adam remembers his relationship with his father changing and becoming 'closed', though it is not clear at what age.

And this memory comes out:

> *He bought my brother a cricket bat for Christmas and he wouldn't buy me one. He'd say I couldn't play cricket. And things like throwing a ball. How a man throws a ball is different to how a woman throws a ball. I didn't want to throw a ball in front of my Dad because I knew it wouldn't look right, it wouldn't be like the way a good, strong boy should throw it. And once, I remember, I was brave enough to throw it. And he made fun of me and said I threw it like a girl.*

Here the interpersonal emotions are fused with the bodily activity, the skill or lack of it. The split is in Adam's presence and perception. He has learnt how to be both inside his body throwing and outside his body watching its gendered performance ('I knew it wouldn't look right'). The body-reflexive practice of sport becomes the medium of a declaration of difference, with the emotional charge of the oedipal situation behind it.

School added a collective dimension to the differentiation of masculine and feminine, with the boys' nudist colony, the teasing of the girls, the all-male high school. By high school Adam had an idea of masculine and feminine character. The 'eccentricity' of his childhood now became 'silliness', and it was suspect since it was feminine.

> *In primary school there were some real bullies . . . always in a different class . . . and I knew just not to go near them, and that was OK. In high school they were just everywhere . . . They were very strong and you couldn't get in their way [without being bullied]. They were in my particular class as well as being throughout the whole form, so it meant pulling back from my freedom to do whatever I wanted to do. Also I became much more aware of male roles in high school, because there were men who were students*

there. I felt much less free for the feminine parts of my personality to come out and the silliness to come out.

What do you mean, 'there were men' as students?

Well, I'd look at different students, especially in the more senior forms, and see that they were students just like me, but their maleness was very very strong. And I was hesitant to do anything, or some things that might be criticized as being a sissy type of way of behaving.

One could hardly ask for a clearer definition of the relationship between hegemonic and subordinated masculinities. Several mechanisms of hegemony can be seen here at the same time: physical intimidation, internalized constraint and cathexis (for Adam unquestionably desires these 'men', as already noted). And despite the growth-movement jargon that the adult Adam Singer introduces to his narration ('feminine parts of my personality'), the sense of adolescent bodies in interaction is strong.

In the school as well as the family, Adam did not fit the template. It seems that he came to see himself as having a spoiled masculinity. He recalls a moment when such a perception came to him. It is not surprising that it was a moment of sport, informal this time:

We were running around the beach or something, tackling and playing around. And my image, as I looked down at my legs and I saw that my thighs were fat—I was tackling or something—and they'd wobble like jelly. And I'd never noticed them like that before, and that's something I've still got embarrassment about . . . That also went along with being bigger in the hips than other boys, and smaller in the chest . . . Made me feel under-confident as a male at that time.

What is happening here is more than the attaching of a social meaning to a body. There is very specifically a bodily doing, a physical practice in which social meanings are called out, not just received.

Adam's body is subverting Adam's fantasy of his body; it is immediately a limit to his agency. But it is more than just a limit, a negation. The texture, shape and performance of his body become parts of an alternative practice, directing him into another pattern of relationship. Not out into another cultural world—hegemonic images of masculinity remain important to Adam. They are cathected; and that cathexis becomes the main axis of Adam's sexual life.

This story has elements familiar in the politics of women's bodies, especially commercial attempts to create disgust with bodies as they now are and the offer of commercial remedies in the form of diets, exercise regimes, fashion and cosmetic surgery. The rise of men's fashion magazines and the marketing of 'fitness' products to men suggest this dynamic is becoming more explicit and more universal.

Adam's earliest memories are little idylls: lying on a foot-path watching ants; walking on a beach on a hot night looking at the phosphorescence. They are also very physical, which is characteristic of Adam's memories. This is why his interview is so suggestive for a history of bodies. His narrative shows particularly clearly how, in the construction of masculinities, body and society are linked through body-reflexive practices (Chapter 2).

The body-reflexive practices here include symbolism. Adam's representations of his body are both visual and tactile: 'jelly . . . embarrassment', 'bigger in the hips' etc. The theme of being looked at is significant in his construction of self, from childhood exhibitionism to the pleasure he took as an adult in being drawn by a lover who was an artist. Similarly, sexual arousal and disgust (the 'emaciated' lover) are radically social (consider the great cross-cultural variation in what is attractive), but also and inescapably bodily. They involve lubrication, engorgement of erectile tisses, panting, nausea.

Bodies also come into relationship as bodies, not just as means of communication. Body talk is no metaphor in Adam's life. When he travelled with a lover, they slept in the same bed but slept head to foot. Adam was keeping an element of distance in the relationship. He was not symbolizing distance this way, he was doing distance. The body as material object, its activity as material practice, are socially consequential in their own right.

BURNING UP THE BODY: TIP SOUTHERN

Tip Southern is about ten years younger than Adam Singer, and just finishing his professional training. He comes from a more affluent though equally tense family background. His parents separated when he was seven, and he grew up in his mother's care. After a couple of years of economic struggle his mother remarried. Tip's stepfather was a well-off professional and the household moved when he got a senior appointment in another city.

Tip's relationship with his mother seems to have been warm. He tells of camping trips together, and she accepted his adolescent rebellions. His stepfather did not. Tip has a memory of a good relationship with his father and like many children involved in separations could not accept the substitute. He seems to have found more and more reasons to dislike his stepfather.

By the time he moved into high school the conflict was open. His first year there was disastrous: fights with both parents, smoking, sex, and finally getting arrested for shoplifting. (Tip notes that his parents never knew how much he did.)

But his parents' class privilege gave them an overwhelming answer. Tip was 'shipped off' to an elite boarding school. These schools have powerful systems of social control and character formation, vehement regimes, which Tip encountered right away:

> First day I was there, I had just had a meeting with the
> Headmaster, the Housemaster, and all that. And I was in
> my new school uniform and with my mother, and you know,
> I suppose, nervous as hell. But on the other hand I was
> anxious to, you know, make a good impression, and get into
> it, and I wanted to redeem myself for my past naughtiness.
> So I went there, got into the work and I did all right. But

*immediately I was there I was hung upside down by my legs
with really painful rope, I was diked in every single toilet.*

*I arrived there and this master and my mother were there,
and they handed me over to this guy called Peter Sinclair,
who was in Third Form [Year 9], a charming young chap,
good family. And you know it was, 'Tip meet Peter', 'How
do you do?', 'Peter take good care of him, show him around
the House, get him a locker, look after him.' 'Yes sir, no
worries sir, nice to meet you Mrs Southern.' They disappear.
Biff bam! [details of the violence follow] I used to have bruises
on my arms, little bruises on my arms all the time.*

Did that happen to all the kids?

*Oh, all of us in First Form [Year 7], and all the people
who had come before us. Occasionally you would get beaten
up badly, at least bad for a schoolkid. You got thrown across
rooms a couple of times.*

There is more, but this extract makes the point. Tip ran
into systematic, institutionalized bullying, which involved a
good deal of physical violence by the bigger boys against the
smaller. A cult of football in this school legitimated masculine
violence, and the staff presumably condoned the bullying as a
means of toughening newcomers and keeping order.

What we see here is the construction of a particular type
of masculinity by a kind of institutionally managed terror.
Where such a regime is working well, the entrants become
recruited into the regime, and this happened to a degree with
Tip. He records not only the terror but also the camaraderie
of boarding-school life, the creation of friendships which were
capable of lasting into adult life. But he did not become
complicit in the bullying of small boys. When he was
appointed head of house in his final year he put an end to the
practice. In this respect he was an agent of modernization.
Private schools have been moving towards more liberal disciplinary regimes and more academic emphases for some time.

In another direction, however, Tip went far beyond what
the most liberal principals would care for. In the senior years

of secondary school he got into a clique of boys who made a name for themselves:

> *Fairly sophisticated, very good families, the people in my group. We were all very radical and into punk music and drugs and cars and the whole scene. Towards the end of Sixth Form [Year 12] it was a very tight little group, full of energy, wild, we just partied on. It was really, really good, it was ideal, sort of thing, just the energy, it was unbelievable the things we got up to, we had a really good time. We were called the Sick Patrol, and we used to dress in the most outlandish clothes imaginable, and crash parties and get kicked out and be completely offensive and monopolize these parties totally, arrive in a fleet of cars. And we always had this fan club of women, not so much in a sexual sense but just . . . we were good friends of a lot of the girls but there was a lot of solidarity between the boys. In a really good sense, it wasn't a very masculine trip, in terms of friendship it wasn't ocker . . . and we used to get pissed when we partied together but . . . we were more into music . . . we just had a really good time, we were all radical rebels and didn't agree with the system, smoked lots of dope and we still all did fairly well at school, they were a good bunch.*
>
> *We were pretty radical, rebellious, angry young men. Men with a mission but partying full on all the time. Towards the end it was just one big blur. Binge after binge after binge . . . It was just full on, we were getting pissed all the time; really, really drunk but handling it because we were so full of energy. You don't get hangovers when you are that young and that much on the go. Every day was a new challenge, a new party. Go for days and days and days pissed as farts, and just be having a good time. Very interesting.*

It is a remarkable picture of a bunch of rich and irresponsible kids being as obnoxious as they knew how. Yet there is something more to it as well, an element of social protest and critique of 'the system'. In an earlier generation Tip would have seen himself as part of a student movement. Tip's protest was politically disconnected, almost privatized. 'Radical' no longer meant left wing.

At a loss what to do after leaving school, Tip went home. Wearing punk haircut and earrings he was not likely to impress his stepfather, and they fought. After a few months of that, Tip set off for a famous university overseas. He soon made the right connection:

> *In a very sleazy part of town, all these prostitutes . . . I had to walk through there to piss, and in the toilet some guy turns round to me and says 'Do you want to buy some hash?', and I just went 'You beauty' . . . And from that moment on the city was divine. It was just full on, going out all the time, bars, drinking lots of nice stuff, having the wildest parties at the flat—really, really heavy, wild parties, and punking around. I had bright red hair, dyed, wore outrageous clothes and lived in a shit mess in this flat with my pet rat . . . This girl in the flat used to make the wildest punch you can imagine . . . My God, all these young American girls who'd come to these parties fresh out of college . . . they went away ruined people . . . One night we had about five girls in the bed and we couldn't go in there because all these girls had died in the bedroom after this punch. I could hardly stand up at the time and it was really disconcerting to pass out and go to sleep.*

At this point Tip was defining himself in rebellion, doing reasonably dangerous things with drugs, trading on his physique and youthful energy. It was a public display of recklessness that was a kind of exemplary masculinity; he sardonically refers to himself at this time as a 'man on the move'.

The display has an interesting relationship with the display of exemplary masculinity by Steve Donoghue, the 'iron man' discussed in Chapter 5. Tip was doing everything Steve could not do because of his training regime and his fame. Where Steve felt trapped in his public image, Tip let go and constructed an image out of his uncontrollability. There is a polarity within hegemonic masculinity between the wholesome and the unwholesome, the beach hero versus the pet rat.

Since it is easy to see the sex-drugs-and-rock'n'roll number as an individual choice of Tip's, I would emphasize again the collective dimension. The Sick Patrol as a group crashed the respectable parties; and Tip's overseas adventures did not really begin until he connected with a network. It was a collective practice that constructed men as central and women as peripheral, as Tip himself notes in wrestling with the idea of the 'fan club'. This was not a straightforward institutionalized patriarchy—the girls were expected to have a good time themselves. But that was up to them. Tip still talks of girls in terms of the supply: 'plenty of girls'.

Following the classic sowing-wild-oats script, Tip dropped out of his courses and ran out of money. He went home again, was sent to another college, ran round the same cycle. And then the life-support system was switched off. His mother left his stepfather, the money ceased to flow and Tip washed ashore in the big city needing to earn his living.

> *I tried to get jobs. 'What are you qualified for?' Nothing. I didn't have any good clothes with me because I had been roughing it for a long time . . . So I never got jobs. I don't think I looked like the most respect—I mean, I was very undernourished in a general way, I was taking a lot of drugs, a lot of acid, drinking a lot. I have got this picture of me in my room hidden away of myself in the worst state that you can imagine: big stoned, swollen red eyes, a huge stye in this eye, and just the most pallid face. I was drinking far too much, taking really nasty drugs, really dirty acid, eech! And just got real bogged down with it all. And finally I just knew I had to do something drastic.*

So Tip, having traded for years on his body's resilience and energy, finally found its limits; and these limits made a personal and relational crisis.

What he did was not as 'drastic' as he suggests. He enrolled for a degree, with a friend from school. He re-established friendship with his mother. He has gained some academic success. And he has established a relationship with a young woman, another student in the same program, which has already lasted much longer than any other in his experience. They have to 'work on' the relationship, but it is working for Tip. 'I have settled down in many ways.'

Tip's rehabilitation was partly physical, a matter of getting off the drugs and doing some physical labour. This bodily change was sustained by a class and gender practice. His access to university was guaranteed by his elite educational background, and actually mediated by the ruling-class network (the friend from boarding school).

His shift from the world of the Sick Patrol and the pet rat was also a matter of gender. He moved from a masculinized world where women were peripheral into one with a stronger presence of women (his mother, his new lover). At the time of interview there was still a sense of fragility about this accomplishment; Tip was worried that 'at the end of the year everything falls apart'.

His remaking was not a politicized reformation of masculinity in the style of the men's movements discussed in Chapter 11. It was more a remodelling after de-toxification.

That may be a useful metaphor for certain kinds of reconstructions of masculinity, for instance the limited changes often seen by those who work with violent offenders. But it leaves open the question of the gender practice that is to follow the remodelling, and the kinds of collective practice that might sustain more profound reconstructions.

REFLECTIONS

Freud writes of 'somatic compliance' in hysteria, the complicity of the body in producing the symptoms needed to communicate distress. In these two cases we seem to see the inverse: two illustrations of somatic non-compliance in the project of hegemonic masculinity.

With Adam Singer we see bodily performance (throwing like a girl) and body shape and texture (jelly) provide cues to difference from hegemonic masculinity. They do not *determine* a different masculinity, since the cues may or may not be taken up in practice. In Adam's life they were taken up, especially in a sexual practice addressing hegemonic masculinity as an object of desire.

With Tip Southern we see the youthful body first energizing the display of exemplary masculinity, then undermining it. The display itself undermined the body (red eyes, pallid face, stye) and made the practice impossible to sustain.

These departures from hegemonic masculinity are by no means free-form. They take definite shapes; and structures of social relations are crucial to the shapes they take.

Thus the historically recent restructuring of cathexis that produced a straight/gay dichotomy, and gave a strong social definition to the 'gay' location in these relations, are major determinants of the course Adam's life has taken. The structure of class relations defined the possibilities followed by Tip. His remodelling was undertaken through a class practice, just as the construction of masculinity in the vehement regime of his school was a consequence of the collective class practice of families and institution. There is a close parallel in the class/gender practices studied by Heward (1988) in the case of an English boarding school.

So the construction and reconstruction of masculinities is far from being a question of occupying positions in a purely discursive space. The discursive construction of masculinity is hemmed in from two directions; or, to change the metaphor, is only one dimension of a process which also operates in the dimensions of body-reflexive practice and of social structure. Indeed we could not speak of hegemonic masculinity, we could not define the discursive position itself, without the dimension of structure.

Accordingly the political significance of the disassembling of hegemonic masculinity cannot be understood just as a matter of transgression, of violated positioning. It is a question of where the transgression is heading: whether it is, for instance, as self-limiting as the adventures of the Sick Patrol. To define a transformative project, from the point of view of ending oppressive constructions of gender, requires a structural concept—the concept of equality.

The concept of equality has become an unfashionable point

of departure for social theory, but it still has its use. A major problem in the past has been that emphasis on equality has gone together with a monolithic view of social structure. This is unnecessary, and is being transcended in contemporary thinking. Current theory recognizes a considerable diversity of structures. It is possible to discuss the state of inequality in several structures at the same time, even to measure them comparatively. The criterion of equality, without homogenizing difference, gives a generalizable point of reference for talking about the politics of transgression.

From this point of view, Adam's gender practice, unpolitical as it is, has an egalitarian potential that Tip's, as yet, does not. There is not much in Tip's history that militated against the reproduction of the inequalities of class and gender with which he began. Indeed the bodily effects looked more like ending the transgressor. Tip's negotiation of more peaceable relationships with women in the most recent phase of his life does, however, point to new possibilities.

Adam's practice more vigorously disconnects elements of the hegemonic construction of gender. To that extent his practice exerts pressure on gender hierarchy. Adam himself is unlikely to turn this into a program of reform. But what he and others like him are doing opens possibilities that others may pursue. The politics is implicit, but the direction of movement is clear.

Far from being the natural object invoked by many current celebrations of true masculinity, hegemonic masculinity is a complex articulation of social structure, discourse and bodily activity. These two cases show how the bodily activity in particular can play a part in forcing a dis-articulation that is experienced as crisis or failure of masculinity, and that may lead to different patterns of gender practice.

To recognize this is to see that the project of reforming men's gender practice is more complex than most masculinity-therapy assumes. But it also suggests that there are more points where the project of reconstruction can be launched, or gain purchase, than is usually recognized.

7

Man to man: Homosexual desire and practice among working-class men

Written with M.D. Davis and G.W. Dowsett

In contemporary Western society, the most symbolically important distinction between masculinities is in terms of sexuality.
Hegemonic masculinity is emphatically heterosexual, homosexual masculinities are subordinated. This subordination not
only involves the oppression of homosexual boys and men,
sometimes by violence, it also involves the informal policing
of heterosexual boys and men. Homophobia, in the sense of
cultural abuse of homosexuality and the fear of being thought
homosexual, is an important mechanism of hegemony in gender
relations.

This is the pattern of prejudice which gay politics has
attacked and, to a certain extent, overcome. Anti-discrimination
laws exist in a number of Western countries and criminal
sanctions against homosexual sex have gradually, though irregu-
larly, been disappearing from the statute books. Gay and lesbian
communities are now fairly widely accepted as part of the social
scene in cities like Sydney, New York, Berlin and Bangkok.

These communities, however, do not include all men (nor
all women) who have homosexual sex; it appears that they

have a limited class composition. Surveys have regularly found respondents from gay community venues to be highly educated and affluent in comparison with the general population (Kippax et al. 1993).

This defines a practical problem of some importance. Urban gay communities have produced a strong response to the HIV/AIDS epidemic, in the form of safe sex strategies and community activism in prevention and care (Altman 1994). Such programs, however, may never reach a large proportion of men who have sex with men—those who come from working-class backgrounds.

There are exceptions, certain outreach activities such as work at 'beats' (Dowsett & Davis 1992). It seems important to support such programs with research about working-class men. How do the conditions of working-class life affect sexuality? What is the shape of sexual experience and current practice? What is the character of desire and how is it linked to identity? How has the HIV epidemic impacted in working-class settings, and what prevention strategies might work there?

The interplay of class and sexuality is by no means a novel issue. The pioneer sexologist Krafft-Ebing (1988) was acutely aware of the class contexts of sexual activity. Mid-Victorian upper-class diarists and moralists in Britain were fascinated by sexual contact across class lines (Marcus 1966). Twentieth-century radicals such as Reich (1972) and Marcuse (1955), blending Freud and Marx, saw class domination take shape as sexual constraint. The Kinsey reports in the United States mapped class differences in the frequency and occasion of orgasm (Kinsey et al 1948). American urban ethnographers recorded the heterosexual values or 'sex codes' of slum dwellers (Whyte 1943) and working-class couples (Rubin 1976).

Working-class men who have sex with men, however, remain a little-researched group. It is not obvious whether they resemble the middle-class groups in gay community surveys, or working-class straight men—or neither. And it is not obvious what health or prevention strategies would be most relevant to their experiences and needs.

We explored these questions in an action-research project

undertaken in two Australian cities in 1989 and 1990. Part of the work was done in western and south-western Sydney, part in a regional city we call 'Nullangardie'. The project was designed to collect evidence from working-class men about male-to-male sexuality and its social context, and to pilot educational strategies with those men as co-workers. Information was gathered by field observation in the relevant social networks, by group discussions about AIDS education materials, and by 21 life-history interviews.

THE WORKING-CLASS SETTING

We first need to explore the nature of social class. In the social relations that form the class structure of modern society, the key role is played by the labour market, the underlying division between capital and labour (Connell & Irving 1992). There are complexities on both sides of that division. In particular, among working-class people, those dependent for their livelihood on a wage (or a wage-substitute like a benefit or pension), there are important divisions of gender, ethnicity, age and educational background.

Economics is the necessary starting point. To be in the working class is to be in a social group where income comes mostly through an employment relation. Some income comes from self-employment (for instance, Barney Sherman, one of our research participants, is a self-employed electrician), and some comes from pensions or benefits (Andy Wilson lives on sickness benefits). Most comes directly from wages. This means that working-class livelihoods are dependent on hiring by employers. Most employment is with companies or small businesses whose economic logic is the pursuit of profit.

Important consequences flow from this employment relation. Working-class incomes are dependent on a labour market. Individual employers do not fix wages individually, they pay the going rate. For unskilled or uncredentialled labour the going rate is low. It is easy for an employer to replace such labour, especially when more workers are looking for work than there are jobs on offer. Those who cannot earn a wage—being unemployed, or dependent on a benefit such as the age pension, sickness or supporting parent's benefit—have lower incomes again. These are the groups most often in severe poverty. Poverty is a scarring experience (Embling 1986), which is increasingly common for young people.

For many working-class people, then, the realities of life centre on economic vulnerability and constraint. Incomes are the lowest the economy offers; housing is the worst the society provides; the material facilities for bringing up children, for education, for social and cultural life are the worst. In working-class life there is generally no 'career', in the sense of life-time advancement familiar to professionals, managers, and some groups of administrative and clerical workers. One's earning capacities (through overtime or piecework) are likely to peak around age 25 or 30. Income may be suddenly cut by a change in corporate strategy such as a plant closure, a shift in the economy, a company failure or an industrial accident.

A good deal of the work done in working-class circumstances is manual work—assembling refrigerators, making steel, cleaning floors, serving food, driving trucks, cutting coal, sewing dresses. Class used often to be named by speaking of 'blue-collar' versus 'white-collar' jobs; opinion polls still often rely on this distinction. 'Pink-collar' jobs for women in service industries (Williams, 1988) need to be included in our understanding of manual work.

Manual work certainly defines a familiar kind of working-class experience. Among the men in this study, Neil Dayton's father was a storeman, his mother a dressmaker, his two brothers a policeman and a mechanic. Neil distanced himself from the 'rough' suburb where he grew up. Peter Farthing's father was a driver and his brother a fitter and turner. Peter rejected 'grease monkey work' and aimed for a 'collar and tie' job in an office.

The class distinction signalled by this language is, however, blurring. For at least a generation past, routine clerical work has resembled manual work in every respect except the amount of sweat and dirt involved: time-keepers, check-out operators, site clerks, cashiers, receptionists, salespeople etc.

Increasingly the key division in the labour market has become that between credentialled and uncredentialled labour. Peter Farthing got his 'collar and tie job' 30 years ago though he left school at the minimum age; he could not do so now. This points to the importance of the education system in shaping modern class relations. Formal schooling is the route to credentials; and as a considerable body of research shows, the schooling system spits out the bulk of working-class students before they get advanced credentials (Welch 1996).

A famous US study of working-class life spoke of 'the hidden injuries of class' (Sennett & Cobb 1972). Cultural exclusion through inadequate education is only one of the ways a capitalist society erodes the self-confidence of working-class people. Disdainful treatment in hospitals, surveillance by welfare agencies, media hostility to strikes and community actions, and blocked promotion structures are all familiar experiences for them.

The damaging relationship between educational authority and many working-class families parallels other interactions between working-class people and the state. Policing bears much more heavily on working-class people than on more privileged groups; a simple measure is the fact that the overwhelming majority of prisoners in gaols are working-class men. These interactions are an important site for the shaping of a combative working-class masculinity, as illustrated in Chapter 8.

In the face of economic constraint, cultural exclusion and state authority, working-class people have not been passive. Employers' power in workplaces and labour markets has been met with industrial struggle and the creation of unions. From unionism grew political action, the historical origin of labour and socialist parties. In Australia, the Australian Labor Party long was, and is still sometimes seen as, the expression of working-class aspirations to use the state to restrain capital and expand welfare measures.

Both unionism and labour politics drew on, and reinforced, notions of working-class solidarity. They were strongest where working-class people were linked in a closely knit community and shared a common culture. Dwyer et al. (1984) have characterized this culture as emphasizing informality (as against the formality of the state and of mainstream schooling); a commitment to productive labour; solidarity and mutual support; and lived experience rather than abstract knowledge. Other studies have emphasized the importance of the family as the central institution in working-class life (Bryson & Winter 1999). Family relationships provide both economic and emotional support against the pressures of labour market and workplace. For many working-class people 'the family' is the core of what they most value in life; family ideology is very strong. The family-household, as Donaldson (1991) calls it, is traditionally organized around a gender division of labour in which women are responsible for child care and most of the housework, and men are responsible for supporting the household by bringing home a wage. This broad division of labour has survived the return of most married women to the paid workforce. Women's earnings are generally lower than men's, as a result of less training, interrupted employment, part-time employment, lower wage rates, and sexism on the part of employers; they are therefore often regarded as supplementary to the wage earned by a husband/father.

As these remarks already indicate, the relationships that organize working-class life are far from static. The working class as such came into being less than 200 years ago. It was made, as a social unit, by the responses of working people to the growth of market relations and industrial capitalism (Thompson 1968). The working class has continued to change throughout the capitalist world. In the case of Australia, the working class has been dramatically reshaped, first by the rise of heavy industry and the emergence of an industrial as well as a commercial and pastoral labour force; then by massive European labour immigration and ethnic diversity. A fresh round of changes is now occurring as a result of prolonged unemployment, economic restructuring, the globalization of markets and firms, immigration between countries, and renewed credentializing of labour markets.

These developments have been, on the whole, corrosive of working-class solidarity. For good and ill, the traditions of working-class life and labour politics are now very much under challenge: internally from working-class feminism, from the unemployed and from the Aboriginal movement, and externally from the new right, from the relentless pressure of corporate mass media, and from the neo-liberal state.

THE SOCIAL FRAMEWORK OF MALE-TO-MALE SEX

In the endless discussion of teenage sex, remarkably little is said about homosexual experience. Researchers, too, have been coy about this issue, partly because of moral panics about 'pedophiles'; Leahy's (1992) study of intergenerational sex being a notable exception. Our interviewees reported patterns of childhood or adolescent sexuality in which male-to-male contact was common. Lyle Canham and his teenage mates went off to masturbate together in the sandhills almost every day. Peter Farthing called it 'fiddlies'. He recalls that he 'fiddled with' a variety of boys, for instance, being played with by his older brother's mate at the movies while his brother 'had it off' with a girl in the back row.

This 'fiddling' was not socially labelled homosexual or gay. It was, rather, a familiar part of a milieu in which erotic experience was easily gained, principally with age mates of both sexes, and with slightly older boys. Sexual contact, mostly involving mutual masturbation but sometimes penetration, was likely to be unspoken. It was known to be 'naughty', hence concealed from adults, happening in the sandhills, the movies and the vacant blocks. But no extra naughtiness was attributed to relations between boys. In a gender-divided community (many of our interviewees went to single-sex schools) sexual relations with other boys were, indeed, often easier to start and maintain than sexual relations with girls.

This free-form, easy-access, wordless erotic life of peer groups was, for about half our interviewees, the reported occasion of their first homosexual experience. Some aspects of it continued into working life. The monotony of factory work and labouring is countered by ribaldry: smutty jokes, boasting about sexual conquests, innuendo, groping and horse-play. There is a substantial homoerotic content to this (in gender-segregated workplaces, which are usual), though the public language is heterosexual. Two respondents described ribald initiation rituals when they first went to work, in which the other men grabbed them and painted their genitals with ink or soft soap. (Grease is used for this purpose among miners: Couch 1991.) Sexual partners were often found at work or in work-related social settings.

We must recognize, then, a continuum of homoerotic experience among working-class men in a number of social settings. At the same time we must acknowledge that this experience is silenced, that the public language of the peer group and the workplace is heterosexual. Moreover, it is often seriously homophobic. 'Poofters' are an object of derision, some-times of hatred.

Several of our respondents have been bashed in homo-phobic attacks, two have been raped (one by police). All found difficulty in coming out to their parents, expecting a hostile response, and often the response was what they expected. Andy Wilson was thrown out of his church and verbally abused by his parents when identified as a sodomite. Josh Foster as a young man attempted suicide, and in hospital was taken in hand by psychiatrists who told his mother he was homosexual and pressed him to accept aversion therapy. The result of this 'treatment' for his homosexual desires was another suicide attempt. Several of our respondents have lost jobs or job opportunities because of discrimination. Almost all find it necessary to be cautious about disclosing their homosexuality, concealing it from neighbours as well as workmates and family.

This widespread homophobia has two key cultural sup-ports. One is the traditional ideology of the family already mentioned, with a clear gender division of labour and strong links between generations. The other is an ideology of mascu-linity in which physical prowess and social power are fused with aggressive heterosexuality. 'Poofters' are culturally supposed to be contemptibly inadequate, feminized men. The actual gender identity is much more complicated, as will be seen below, but this is the popular conception, reflected in endless 'poofter' jokes.

However, this picture has to be qualified in significant ways. Many of the parents did adjust to the news about their sons, some becoming quite supportive. The working-class family, despite heterosexual ideology, may be flexible enough in practice to embrace a male lover, not quite as a wife but still as part of the network (perhaps like a close family friend).

Alongside religious bigotries and hypermasculinities, working-class traditions include a broad current of sexual explicitness (for instance, the workplace ribaldry mentioned above) and sexual tolerance. This can work to the advantage of homosexual men. Most of our respondents feel secure in their neighbourhoods, and some are 'out' at work. Those who have suffered employment discrimination or aversion therapy were of course encountering the homophobia of employers and doctors, not the working class. We should not neglect the fact that class power means that the homophobia of the privileged impinges on working-class people.

It is still the case that acknowledging a sexual preference for men is likely to be hard, so entry into networks where that sexual preference is easily realized is a major step. This step generally follows a certain amount of sexual activity with men in the undifferentiated milieu of youth eroticism.

The most common occasion for this step in our respondents' life histories was the discovery of 'beats' (public meeting places for casual sexual encounters) and the possibility of frequent, free sex with a range of partners. For some boys the fact that it was male-to-male sex was probably incidental, and an object choice crystallized out of the practice; for others a sexual preference was already formed. The beats fitted in with working-class traditions in significant ways: informal, egalitarian, self-made, communal (being based on mutual support), anti-authoritarian.

The next most common path of entry was a relationship with an older man who acted as mentor both sexually and socially. This might be a neighbour, a male relative, or a man met at a beat with whom a personal relationship developed. Beyond beats and mentors was a wide variety of entry paths: church youth groups, a choir, seduction at work, advertisements or announcements in newspapers, visits to gay community venues like bars and nightclubs, and so on.

Contact or entry was most often experienced as happenstance, so our respondents' narratives emphasize the accidental character of most of these contacts. But what is chance from the point of view of the individual life may be quite systematic from a social point of view. Homosexual desire is produced systematically in the gender order of contemporary Western society, and it is no accident that its realization takes the social form of the diverse recruitment of individuals into a social network existing on the margins of institutionalized heterosexuality.

The form taken by this social network is in turn shaped by class relations. The two settings in which we did our fieldwork have different class histories. 'Nullangardie' is a provincial city with a history of bitter industrial conflict, male working-class militancy and working-class community solidarity. Now in recession with the decline of its major industries, its mostly Anglo-Australian population sustains a tradition of local and often dissident labour politics. Western Sydney by contrast is bigger, newer, more socially and politically diverse. Products of massive postwar urban-fringe expansion, these outer suburbs now hold over a million people from a wide range of ethnic backgrounds. The region is seriously short of public services and social facilities. The dominant political force is right-wing Labor Party and the level of community mobilization is low.

Homosexual men in Nullangardie have created a community setting which in obvious ways reflects the character of the regional working class. Key venues for networking are the pubs, whose traditional importance in working-class life is familiar. There is a sense of intimacy and personal knowledge in the moderate numbers involved. Beats in Nullangardie are by no means anonymous. One runs into relatives and old friends. Nullangardie men contrast the relaxed, friendly quality of their network with what they see as the cliquey, bitchy scene in Sydney.

Most of our respondents from western and south-western Sydney lack this connectedness or sense of community. Some are, indeed, seriously isolated. Their situation is clearly structured by the presence of the inner-city gay community based in the eastern suburbs. The area around Oxford Street in east-central Sydney is the city's gay quarter, with a range of commercial venues, political/cultural institutions and informal networks making up gay community life. The community is often informally called 'Oxford Street'.

Other survey work done by us in the gay community centred on Oxford Street found a high proportion of professional workers and above-average incomes. There is room for argument about the extent of working-class participation in this commercial and social scene. There is clearly some participation, as our interviews document; possibly quite extensive. But the interviews also say something about the terms of this participation. A number of them reveal a strong sense of class distance from 'Oxford Street', an experience of exclusion, whether cultural or economic. Some of our respondents had made efforts to create networks more to their taste in their own suburbs, ranging from dinner parties and dance parties to car clubs and sex clubs.

Interwoven with the creation of social and sexual networks is an economic strategy. There is not much money around. Some of the men we interviewed were in poverty; few owned a house. Economic survival is a problem.

Most homosexual working-class men have work histories little different from heterosexual working-class men. Our respondents included some licensed tradesmen (a boilermaker, an electrician), some men who have worked up to a supervisory position, as well as some who have knocked about picking up whatever wage was going—labouring, clerking, sales, driving etc. The interchangeability of unskilled jobs is such that Jerry Spencer, for one, simply cannot remember what all his jobs have been.

But openly homosexual men have extra vulnerability, and some therefore gravitate into occupational niches which are recognized as relatively safe. The hotel trade, theatre and entertainment, and health work, are important cases. On occasions groups of homosexual men have set up small businesses together (e.g. a sandwich bar). This is a fragile strategy given the lack of capital that is a defining feature of working-class life.

The theme of economic strategy is surviving rather than getting rich. As we noted before, there are few 'careers' in working-class employment. The economic ambition of most of our respondents is to own a home and have a secure income. A good car on top is cream. This suggests a highly realistic appraisal of economic constraints; the International Monetary Fund should be proud of them.

But there is also a darker side, a sense of personal constraint and closed horizons, illustrating Sennett and Cobb's (1972) phrase 'the hidden injuries of class'. The sense of cultural exclusion from the Oxford Street quarter is a class injury. Occupational niches may give some protection, but they are niches not breakthroughs; and they, too, are vulnerable to class power.

For instance, Chris Garwood was employed in a large hotel along with about a dozen other gay men. When a new boss came in who was homophobic, Chris found himself back on the street. Andy Wilson, after a terrible struggle to find and hold a job, with ill-health and no credentials, found a niche in a publicly-funded theatrical organization. But after a year or two the organization concerned lost its public funding, and it was branches in working-class areas which were closed down. 'I just feel like I must have killed six Chinamen,' Andy remarked, proverbially worse than breaking mirrors. But it is a social dynamic that is damaging him, not chance.

A homophobic culture means that the resources of working-class militancy in unions and labour politics, which counter class put-downs by asserting working-class solidarity and agency, are not available to this part of the working class. A sense of constraint and stress comes through in many of the interviews, even with men who might be seen as having made a resounding success of their sexual and social life.

Keith Winter is one. He told us the story of coming out to his family at his father's birthday party—when his Aunty

remarked, seeing Keith eating cocktail frankfurts ('little boys'),
'Oh, you like little boys'. Then he went on:

> You know, I didn't totally realize what it was to be gay.
> I mean it's a bastard of a life. If ever I could help someone
> get out of it, or talk someone out of it, if they were able to
> be talked, I would . . . didn't pick this life. I've always
> been this life.

SEXUAL PRACTICE

The two main settings of sexual activity are beats and homes,
and these correspond to different relationships and often different erotic practices. Venues (bars, clubs etc.) are much more
a setting for the social pleasures of conversation, joking and
drinking than directly an occasion for sex.

The beats are a common point of entry, and they remain
important for many men whatever else is going on in their
lives. Erotic practice is generally masturbatory or oral-genital,
not often anal. As already noted, the beats in Nullangardie
especially are not anonymous: friends, acquaintances, relatives
may be met there. Men who meet at a beat sometimes go off
for a drink together at a pub. Occasionally this develops into
a sustained relationship.

For most of the respondents, beat sex, while pleasurable,
is not enough. Much greater value is placed on sex in relationships. Bill Markham puts this concisely. What he wants is a
stable couple relationship with 'a wonderful, loving, caring
guy'—no matter what he looks like.

Monogamous, stable couples are the hegemonic rather than
the normal thing. Not everyone has one, indeed the majority
do not have such relationships. But most admire them and
would prefer to live in them. Well-established couple relationships are consummated by living together and buying and
fixing up a house together.

Given such a relationship, other links can be a source of
jealousy. Bill Markham for instance was 'tormented' when he
found his partner secretly going to beats, and this led directly

to the end of the relationship. It is impossible to miss the similarity with heterosexual marriage, and there is of course much joking about husbands and wives. There is also a more serious romantic principle of 'being the only one' for your partner. When an established couple breaks up the emotional consequences are heavy.

Anal-genital practice is much more likely in relationships than at beats. In sharp contrast to folklore about 'fast-lane' sex, for these men anal sex is associated with intimacy and trust. It is a vehicle of relatedness. Peter Farthing recalled his early experience of anal sex: '. . . I knew that by doing it with him, I still—I had a friend. Whether you'd call it a friend—I had somebody of my own. All I wanted was something of my own. I think that's what I mean about "mate".'

The communicative function of sex is very strong here. This meaning was dramatized by one respondent in the story of a visit to a sauna in the Oxford Street quarter. He saw a man to whom he was attracted walk up to a couple engaged in sex and penetrate one of them; in that moment his attractiveness dissolved. What upset the observer was not the action, but its lack of relational context.

This has consequences for safe sex strategy. To the extent that safe sex is identified with using condoms for anal sex (a very common understanding), and anal sex is identified with intimacy and relationship, then the less intimate sexuality of the beat may seem not to require precautions. On the other hand, sex in a relationship, connected with an ideal of monogamy ('being the only one'), may be felt as safe *because of the relationship*. Most of the respondents who are currently in couple relationships practise unprotected anal sex with their lovers whether or not they are sure their partners have no other sexual contacts. Where the medical definition of prevention conflicts with the social definition of relationships and practices, the social meanings prevail.

Anal sex is more than an expression of relatedness. It is a political arena, in which there is a struggle to define the kind of relationship involved. On the one hand there is an egalitarian relationship emphasizing what is common between the partners. Homosexual sex between men allows for reciprocity, since each partner can both penetrate and be penetrated in the same way. Several of our respondents had phrases for this: 'give and take', 'a two-way street', 'tit for tat', 'a ride there for a ride back'. That is to say, the partners took turns at fucking and being fucked, or at least acknowledged a right to do so. Jerry Spencer put it crisply:

> I mean it's a two-way street. I mean, you'll fuck him and he'll fuck you, and it's really the exchange that's good. Whereas you are not so cool about the other guy wanting to fuck you and that's it, or the other guy wanting to be fucked and that's it.

But fucking and being fucked in our heterosexist culture also carry connotations of dominance and submission, active and passive, and some of our respondents also acknowledged this. Anal sex allows one to be a 'total man', as Neil Dayton put it. The most common imagery for this is the gender imagery of masculine/feminine. Keith Winter also revealingly used a class imagery for anal intercourse, speaking of 'doers and do-ees . . . employers and employees'. The implications of power are unmistakable. Thus two social definitions of anal intercourse, with different political implications, co-exist in the milieu. They may even co-exist in the same relationship as the framework for day-to-day negotiation.

However, we should not exaggerate the explicitness or formalization of these meanings. Sex research tends to reify behaviours or practices like anal intercourse and talk as if they were discrete items. The reality is more likely to be a continuous flow of interaction, both verbal and physical, in which erotic experience arises. Andy Wilson, questioned about being fucked, perceptively remarked that 'nine times out of ten it's a thing that follows on from other things, it's not a standard thing'.

His small group of friends do not negotiate in advance about anal sex because that is not how sex is organized in their interaction. To the extent that negotiation occurs, it takes the form of directing the flow, indicating what one does or does not want to happen next, giving out cues which the others respect because the flow is in the context of, and instantiates, their friendship. Any discussion of safe sex in such a context is necessarily a discussion about redesigning relationships.

Anal intercourse, like other sexual practices, has a technique to be learnt. Among the most interesting parts of the interviews are accounts of how the men acquired or developed sexual skills. Generally this happened on the job, so to speak, with sexual skills building up from relationship to relationship. In some cases an older man taught sexual techniques, which include the choreography of approach and courtship as well as the physical techniques of making love. Bill Markham, for instance, was taken in hand by his first lover:

> *That's where I got most of my education from . . . He taught me a lot about making love . . . A lot of older people say that when you get young guys into bed they don't know what they are doing. But there are lots of people who tell me that I know what I'm doing, but that was due to the fact that he'd taught me all this at such a young age . . . He showed me Oxford Street, we drove up and down Oxford Street, and pointed out a few of the nightclubs sort of thing, and showed me Campaign [a Sydney gay newspaper] and we read it; and just introduced me to a social life of being gay, that there was a gay community out there.*

Sometimes a peer group would set out to acquire knowledge to inform its own practice. Thus Andy Wilson's friends conducted their own consumer research on brands of condoms. Information about HIV/AIDS is often acquired and disseminated in this informal person-to-person way.

Sexual skilling can occur at any age. Among our respondents, entry and skilling mainly occurred at two markedly different stages of life, which point to two broad types of sexual careers. In the first, a young man emerging from the matrix of childhood or youth peer eroticism makes contact, via beats or mentors, with substantially homosexual networks. Early on he consolidates an erotic interest in men and a sense of social difference. In the second, a young man emerging from the same matrix settles into heterosexual relationships and marries. Ten to twenty years later, the marriage ends and the husband, generally via beats, enters or re-enters homosexual networks.

On the evidence of our interviews and observation, few adult men sustain both heterosexual and homosexual relations at the same time for long. 'Bisexual' is not a recognized identity in these milieux, nor is there any valuing of the instability of sexual identities proposed by queer theory. Some of our respondents are actually hostile to men who will not choose to be one thing or the other.

Variations on these careers mainly concern the balance between relationships (ideally monogamous, and generally so in the sense that only one relationship runs at a time) and casual sex at beats or on social occasions. A small number of men become involved in commercial sex; two of our respondents have worked as prostitutes at some stage.

DESIRE AND IDENTITY

In another report we have suggested on the basis of survey data that, in the context of working-class life, homosexuality is less separated out from the heterosexual social matrix than it is among more privileged groups (Connell, et al. 1991). At the level of practice this is neatly illustrated by Neil Dayton's introduction to gay social life, which was accomplished by his girlfriends. Even his first homosexual experience was with the boyfriend of a girlfriend, in a sleeping bag on the floor. At the level of identity the lack of separation is confirmed by the reluctance a number of these men have to identify as gay.

There is no explicit alternative, and it is reluctance not refusal. Yet one gathers that the term 'gay' is disliked because it connotes effeminacy, or class privilege, or both. Those are exactly the connotations of 'poofter', which can be a class insult to office workers as well as a sexual insult. Men like Alan Cunningham have a conventional masculine presence and would heartily dislike any imputation of effeminacy. They can even reinterpret homosexual desire in a framework that affirms masculinity: as Alan put it, 'man to man' sex is best.

It is still true that in the wider culture the key definition of homosexuality is being gay in the sense of the big-city communities. Since working-class men are aware of, and sometimes visit and participate in, these communities, this identity is also available to them. A few of our respondents are actively pursuing it and urge it on other men in their networks. Its main consequences seem to be a commitment to organized larger groups rather than informal networks alone, and a tendency towards separatism tinged with antagonism to women. This is exceptional, because positive relationships with women—mothers, girlfriends, wives, housemates—are common in most of our respondents' lives. There is a historic trend in working-class life towards breaking down old and deeply entrenched patterns of gender segregation; and the social life of homosexual men is, perhaps unexpectedly, a case in point.

The muted 'gayness' of our respondents seems to correspond to another aspect of their sexual style. Richard Cochrane is very experienced sexually and has a wide repertoire. His favourite sexual fantasy, one of the more adventurous, is being fucked mid-air while parachuting. He has been both top and bottom in a leather scene. But when it comes to the crunch he can let all that go:

> *I've been there, done that, now it's a case of just get in there and have a good time. Forget the games, you know, gets you nowhere. Waste of time when you could be fucking.*

'Forget the games' could be the theme song for most of these narratives. There is a matter-of-fact quality to their discussion and enjoyment of sex, with obvious bases in working-class practicality and ribaldry. There is a lack of the fixation (in the Freudian sense) or fetishism that is familiar in other sexual cultures, a familiar example being the turnover of styles and attractiveness in inner-city gay communities. Huey Brown joked about going into an Oxford Street SM bar—'SM' meaning 'Same Models', all the inhabitants being young, pretty and this year's style. He likes more of an assortment.

This is not to deny that particular men have special preferences (they do, including hairy chests, 'European' men, noses of a certain shape). It is to suggest that sexual desire in this milieu is broadly not narrowly focussed, that subcultural sexuality has little grip. Sex as such is treated as an adventure, as always a bit naughty; there is pleasure in its routinely transgressive character.

This throws the emphasis back on gender itself as the structuring principle in desire. The thing that remains after styles and fixations are gone is the 'homo' in homosexuality. And here the relatively relaxed and unproblematic picture of vanilla sex in the working-class suburb begins to break down. ('Vanilla' is the evocative slang for bland, straightforward sex compared to subcultural sex.) We have emphasised the importance of families and the strong sexual division of labour within them. The folk understandings of sex in this milieu are uncompromisingly heterosexual: to be masculine is to fuck women.

It follows from this that to desire a man, and even more to be desired by a man, is very probably to experience oneself at some level as feminine. This is certainly true for the two of our respondents who worked at various times as drag artists. Drag shows rely heavily on double entendres and broad erotic humour. Their popularity with (notionally) heterosexual audiences in working-class venues such as Returned Services (veterans) and Rugby League (football) clubs is a pointer to the strength of the gender dynamic being tapped here—if we place any credence in Freud's idea that humour is a guide to unconscious conflict.

The sense of difference some boys experience in adolescence on their route towards homosexual identity is often immediately interpreted for them in gender terms. Ed Johnson, for instance, did not like football, did like knitting and cooking, and thereby aroused deep suspicion in his father's mind.

Coming out, it seems, is not the straightforward acknowledgment of identity that gay liberation once thought it. For these men in these settings, it means, rather, entering a kind of gender reversal, perhaps more exactly a gender split. They are now sustaining masculinity at the level of social interaction and economics, while experiencing an unacknowledgeable femininity at the level of fantasy and bodily desire.

This contradiction allows various resolutions, and the life stories diverge from the point where this dilemma is confronted.

A drastic resolution is to tip completely over into femininity, via drag into transsexual status. Huey Brown went that way, setting up as wife to an aggressively masculine young man, getting breast implants, working in drag as a woman prostitute, stopping just short of the operation.

A less drastic resolution in the same direction is to move into gender-structured couple relationships where a masculine/feminine pattern is played out in the household. Josh Foster went down that track, playing the 'female role' to his lover. He does the housekeeping, and he is the one penetrated in anal intercourse. Though he would prefer 'give and take', he cannot get it: his lover is committed to the enactment of dominance.

As Josh Foster recognizes, this is to limit the erotic possibilities of the male body; and anyway that enactment of female roles is under criticism in the culture at large. An alternative resolution of the gender contradiction is to emphasize maleness, not as one term in a masculine/feminine split, but as the social grounding of all interaction in the milieu. In pre-AIDS days this masculine emphasis took the form of the 'Castro Street Clone'—the San Francisco uniform of jeans, T-shirt, moustache, cropped hair etc.—as an erotic style. The assertion of gay identity in the form mentioned above seems to mark out a male preserve, a world of domestic, social and sexual life in which there are no women and no assertions of femininity.

Some part of this strategy is attractive to most of the men we interviewed. They repeatedly expressed a dislike of queens ('I couldn't cope with queens en masse,' said Jack Sayers), a dislike of flamboyance and campness. Their desired social style is not hypermasculinity (Lyle Canham's comment on football: a 'mindless, aggressive sort of game') but is comfortably, conventionally masculine.

Yet to construct a male preserve in reality would cut off supportive relationships with families and women friends, which are often important. It would also make gay networks and households more conspicuous and thus more vulnerable to homophobic attack. So the largest group among our respondents does not go far down that track either.

Their sexual identity is, rather, constructed as a series of pragmatic compromises, the terms of which vary from person to person and from time to time. Alan Cunningham has disclosed his sexual preference widely, not as a political gesture but because in practical terms he finds living in the closet harder. Lyle Canham, who has worked for the same company for 32 years, lived all his life in the same area, and has a low-key involvement in homosexual networks, remarked, 'I'm pretty well adjusted to my maladjustment.' The principle of erotic reciprocity, the 'tit for tat' of anal intercourse, fits well with such a strategy of compromise and adjustment.

THE HIV/AIDS EPIDEMIC

Cross-sectional social research—whether it uses surveys, participant observation or other methods—tends to fix a set of relationships in one point of time. It is important to register that the social relations involved in sexuality are historical, they do change over time.

The older respondents (seven are 45 or older) grew up in the 1940s, 1950s and 1960s, before there were visible gay politics, a visible gay community, or a gay commercial scene (Wotherspoon 1991). There were beats, and there were subterranean networks which a young man might encounter more or less by accident. Barney Sherman recalls his early sexual encounters being mostly with older men in uniform, which must have been common in the 1940s. He and Jerry Spencer recall the Sydney nightclub scene in the 1950s and 1960s, where a small homosexual milieu existed as an aspect of King's Cross bohemia, blurred with heterosexual drag, avant-garde art and literature, and the sex trade.

The 1970s, with the advent of gay liberation and the creation of a specifically gay commercial centre (bars, saunas, hotels, clothes shops, bookshops etc.), split this older bohemian milieu and profoundly redefined homosexual practice and identity. Yet this redefinition was uneven, given the class composition of the emerging inner-city gay community and the reaction of significant numbers of men against the commercial scene, the new (mainly US-derived) gay styles and the political mobilization.

This history is important in understanding the HIV/AIDS crisis. The HIV epidemic did not arrive from outer space to disrupt a static community. It arrived through sexual practices already being reworked, into a set of social relations already in motion, indeed substantially reshaped in very recent history. The response to HIV/AIDS was therefore likely to be diverse, reflecting the unevenness of the changes and the variety of men's life situations. Given this history, the very emphasis on gay community and gay identity which was the basis of the most successful prevention education work in the 1980s (Dowsett 1990) could be expected to increase divisions on class lines among homosexual men—and thus create difficulties for further prevention work.

As news of the epidemic spread, the first response among our older respondents seems to have been a defensive drawing in behind boundaries. Some gave up the beats, or reduced their use. This could imply a withdrawal from sexual activity and social networks altogether, or it could mean a renewed emphasis on couple relationships. Since this is in any case the most valued sexual practice, such a response can make the epidemic seem almost a blessing:

> But AIDS is probably the best thing that ever happened to the gay scene in my view. It's the thing that got the people saying, 'Hey, let's stop screwing around, let's get together, let's settle down, let's shack up, or let's curb our thing.' I think it did the best for us. It gave us a lot of hurt and harm, hurt and hassles too. But I think if you look at the last five or six years, just how many people have either been in a relationship, or got one. And 90 per cent of the time stayed in it.

That is Keith Winter's opinion. Richard Cochrane did not get a relationship. He got AIDS. In consequence he has no sex life, and little admiration for the 'gay scene'. He has come home to his family while dying.

In due course another response developed among working-class men: a renewed attempt at building community in the face of HIV/AIDS. Prevention education and care of people living with AIDS became central to energetic people in the milieu. To put it another way, local people became HIV/AIDS activists organic to their own communities. The key was the articulation of safe sex principles in the mid-1980s which, unlike conventional health education models, allowed and even required the empowerment of the affected group.

Working-class communities and households broadly lack access to scientific information and skills in handling it, a significant consequence of their class disadvantage in education. In consequence their HIV/AIDS information is likely to be at best approximate. (For instance, the meanings of 'positive' and 'negative' HIV-antibody test results get reversed. Also the idea that there are safe partners rather than safe practices is common.) In both Nullangardie and western Sydney certain local men set themselves the task of disseminating HIV/AIDS information and safe sex principles, and seeing to it that the principles were followed. Safe sex became a means by which the individual could have an effect in the face of the epidemic, and a basis on which a collective response could develop.

This goes against the broad trend in HIV/AIDS work towards professionalism, a trend which in working-class settings gives authority to men like Michael Swanston. Michael is a student and part-time health worker, who, while living and gaining his sexual experience in working-class communities, has maintained a sense of class difference stemming from his family background. He is interested in HIV/AIDS work as a possible occupation, and will be qualified to enter it when he completes his studies.

The same set of social relations that authorizes Michael Swanston de-authorises Huey Brown. Huey has considerable but uncredentialled expertise as a former sex worker, and has vigorously maintained for years a strict safe sex regime. Huey commented on the amount of unsafe sex he sees at beats. Asked why he did not apply for a job as an HIV/AIDS outreach educator, he replied that he could not since he was a 'known homosexual' (i.e. known to the police). His reputation would make it impossible for official organizations to trust him enough to appoint him to such a job.

Huey Brown not only has an accurate knowledge of safe sex strategy, he already works as an energetic and effective community HIV/AIDS educator. He is one of the organic activists mentioned above. Another side of this informal networking is apparent in a story told by Bill Markham. Growing up in a country town, Bill was taken for a drive by an older acquaintance who had been away for several years:

> And all afternoon we just talked about safe sex, and he was telling me what to do and what not to do. [Why?] Well that's what I couldn't work out. Like it was just like a normal conversation, but he was so persistent to talk about this safe sex . . . He really went through everything. Told me the ins and outs. And that was the first lecture I had on safe sex.

Bill later heard that this man had AIDS—and later again, that he was dead.

These episodes point to an active informal HIV/AIDS education process in which particular men function as barefoot doctors, to use the Chinese expression—perhaps better, barefoot educators. Such people are known in other cities too (Frowner & Rowniak 1989).

The occasions of this work are as varied as social and sexual life itself. Peter Farthing and his partner sometimes pick up other men for threesomes. If the pick-ee wants unsafe sex, he gets a good talking to. Bill Markham went off for a dirty weekend in Sydney and climbed into bed with a nurse, who got ready to be penetrated but had no condom at hand. Bill laughs at the subsequent scene: he stopped the action, got coffee, and delivered a lecture on safe sex principles and community resources to the older, professional man.

Here is an educational enterprise that is organic to the working-class setting, that works through relationships and networks and disregards credentials. The barefoot educator is, we would suggest, the key HIV/AIDS prevention resource for working-class men. This is a means by which a process of collective empowerment can occur in this milieu as it has done in the affluent gay communities. It is a means by which information can get around without the class put-downs and disempowerment that are the usual consequences of pro-fessional intervention.

This is not to imply the strategy is problem-free. David Booth, eighteen at the time of interview, provides an example. He has been given sexual skilling and lots of safe sex advice by his barefoot educators, an older relative and a friend met at a beat. He has high safe sex awareness. But when quizzed about the details of safe sex he turned out to be dangerously vague about both the practice and the principles on which it is based. It seems that the mentoring has cotton-woolled him; he has not had to take responsibility for learning the details himself.

Such problems have solutions; they signal not that the strategy is flawed but that it has to be thought out, developed, and resourced. To develop these possibilities requires an approach which is closer to that of adult literacy work (Lankshear 1987) than the usual top-down, individualized model of health education and behaviour change. A price in lives has already been paid for the class selectiveness of pre-vention strategies. Working-class people deserve something better in future.

REFLECTIONS

It is important to consider the whole social matrix of sexuality, not just its immediate interpersonal context. The structure of class as a whole means that sexual practice, for men like our respondents, reflects economic vulnerability and social con-straint. Yet these constraints do not fix the outcomes. Different collective responses can be made to them, as we see in the different experiences of Nullangardie and western Sydney.

In both cities the hegemonic construction of masculinity is important. But working-class masculinity cannot be taken as a fixed social form. It is at issue, under tension, and in some of these lives, directly challenged. Here working-class homo-sexual men are involved in a wider politics of gender which is still open-ended.

Given the need to deal with economic vulnerability, tensions about masculinity, homophobia and the HIV epidemic itself, it is no wonder that these men place emphasis on the most supportive type of relationship they know, the stable couple. This is, however, a solution not available to all. And for reasons we have noted, it provides imperfect shelter from the epidemic. That haven in a heartless world is no more storm-proof than the corresponding heterosexual household.

This study also suggests directions for HIV/AIDS prevention strategies. The professionalization of community-based HIV/AIDS service organizations has been noted overseas (Patton 1990). Clearly, many of the men in this study are educators in their own right and have already made a contribution to stopping the HIV epidemic. The task facing gay community HIV/AIDS agencies is to find ways to include such men in their programs, and to provide support and back-up for their work.

Similarly, an emphasis on younger working-class homosexually active men, who do not claim or want a 'gay' identity, is warranted. Outreach strategies and peer education programs and techniques are needed which rely more on the informal social networks of the men themselves than on abstract social categories such as ethnicity, age or sexual identity (e.g. bisexual). Programs which assume that attaching these men to existing gay communities is the easy way to increase compliance with safe sex, must take into account the very mixed experience the men in the study report in their dealings with gay communities. It is important to take preventive education activities to the places where working-class men are more likely to be found—their workplaces, their local clubs and hotels, and the networks and relationships they have themselves constructed in the face of economic hardship and cultural exclusion.

PART 4

PRACTICALITIES

8

Cool guys, swots
and wimps

Schools have often been seen as masculinity-making devices.
In the nineteenth century Dr Arnold saw his renovated Rugby
School as a means of forming Christian gentlemen. Other
reformers in the years since have given other schools the task
of forming sober and industrious working men, technocratic
competitors, and exemplars of the New Soviet Man.

Research in the 1970s and 1980s, inspired by the new
agenda of feminism, suggests that Dr Arnold was right. Schools
do not simply adapt to a natural masculinity among boys or a
natural femininity among girls. Schools are active in the matter,
constructing particular forms of gender and negotiating relations between them.

Research and policy discussion in the 1970s (epitomized in
the remarkable 1975 report of the Australian Schools Commission, *Girls, School and Society*) found conventional gender
stereotypes spread blanket-like through textbooks, career coun-
selling, teacher expectations and selection processes. This was
theorized as the transmission of an oppressive or restrictive 'sex
role' to girls. It followed that girls would be benefited by
modifying the sex role or even breaking out of it. This led easily
to an educational strategy: a program of compensation and

redress to expand girls' occupational and intellectual horizons, affirm women's worth, and write women into the curriculum.

At the start, almost all this discussion was about girls and their restrictive sex role. By implication, the boys were getting one too. But here the sex-role approach does not translate smoothly into educational reform. Since men are the privileged sex in current gender arrangements, it is not obvious that boys will be advantaged by teachers' efforts to change their 'role'. On the contrary, boys may resent and resist the attempt. A puzzled literature on the 'male sex role' in the 1970s scratched pretty hard to find ways by which men are disadvantaged or damaged by their sex role. No convincing educational program ever came of it. Teachers grappling with issues of masculinity for boys now seem to be reaching for concepts beyond that of 'role', and are expecting to face a politicized and emotionally charged situation.

This is very much in accord with the development of research since the 1970s. More intensive research techniques and more sophisticated theories of gender have found complexities and contradictions in the 'stereotypes', as shown in Chapter 1, and have highlighted instead the institutional practices of gender which children encounter in schools. Thus Thorne (1993) shows how situational is the segregation of the sexes in primary schools. Messner (1990) shows how the formal structure of organized sport provides a temporary resolution for developmental problems of masculinity. Kessler et al. (1985) point to the ways curricula and school organization separate out different kinds of femininity and different kinds of masculinity within the same school.

It is clear that the sex-role model will not work; but it is not so clear what way of thinking about the making of gender should take its place. It is plain that the strategy of providing 'compensatory' programs for the disadvantaged has little relevance to the privileged gender; but it is not so plain what other shape should be taken in educational work with boys.

This chapter is relevant to both the conceptual problem and the practical one. Unlike most discussions of the topic it is not based on research in schools. Research on schooling is usually confined to schooling, and thus has difficulty seeing where the school is located in a larger process. This chapter is based on life-history interviews with adults that cover family, workplace, sexual relationships, friendships and politics, in addition to schooling, as settings for the construction of masculinity. I hope this will give a useful perspective on events in school.

Rather than following individual narratives, my approach is to identify some key moments in the collective process of gender construction, the social dynamic in which masculinities are formed. In such moments, the formation of the person and the history of the educational institution are simultaneously at issue.

The evidence is drawn from two groups of interviews in a larger study of contemporary masculinities: (1) a group of young men from the working class, recently out of school, growing up in the face of structural unemployment and in the shadow of the prison system; (2) a group of men, mostly some years older and mostly from more affluent backgrounds, who are involved in 'green' politics, that is social action on environmental issues.

GETTING INTO TROUBLE

Down behind Mal Walton's high school is the bush—the school was built during the post-war suburban expansion of Australian cities—and at the edge of the bush are the school toilets. This is where Mal and his friends would gather:

> In high school [my friends] were real hoods [toughs] too. Like we used to hang down the back. . . we'd sit down there and smoke cigarettes and talk about women, get dirty books out, going through—what do you call it? I can't think of the word. Just the things you do at high school in the first year.

Mal had been placed in the bottom stream, and was evidently regarded by most of his teachers (though not all) as disruptive. The main reason he was in the bottom stream was that he could not read. He was arrested for theft at fifteen, in the year he left school, and has not had a lasting job in the six years since.

Harry the Eel (so called because of his fanatical devotion to the Parramatta football team, 'the Eels'), now twenty and about to become a father for the second time, used to practise his school smoking in the same fragrant setting:

> *I was in a bit of trouble in the last four years of school. I got busted for—what was it? Second Form* [Year 8] *it was selling porno books. Third Form it was getting drunk at the school fete, and allegedly holding another bloke down and pouring Scotch down his throat—which we didn't do, he was hassling us for a drink . . . They found him drunk and they said where did you get it? and he mentioned our names and biff, straight into it . . . Fourth Form, wasn't much happening in fourth form really, busted in the dunnies* [toilets] *having a smoke!*

Eel started an apprenticeship but his employer went broke and no one else would take over his training. Since then he has been on the dole, with casual jobs from time to time, and has a sideline dealing drugs to finance his motorbike.

Eel has not been arrested, but his mate Jack Harley has. Jack is less of a tactician, and fought every authority figure from his parents on. He thinks he was labelled a troublemaker at school because of an older cousin. He clashed early and often with teachers: 'They bring me down, I'll bring them down.' He was expelled from at least one school, disrupting his learning—'I never did any good at school.' Eventually he assaulted a teacher. The court 'took the teacher's word more than they took mine', and gave him a sentence in a juvenile detention centre. Here he learnt the techniques of burglary and car theft. About three years later he was doing six months in the big people's prison. At 22 he is on the dole, looking for a job to support his one-year-old child and his killer bull terrier.

These three young men come from labouring families, in Mal Walton's case from a very poor family. Their experience of school shows the relationship between the working class and education at its most alienating.

What they meet in the school is an authority structure, specifically the state and its powers of coercion. They are compelled to be at school and once there—in their own view—they are ordered about arbitrarily by the teachers. The school is a relatively soft part of the state, but behind it stands the hard machinery of police, courts and prisons. Push the school too far, and, like Jack Harley, one triggers an intervention by the enforcers.

Up against an authority structure, acts of resistance or defiance mean 'getting into trouble'. This is one of Jack Harley's most common phrases, and indicates how his actions are constantly defined in relation to institutional power. Fights with other boys, arguments with teachers, theft, poor learning, conflicts with parents are all essentially the same.

One can try to retreat beyond the routine reach of institutional power, as Mal Walton and his friends did in their idyllic moments in the toilet block on the edge of the bush. Even there one will be 'in trouble' when the authorities raid the retreat, as Eel found.

At the same time, trouble has its attractions and may be courted. Mal Walton, for instance, was caned a lot when he went to a Catholic primary school. So were his friends. In fact, he recalls, they fell into a competition to see who could get caned most, though no one would win: 'We just had big red hands.'

Why this competition? 'Nothing to do; or probably proving that I was stronger than him or he was stronger than me.' A violent discipline system invites competition in machismo. More generally, the authority structure of the school becomes the antagonist against which one's masculinity is cut. Jack Harley, in the comment on teachers quoted above, articulated an ethic of revenge which defines a masculine pride common in his milieu. But he lacked the judgment to keep it symbolic. Teachers often put up with verbal aggression as part of their jobs, but they are hardly likely to stand still when physically attacked.

So the courting of trouble calls out an institutional response, which may push an adolescent assertion of masculine pride towards an early adult criminal career.

'Trouble' is both sexualized and gendered. Getting the 'dirty books' out and 'talking about women' are as essential a part of the peer-group activity as smoking and complaining about teachers. In the mass high-school system, sexuality is both omnipresent and illicit. To act or talk sexually becomes a breach of order, a form of 'trouble' in itself.

But at the same time it is a means of maintaining order, the order of patriarchy, via the subordination of women and exaltation of one's maleness. Patrick Vincent, currently on probation for car theft, succinctly explained why he liked being sent to a co-educational high school after being expelled from his boys-only church school: 'Excellent, chicks everywhere, good perve'. He boasts that within a week all the girls in his class wanted to climb into his bed. The treatment of young women by these young men is often flatly exploitative.

KNOWING WHERE YOU STAND

To other boys, the hoods in the toilet may be objects of fear. Danny Taylor recalls his first year in an urban working-class high school. Despite being big for his age, he hated the physical contest:

> When the First Form [Year 7] joins and all comes together from all different [primary] schools, there's this thing like sorting out who was the best fighter, who is the most toughest and aggressive boy in the form, and all the little mobs and cliques develop. So it was like this pecking order stuff . . . and I was really frightened of this.

He did not enjoy high school until Form Four (Year 10, about age sixteen), when 'all the bullies left'. This is not peculiar to urban schools. Stewart Hardy, the son of a labouring family in the dry, flat country in the far west of New South Wales, makes the usual contrast between city and country, but paints the same kind of picture:

In the country . . . it was easier for us to get along with each other, although there was the usual dividing: the cool guys hang out together, and the cool girls hang out together, and there was the swots and the wimps . . . You knew where you stood, which group you belonged to.

Stewart and Danny joined the wimps and the swots (the academic triers) respectively. Both managed to use the education system to win social promotion (though in both cases limited) out of their class.

The process of demarcating masculinities in secondary school has been noticed in ethnographies of working-class schools in Britain (Hargreaves 1967, Willis 1977) and Australia (Walker 1988). We have seen a similar sorting in a ruling-class private school, between the 'bloods' (hearty, sporting) and the 'Cyrils' (wimpish, academic) (Kessler et al. 1985)

This suggests a typology of masculinities, even a marketplace of masculinities. To know where you stand, in Stewart Hardy's phrase, seems to mean choosing a masculinity, the way one might choose a football team (the Eels) to barrack for.

It is important to recognize that differing masculinities are being produced. But to picture this as a marketplace, a free choice of gender styles, would be misleading. These 'choices' are strongly structured by relations of power. In each of the cases mentioned, the differentiation of masculinities occurs in relation to a school curriculum which organizes knowledge hierarchically, and sorts students into an academic hierarchy. By institutionalizing academic failure via competitive grading and streaming, the school forces differentiation on the boys.

But masculinity is organized, on the large scale, around social power. Social power in terms of access to higher education, entry to professions, command of communication, is being delivered by the school system to boys who are academic 'successes'. The reaction of the 'failed' is likely to be a claim to other sources of power, even other definitions of masculinity. Sporting prowess, physical aggression, or sexual conquest may do.

Indeed, the reaction is often so strong that masculinity as

such is claimed for the cool guys, with boys who follow an academic path being defined as effeminate ('the Cyrils'). When this situation is reached there is a contest for hegemony between rival versions of masculinity.

The school, though it has set this contest up, may be highly ambivalent about the outcome. Many school administrations actively seek competitive sporting success as a source of prestige. The First Fifteen, or the school's swimming champion (see Chapter 5), may attract as much honour and indulgence from the staff as the academic dux.

The differentiation of masculinities, then, is not simply a question of individual differences emerging or individuals' paths being chosen. It is a collective process, something that happens at the level of the institution and in the organization of peer group relationships. Indeed, the relationship of any one boy to the differentiation of masculinities may change over time.

Stewart Hardy remembers being terrified on his arrival at high school (and even before, with 'horror tales' about high school circulating in his primary class). He and his friends responded by 'clinging to each other for security' in a wimpish huddle in First Form (Year 7). But then:

> Once I started getting used to the place and not so afraid of my own shadow, I felt here was my chance to develop a new identity. Now I can be a coolie, I can be tough. So I started to be a bit more belligerent. I started to get in with the gangs a bit, slag off teachers behind their backs, and tell dirty jokes and stuff like that.

But it did not last. After a while, as Stewart got older, 'I decided all that stuff was quite boring. It didn't really appeal to me, being a little shit any more, it didn't really suit my personality.' This was not just a matter of Stewart's 'personality'. His parents and his teachers put on more pressure for academic performance as the School Certificate (Year 10) approached. Indeed, his parents obliged him to stay on at school to Fifth Form (Year 11), long after the 'gangs' had left.

OVER THE HUMP

The labour market in modern capitalist economies is segmented and stratified in a number of dimensions. Perhaps the most powerful division in it is not any longer the blue-collar/white-collar divide, but the distinction between a broad market for more or less unskilled general labour, whether manual or clerical; and a set of credentialled labour markets for specific trades, semi-professions and professions.

The public education system, as the main supplier of credentials (certificates, diplomas, degrees), is deeply implicated in this division. When Stewart Hardy's working-class parents ignored his protests and made him stay on in high school, they were pursuing a family strategy to get him over the hump between these two labour markets and into the world of credentialled labour.

For Stewart it was a rocky path. He resented the pressure, slacked off at school, got involved with a girlfriend, and did 'miserably' at the Higher School Certificate (final-year certificate). Soon after that he ditched the girlfriend and got religion. But after he had been a while in the workforce, his parents' pressure bore fruit and he took himself to a technical college to have a second try at the Higher School Certificate. This time he did so well that he qualified for university.

He is now (aged 24) doing a part-time arts degree, and at the same time a computer training program organized by his employer, a big bank. He does not see computing as a career, but as a fallback: 'If things get tight I can always go back to being a programmer, because there are always jobs for that.' He may get into a career through his degree.

Stewart has got the message about qualifications, with a vengeance:

All the time I wasted before, I could have been at university getting a degree. Seven years out of school and I have absolutely no qualification at all. All I did was bum around and take whatever jobs came up.

The contrast with Mal Walton, Jack Harley and Patrick Vincent is stark. They are glad of 'whatever jobs come up', and expect to be at the mercy of such economic chances as far as they can see into the future. To them it is not 'time wasted', it is life.

Through the mechanism of educational credentials, Stewart Hardy has bought into a different construction of masculinity. This is much closer to the hegemonic masculinity of the middle-class world described by Roper (1994), though it may seem a shade old-fashioned beside the transnational business masculinity discussed in Chapter 3. The notion of a long-term career is central. A calculative attitude is taken towards one's own life; a passive and subordinated position in training programs is accepted in order to provide future protection from economic fluctuations. The life course is projected as if up a slope, with periods of achievement distinguished from plateaux of wasted time. The central themes of masculinity here are rationality and responsibility rather than pride and aggressiveness.

Young men from more privileged class backgrounds are here, so to speak, from the start. Their families' collective practice is likely to be organized around credentials and careers from before they were born. For instance, I come from a family whose men have been in the professions—engineering, the church, medicine, education, law—for several generations. It never occurred to me to do anything but go to university in my turn.

In such a milieu, the practice of credentialling does not even require active consent, merely the non-occurrence of a refusal. As Bill Lindeman, son of an administrator and an academic researcher, put it, getting a little bogged in his multiple negatives:

> Because I'd had three siblings who'd gone ahead of me, so there was that sort of assumption there, that the opportunity was given to me to not question it, to not go to something else. And I didn't have strong interests: the strongest interest I had was surfing, in the Sixth Form [Year 12]. And there was nothing really to motivate me to go off and do anything else. So I went to uni.

Here, very visibly, is a life course being constructed collectively and institutionally, that is, through the education system and families' relationships to it. Of course the young person has to do such things as sit in class and write exam answers: there is a personal practice involved. But to a marked degree it is a passive practice, following an external logic. The person's project is simply to become complicit in the functioning of an institutional system and the privileges it delivers.

There is a painful contrast with the personal investment, and cost, involved in the hoods' doomed assaults on the same institutional system. One begins to feel the reason in all that anger.

DRY SCIENCES

What privileged young men find at the end of the educational conveyor belt is not necessarily to their taste. Bill Lindeman went to university because there was nothing motivating him to go elsewhere. But after he had been there—and I hope it pleases his teachers—he began to think.

When I chose science I chose zoology. My sister and my brother had done exactly the same and my other brother was doing physics, so we were all doing science. There was a strong analytical bent there. I chose life science because—that stemmed from my earlier childhood, enjoying natural places. It wasn't till I'd left uni that I realized I was so bored with 99.9 per cent of it. I just wasn't finding nature in laboratories, cutting up rats and dogfish. The vitality and change that you can learn from nature just isn't there. It was dry. I didn't relate it to the living world.

Bill's critique of the abstractness, the un-lifelikeness of biology as a subject, is a familiar theme in critiques of other disciplines and of academic knowledge in general (e.g. Johnson 1968, Rich 1979). Bill's version is informed by his green politics. He began to resolve the problem in a research project involving long field trips to the Snowy Mountains, and then became deeply committed to environmental activism. In that context he also became concerned with the remaking of masculinity, though he has not specifically linked this theme back to his academic experience.

There is, nevertheless, a connection. The dry sciences of academic abstraction are a particular institutionalization of mascuculinity. Masculinity shapes education, as well as education forming masculinity. This has become clear from explorations of the history of natural science inspired by feminism (see Harding & Hintikka 1983).

The connection of masculinity with science is not a question of maleness in general. The argument would hardly apply, for instance, to the relation of men to nature in central Australian Aboriginal society. It is a culturally specific version of masculinity, indeed a class-specific version. Contrast the hot, loud, messy masculinity of the 'hoods'. Even within one class, as the case of the 'bloods' versus the 'Cyrils' shows, the rational, technical style is not the only style of masculinity on offer.

Yet this is an important, even crucially important, form of masculinity in the contemporary world. Winter and Robert (1980), in a pioneering article, noted the importance of the changing scale and structure of the capitalist economy for the dynamics of masculinity. The dry sciences are connected on the one hand to administration, whose importance is obvious in a world of enormous state apparatuses and multinational corporations. On the other hand they are connected to professionalism, which is a synthesis of knowledge, power and economic privilege central to both the application of developing technologies and the social administration of modern mass populations.

In both respects science is connected to power. But this is not the crude assertion of personal force that is all the power a young man like Jack Harley can mobilize. Rather, it is the organized collective power embodied in large institutions like companies, the state and property markets, the power which delivers economic and cultural advantage to the relatively small number of people who can operate this machinery. A man who can command this power has no need for riding leathers and engine noise to assert masculinity. His masculinity is asserted and amplified on an immensely greater scale by the society itself.

READING FEMINISM

The men in the study who are involved in counter-sexist politics, or who have at least adopted some feminist principles, have almost all read feminist books. Indeed, some say this is their main source of feminist ideas, alongside personal relationships with feminist women. In contrast, mass media seem to be the main source of information about feminism among men who have not moved towards feminism.

Contemporary feminism, at least self-identified feminism, is a highly literate political movement. The mobilization of the 'second wave' was accompanied by a vast outpouring of writing: new books, new magazines, special issues of old journals and so on. Students and teachers made up a high proportion of activists. Writers occupy a central place in modern feminism, and the conflict of texts is central to the definition of its various currents. To become a feminist does not absolutely require a higher degree in literature, but it is certainly usual that someone becoming a feminist will read a lot.

Many people cannot read. This is true absolutely for Mal Walton, whose alienation from school was described above; he was tipped out into the labour market at fifteen unable to read a job advertisement. He is desperately disadvantaged by illiteracy, tries to conceal it from the employment service as well as from employers, and is currently asking his girlfriend to teach him to read.

Illiteracy in first-world countries tends to be concentrated among poor and marginalized groups (Hunter & Harman 1979). In a case like Mal's it is easy to see its connection with 'getting into trouble', the war on school in which Mal's embattled masculinity was shaped.

More commonly in Australia young people do learn to read, in the sense that they can decode the letters and spell out the words, but do not put this skill to use for anything much beyond job advertisements and sports results. I think this is true for Eel and for Jack Harley. Patrick Vincent is in between, he can read reasonably but has difficulty in writing. None of these young men ever mentions *ideas* they have got from print, only those that come from talk and television.

There is a level of political literacy where reading opens up new ideas, poses alternatives to existing reality, explains what forces are at work in the wider world. These young men have not entered this world, and are only likely to if there is a major politicization of the Australian working class and a massive adult education initiative. Since the mass communication system which they are plugged into, commercial television, is totally opposed to such a change, the strong likelihood is that they never will reach political literacy.

The men who do grapple with the textual politics of feminism are likely to be from privileged class backgrounds, like Bill Lindeman, whose political literacy is an aspect of his easy insertion into higher education. Or they are men who, like Danny Taylor, have used the education system to escape a working-class milieu.

In neither case is the reading likely to be uplifting and enjoyable. The literature they are most likely to encounter, the 'public face' of feminism as Segal (1987) puts it, is sharply critical of men and little inclined to make distinctions between groups of men. The man reading feminist writing is likely to encounter pictures of men as rapists, batterers, pornographers, child abusers, militarists, exploiters, and images of women as targets and victims. Young men who read much of this literature and take it seriously seem to have one major reaction: severe feelings of guilt. Barry Ryan summed it up:

> *After university I was at the stage where I could understand academic literature, and I read some pretty heavy stuff, which made me feel terrible about being male for a long time.*

Guilt is an emotion with social effects, but in this case they are likely to be disempowering rather than positive. A young man 'feeling terrible about being male' will not easily join with other men in social action, nor can he feel solidarity (except at some symbolic level) with women. Thus guilt implies that men's personalities must change but undermines the social conditions for changing them, an enterprise which requires substantial interpersonal support. There is of course some backlash literature designed to assuage the guilt feelings of men affected by feminism (e.g. Farrell 1993). This is almost as demobilizing as the guilt itself.

This is a situation where an educational effort concerned with gender issues for boys might bear rich fruit. Barry Ryan is the only one of our respondents to describe a course of this kind, in a progressive private school:

> The teachers at that free school were the ones who decided to implement that sexism program and we [the students] were involved in it. I remember having to go and make a verbal submission . . . We got this course together. I remember having all-male groups and the women having all-women groups, and talking about sexism, and that was basically it. We did a lot of discussion about sexism and how we communicated about women. I didn't learn that much in the course itself, it just taught me that it was something that I was going to have to think about. And so from then on I was always thinking about it.

On Barry's account, the organizing framework is 'sexism', which would imply a focus on attitudes and perhaps a moralization of the issue. Two other interviewees described meeting feminist content in tertiary courses, though not as focussed as Barry's school course. Both had come back to education after a period in the workforce, with a project of personal change in mind; this may explain why they were in courses dealing with such issues. There is a marked sexual division of labour in Australian higher education. Material on sexual politics is rare in courses with high proportions of male students.

REFLECTIONS
The part played by schooling in the formation of masculinity, looking down the perspective of these life histories, is more

conflictual and more contradictory than the idea of the school as an agency of 'sex-role socialization'.

The school is not necessarily in harmony with other major agencies—the family, the media, the workplace—and it is not always in harmony with itself. Some masculinities are formed by battering against the school's authority structure, others by smooth insertion into its academic pathways. Others again are formed by a tortuous negotiation of possibilities. Teachers' characters and sexual politics are not brought into focus in these interviews, but they are no less complex than the sexual politics of the pupils, and are also important in shaping what happens in schools.

There is some explicit educational treatment of masculiity documented here, including the counter-sexist course described by Barry Ryan, and the influence of organized sport mentioned by many of the respondents. On the whole, however, it is the inexplicit, indirect effects of the way schools work that stand out in the long perspective on masculinity formation.

A stark case is the way streaming and 'failure' push groups of working-class boys towards alienation, and state authority provides them a perfect foil for the construction of a combative, dominance-focussed masculinity. Equally clear is the role of the academic curriculum and its practices of selection in the institutionalization of a rationalized masculinity in professions and administration.

To put it in more familiar language, the 'hidden curriculum' in gender relations is more powerful than the explicit curriculum. This creates a dilemma for those concerned with democratizing gender relations in the schools. What the school acknowledges as its activity in relation to gender, and may therefore be willing to discuss under the heading of 'equal opportunity' or 'anti-discrimination', is less significant than what it does not acknowledge.

The school is probably not the key influence in the formation of masculinity for most men. In most cases in the study I would judge the childhood family, the adult workplace or sexual relationships (including marriage) as being more potent.

Nevertheless, schooling is the next most powerful influence across the board, and in some cases and some situations it is decisive. It may also be the most strategic, in the sense that the education system is the setting where an open debate about the democratization of gender relations is most likely to happen, and can gain some purchase on practice.

There is no lack of interest in questions of sexuality, gender and sexual politics among boys and young men—as illustrated by the topics of conversation in Mal Walton's toilet block. For many these topics are matters of absorbing concern. How to respond to this concern will be the subject of the next chapter.

9

Teaching the boys

Several troubling issues in education concern boys, men and
their place in gender relations. Discipline problems in schools
most often concern boys, and violence in schools is mainly
enacted by boys. Boys are widely thought to lag in literacy.
The spread of affirmative action programs for girls, as well as
the contemporary backlash against them, raises questions about
their impact on boys, and whether boys need special programs
of their own. Agendas of school restructuring constantly raise
questions about the teaching workforce, whose most striking
internal division is the gender division of labour. While this
division of labour persists, boys and girls in infants and elementary classrooms rarely have men as teachers.

It is not surprising, then, to find controversies about boys,
men and education bubbling up in a number of countries. In
the United States, a proposal to set up boys-only public schools
in Detroit, as a response to disastrous drop-out rates among
African-American youth, was halted at the last minute in 1991
by legal action that declared them discriminatory. In New
South Wales, after media controversy about boys' academic
'failure' relative to girls, a parliamentary enquiry into boys'
education was launched (O'Doherty 1994). In Germany, edu-

cational programs on gender issues have multiplied outside the schools, both for youth and for men (Drägestein & Grote 1997/98, Kindler 1993). This is not the first time such issues have been aired. At the end of the 1960s, for instance, there was a minor panic in the United States about schools destroying 'boy culture' and denying boys their 'reading rights', because of the prevalence of women teachers and the 'feminine, frilly content' of elementary education (Austin et al. 1971, Sexton 1969).

The context, however, has changed. Second-wave feminism has now influenced public thinking for three decades, and one of its long-term consequences has been to unsettle traditional ideas about men and masculinity. In previous chapters I have discussed the emergence of 'men's movements' and policy debates about masculinity. Some pop psychologists work up statistics of men's troubles (such as earlier death and higher rates of injury) into claims that men, not women, are the truly disadvantaged sex (e.g. Farrell 1993).

Similar claims are increasingly heard in education. Discrimination against girls has ended, the argument runs. Indeed, thanks to feminism, girls have special treatment and special programs. Now, what about the boys? It is boys who are slower to learn to read, more likely to drop out of school, more likely to be punished, more likely to be in programs for children with special needs. In school it is girls who are doing better, boys who are in trouble—and special programs for boys are needed.

More heat than light has been generated by these claims. In education, counter-claims are made: that for girls, success in schooling does not translate into post-school equality; that boys get more attention in school than girls at present; that programs for boys would entrench privilege, not contest it. As Gilbert and Gilbert (1998) note, the media love to turn the issue into a pro-girl versus pro-boy (or pro-feminist versus anti-feminist) shoot-out.

But the educational issues are far more complex. How real is the formal equality provided by co-education? Are girls benefited in some ways, boys in others? How far can we make generalizations about 'boys' as a bloc? If boys are having trouble in school, which boys, and what are the sources of their trouble? How far can schools affect masculinity and its enactment? If at all, through what kind of programs, and what kind of pedagogy, should they try?

It is clear from current debates that many teachers and parents see these issues as urgent. Schools are launching 'programs for boys' whether researchers and policymakers give them guidance or not. Some of the resulting efforts are, unfortunately, little informed by accurate knowledge or careful thinking about masculinity. Equally unfortunately, researchers have not done a great deal to help the schools. It is time for this situation to change. It can change, because the masculinity research introduced in Chapter 1 allows a fresh understanding of the issues in education.

The purpose of this chapter is to provide a framework for thinking about gender issues in the education of boys, focussing on the industrialized countries. First I will consider the relationship of schools to the structure of gender. In the light of the recent work on masculinities I will examine educational research, especially ethnographies, for evidence on the making of masculinities in schools: first looking at schools as agents, then at pupils as agents. Using the results of this analysis I will explore the logic of educational work with boys, then return to the public controversies about boys' education and consider the groups and interests in play, and the prospects of changing gender relations in and through schools.

SCHOOLS AND GENDER

Since schools are routinely blamed for social problems of every description, from unemployment to godlessness, it is not surprising that they should also be blamed for problems about boys. It is, therefore, important to say that the school is not the only institution shaping masculinities, and may not be the most important. Psychoanalysis has made us familiar with the emotional dynamics of the family as an influence on gender, an argument recently renewed—and carefully located in the history of gender relations—in Nielsen and Rudberg's (1994) developmental model of gender. The sociology of culture makes us aware of the importance of mass communications in the contemporary gender order. Media research documents what we know intuitively, that mass media are crammed with representations of masculinities—from rock music, beer commercials, sitcoms, action movies and war films to news programs—which circulate on a vast scale (Craig 1992).

Given these forces, why pay attention to the school? Teachers discussing problems about boys often suggest that they are confronting intractable patterns fixed outside the school. Certainly children bring conceptions of masculinity into the school with them. Jordan (1995) has wittily documented the 'Warrior Narratives' brought into an Australian kindergarten, where some of the boys disrupted a carefully non-sexist regime by playing games involving guns, fighting, and fast cars. This is hardly an isolated experience. Witness the Ninja Turtles and X-Men of the American Grade 2 classroom studied by Dyson (1994). Such a feeling among teachers is reinforced by the two most popular explanations of masculinity, biological determinism, which emphasizes the body, and sex-role theory, which emphasizes broad cultural expectations.

That the school is an important player in the shaping of modern masculinities can be suggested, but not demonstrated, by research within schools. It is more strongly demonstrated from outside, for instance by life-history studies of masculinity such as Messner's work on US athletes, or my research with groups of Australian men (see Chapter 8). Schools figure significantly in autobiographical narratives, for instance in the preparation and choice of an athletic career.

Further, we should not ignore the practical judgment of parents about the importance of schooling, reflected in the demand for 'boys' programs'. Though we will never have a simple way of measuring the relative influence of different institutions, there seems to be good warrant for considering schools one of the major sites of masculinity formation.

A 'site' can be understood in two ways. It can be examined as an institutional *agent* of the process. To understand this, we must explore the structures and practices by which the school forms masculinities among its pupils. Alternatively, we can examine the school as the *setting* in which other agencies are in play, especially the agency of the pupils themselves. Both aspects are explored later in this chapter.

Since almost all the discussion of gender focusses on gender difference, we should from the start be alert to gender *similarity*. Public controversies over gender differences in educational outcomes ('The girls are beating the boys!') persistently ignore the extent of overlap, focussing on small differences between statistical means and ignoring measures of dispersion.

Many educational practices iron out gender differences. A common curriculum, a shared timetable, and the experience of living daily in the same architecture with the same classroom routines are not trivial parts of boys' and girls' school experience. Teachers may deliberately set out to de-emphasize gender difference, laying their emphasis on individual growth, as King (1978) noted about British infants schools in the heyday of 1970s progressivism. The whole history of feminism shows that education systems can be a force for gender equity as well as inequity.

This issue can lead to serious problems in the interpretation of quantitative research of the very common kind which goes looking for statistical differences between groups of boys and girls. Schools may be having a gender *effect* without producing gender *difference*. The school is having a gender effect, for instance, when it changes gender relations so as to produce more similarity.

A key step in understanding gender in schools is to 'think institutionally', as Hansot and Tyack (1988) have argued. As with corporations, workplaces and the state, gender is embedded in the institutional arrangements through which a school system functions: divisions of labour, authority patterns and so on. These are, as Lingard and Douglas (1999) have recently shown, the sites of a shifting gender politics which provides the context of gender relations in individual schools.

The totality of gender arrangements within a school is the school's *gender regime*. Gender regimes differ between schools, though within limits set by the broader culture and the constraints of the local education system (Kessler et al. 1985).

The theoretical work presented in Chapter 2 allows us to sort out the different components of a school's gender regime. Four types of relationship are involved:

Power relations

These include supervision and authority among teachers; and patterns of dominance, harassment, and control over resources among pupils. A familiar and important pattern is the association of masculinity with authority, and the concentration of men in supervisory positions in school systems. Among pupils, power relations may be equally visible. Prendergast's (1996) ethnography in a British working-class high school shows, for instance, how control over playground space for informal football games was crucial in maintaining the hegemony of an aggressive, physical masculinity in this school's peer group life.

Division of labour

This includes work specializations among teachers, such as concentrations of women in domestic science, language and literature teaching, and men in science, mathematics and industrial arts. It also includes the informal specializations among pupils, from the elementary classroom where a teacher asks for a 'big strong boy' to help move a piece of furniture, to the gendered choice of electives in vocational education at secondary and post-secondary levels.

Patterns of emotion

What the sociologist Hochschild (1983) has called the 'feeling rules' for occupations can be found in teaching, often associated with specific roles in a school: the tough deputy principal, the drama teacher etc. Among the most important feeling rules in schools are those concerned with sexuality, and the prohibition on homosexuality may be particularly important in definitions of masculinity (Frank 1993, Mac an Ghaill 1994). Lingard and Douglas (1999) note how the 'emotional economy' of education can be reconstructed, indeed is being reshaped now under the impact of neo-liberalism.

Symbolism

Schools import much of the symbolization of gender from the wider culture, but they have their own symbol systems too: uniforms and dress codes, formal and informal language codes etc. A particularly important symbolic structure in education is the gendering of knowledge, the defining of certain areas of the curriculum as masculine and others as feminine. Activities such as sports may also be of great importance in the symbolism of gender.

Through these intersecting structures of relationships, schools create institutional definitions of masculinity. Such definitions are impersonal; they exist as social facts. Pupils participate in these masculinities simply by entering the school and living in its structures. The terms on which they participate, however, are negotiable—whether adjusting to the patterns, rebelling against them, or trying to modify them.

Gender regimes need not be internally coherent, and they are certainly subject to change. This is vividly shown in Draper's (1993) account of the 're-establishment of gender relations following a school merger' in Britain, an unusual study which catches gender arrangements in the midst of change. Draper shows how different groups of pupils and teachers involved in the merger had conflicting agendas and interests, with sometimes startling results—from boys wearing eyeshadow to girls subverting school uniform.

Teachers' autobiographies, especially those of feminist teachers, contain many narratives of encounters with oppressive gender regimes in schools and of attempts—sometimes successful—to change them. Children as well as teachers work on the gender regime. In the US elementary schools studied by Thorne (1993), the meanings of gender were constantly being debated and revised by the children, the gender boundaries both enforced and challenged in the playground and classrooms.

Given this background, let us examine how schools influence the construction of masculinities.

SCHOOLS AS AGENTS IN THE MAKING OF MASCULINITIES

Masculinizing practices

There is no mystery about why some schools made masculinities: they were intended to. A fascinating historical study, Heward's *Making a Man of Him* (1988), reconstructs the interplay between Ellesmere College, a minor private school in Britain, and the class and gender strategies of the families who sent boys there. The school defined and enforced a suitable masculinity among its boys through rigidly-enforced conventional dress, discipline (prefects having the authority to beat younger boys), academic competition and hierarchy (emphasized by constant testing), team games, and gender segregation among the staff. In the wake of the 1930s Depression, Ellesmere modified its formula, increasing its academic and vocational emphasis and decreasing its emphasis on sport.

The discipline, dress code etc. can be considered a set of *masculinizing practices* governed by the gender regime of the school. Different circumstances produce a different formula. In another illuminating historical study, Morrell (1993–4) traces the production of 'a rugged, rather than cerebral, masculinity' on the colonial frontier. The white boarding schools of Natal, South Africa, in the half-century to 1930, also used the prefect system and gender segregation. But these schools laid more emphasis on toughness and physical hierarchy among the boys, through masculinizing practices such as initiation, 'fagging', physical punishment and spartan living conditions. This agenda was obviously connected with the context of colonial conquest, and the goal of maintaining racial power over colonized peoples.

These vehement gender regimes show the potential of the school as a masculinity-making device, but such cases are hardly the norm in contemporary public education. The masculinizing agenda has been muted by co-education—but has it been eliminated?

In some ways, co-educational settings make it easier to mark difference, that is, establish symbolic oppositions between girls and boys. School uniforms or conventions of dress, separate toilets, forms of address, practices such as lining boys and girls up separately, or creating classroom competitions of 'the boys' against 'the girls', all do this job. Formal texts may reinforce the lesson from popular culture that masculinity is defined by difference from femininity. As Sleeter and Grant (1991) have shown in a study of textbooks used in US schools up to Grade 8, gender patterns have persisted despite a recent shift by writers and publishers to non-sexist language. Representations of men have remained more stereotyped than those of women.

Broad features of co-educational schools' gender regimes thus sustain particular definitions of masculinity. Does this turn into an active masculinizing practice? Studies of particular areas of schools' work show that it does.

A case in point is the schools' treatment of sexuality. Sex education classes generally teach an unreflective heterosexual interpretation of students' desires, in which masculine sexuality is defined by a future of marriage and fatherhood. This can be seen in Trudell's (1993) detailed ethnography of sex education in a US high school.

Since formal sex education is mostly ineffective, such classes will probably not be a major source of gender meanings for the pupils. But, as Mac an Ghaill's (1994) important British study of school sexuality and masculinity demonstrates, these ideas are backed by a much wider range of practices. A heterosexual construction of masculine and feminine as opposites (as in 'the opposite sex', 'opposites attract') runs through a great deal of the school's informal culture and curriculum content. Homosexual experience is generally blanked out from the official curriculum. Gay youth are liable to experience hostility from school officials and straight youth, while teachers experience heavy constraint in dealing with sexual diversity (Laskey & Beavis 1996).

Co-educational schools, then, typically operate with an informal but powerful ideology of gender difference, and do put pressure on boys to conform to it. In certain areas of the school's gender regime the pressure approaches that of the vehement regimes discussed above, and a regular vortex of masculinity formation can be seen.

Masculinity vortices

Boys' subjects. The first vortex arises in the realm of symbolism through the gender meanings of school knowledge. Most of the academic curriculum is common to girls and boys, and while conveying gender messages, does so diffusely. But in certain areas of study, pathways diverge and gender messages become more concentrated. Grant and Sleeter's (1986) study of 'Five Bridges' junior high school in the United States found that while the school made an equal formal offer of learning to boys and girls, it allowed virtual segregation in some subject areas. These were especially practical subjects such as Shop (Industrial Arts) and Child Development. Indeed the school cued this segregation by its own gender division of labour among teachers.

This is a widespread pattern. System-wide data on enrolments in New South Wales secondary schools show certain subjects with marked gender differences in enrolment. In 1998, for instance, boys in Year 10 made up 90 per cent of the candidates for the elective School Certificate subject Technics I, and 87 per cent of the candidates for Technical Drawing—compared with 50 per cent of the candidates for Science, a compulsory subject, and 26 per cent of the candidates for Food Technology, a subject descended from the old 'girls' subject' of cooking (Board of Studies 1998).

At the Higher School Certificate level, Year 12, there is more flexibility and the gender patterning is more pronounced. At this level in 1998, boys made up 94 per cent of the candidates for Engineering Science, 73 per cent of the candidates for Physics, 69 per cent of the candidates for Design and Technology, and 61 per cent of the candidates for Computing Studies—compared with 36 per cent of Biology, 35 per cent of Visual Arts, 25 per cent of Drama, 21 per cent of Food Technology and 1 per cent of Textiles and Design (Board of Studies 1999).

This degree of segregation does not arise by chance. Particular curriculum areas are culturally gendered. Industrial Arts (Shop) teaching, for instance, is historically connected with manual trades where there was a strong culture of workplace masculinity and where women used to be excluded. As Mealyea's (1993) case study of new Industrial Arts teachers demonstrates, it can be difficult for men with backgrounds in such trades to accept the new policies of gender equity and inclusiveness.

Academic subjects may also have strong gender meanings. It has long been recognized that physical sciences are culturally defined as masculine and have a concentration of men teachers. Martino's (1994) sophisticated analysis of secondary classes in Western Australia shows how subject English, by contrast, is feminized. In the eyes of many of the boys, English classes are distanced by their focus on the expression of emotions, their apparent irrelevance to men's work, the lack of set rules and unique answers, and the contrast with activities defined as properly masculine, such as sport.

Discipline. The second vortex is closely linked to power re-lations. Adult control in schools is enforced by a disciplinary system which often becomes a focus of masculinity formation.

Teachers from infants to secondary level may use gender as a means of control, for instance shaming boys by saying they are 'acting like a girl'. Punishment too is liable to be gendered. When corporal punishment was legal, boys were much more often beaten than girls. Non-violent punishments still bear down more heavily on boys. A pioneering study of suspensions in a working-class area of Sydney found that 84 per cent of the pupils suspended were boys, as were 87 per cent of the pupils with repeat suspensions (White 1993).

These turn out to be typical percentages. A few years later the New South Wales public school system began to release system-wide discipline statistics. In 1998, of 35 755 short suspensions from schools, 81 per cent were of boys. Of 5396 long suspensions, 85 per cent were of boys (*Sydney Morning Herald,* 11 March 1999.) The highest rates were in working-class areas.

Where the hegemony of the school is secure, boys may learn to wield disciplinary power themselves as part of their learning of masculine hierarchy. This was the basis of the old prefect system.

Where hegemony is lacking, a 'protest masculinity' may be constructed through defiance of authority, all too familiar in working-class schools. With corporal punishment, defiance requires bravery in the face of pain, a masculinity test of the crudest kind. Even with non-violent discipline, such as the 'punishing room' in the African-American school studied by Ferguson (1994), the contest with authority can become a focus of excitement, labelling and the formation of masculine identities.

Sport. The third vortex blends power, symbolism, and emotion in a particularly potent combination. Here the schools are using consumer society's key device for defining hegemonic masculinity.

Foley's (1990) superb ethnography of a high school in a south Texas town gives a vivid description of 'the great American football ritual'. He shows that not only the football team, but the school population as a whole, use the game for celebration and reproduction of the dominant codes of gender. The game directly defines a pattern of aggressive and dominating performance as the most admired form of masculinity; and indirectly, marginalizes others. The cheer-leaders become models of desirability among the girls; and their desirability further defines the hierarchy of masculinities among the boys, since only the most securely positioned boys will risk ridicule by asking them for a date.

The only thing wrong with Foley's account is the suggestion that this is peculiarly American. Ice hockey in Canada, rugby in South Africa and New South Wales, soccer in Britain, are heavily masculinized contact sports that play a similar cultural role (Gruneau & Whitson 1993, Robins & Cohen 1978, Walker 1988).

Girls too participate in school sport, though not with the same frequency as boys. Typically the high-profile boys' sports are markedly more important in the cultural life of schools. The coaches of boys' representative teams can be important figures in a high school. Physical education teachers have an occupational culture that, on Skelton's (1993) autobiographical account, centres on a conventional masculinity that is 'not only dominant, but neutralized as natural and good, part of the expected and unquestioned nature of things'.

Selection and differentiation

The masculinizing practices of boys' subjects, discipline and sport each tend to produce, directly, a specific kind of masculinity. But this is not the only way that masculinities are produced in schools. Some aspects of the school's functioning shape masculinities indirectly, and may have the effect not of producing one masculinity but of emphasizing differences between masculinities. The most important case is, undoubtedly, educational selection.

The competitive academic curriculum, combined with tracking, streaming, or selective entry, is a powerful social mechanism that defines some pupils as successes and others as failures, broadly along social class lines. There are strong reactions among the pupils to this compulsory sorting-and-sifting, whose gender dimension has been visible (though not always noticed) since the early days of school ethnographies.

The most clearcut examples are from studies of boys' schools. The famous cases of the 'lads' and the 'ear'oles' in the British working-class school studied by Willis (1977) show a difference not only in conformity to school but in styles of masculinity. The 'ear'oles', defined by the other group as effeminate, are using the school as a pathway to careers, while the 'lads' are headed for the factory floor.

The pattern can also be traced in co-educational schools. Mac an Ghaill, for instance, distinguishes the 'Academic achievers' from the 'macho lads', the 'new enterprisers' and the 'real Englishmen', as subcultures of masculinity in the school he studied. Something like these differences can be seen as early as elementary school, as shown by Warren's (1997) study of boys and differing masculinities in an English classroom. As Garvey (1994) puts it, streaming itself becomes a masculinizing practice.

Sewell (1997), in an illuminating study of black youth in British schools, shows how the interplay of school with popular culture tends to push African-Caribbean boys into a dichotomy of rebellion or overconformity. The academic and disciplinary hierarchy of schools thus influences the making of masculinities, but by producing plural masculinities, in a structured gender order among boys, rather than a single pattern of masculinity.

PUPILS AS AGENTS, SCHOOL AS SETTING

Peer culture

One of the most important features of school as a social setting is its informal peer group life. The peer milieu has its own gender order, distinct though not fixed. There is turbulence and uncertainty as young people try to define their paths in life. With the approach of adolescence, interactions between boys and girls are liable to be sexualized, by flirting, innuendo and teasing. The heterosexual 'romance' pattern of gender relations persists through high school into college, where it can still dominate student life, as Holland and Eisenhart's (1990) intensive study shows.

The romance pattern defines masculinity in general through the masculine/feminine dichotomy. It also feeds into the hierarchy of masculinities, since heterosexual success is a formidable source of peer group prestige. Foley's study of a Texas high school gives an extended account of the parties and other social events at which masculinity is displayed and hierarchies reinforced. In this milieu the interplay of gender and ethnicity constructs several versions of masculinity: Anglo jocks, Mexican-American anti-authoritarian 'vatos', and the 'silent majority'.

Peer culture is now closely linked with mass communication. Mass culture generates images and interpretations of masculinity which flow chaotically into school life and are reworked by the pupils through everyday conversation, ethnic tensions in the playground, sexual adventures and so on. Some are racially based, such as the image of uncontrollable, violent black masculinity that is familiar in white racism—and has now been seized by young black men (for instance in rap music) as a source of power. Some of these representations are at odds with school agendas. Others (such as interest in sports) are likely to mesh; we should not assume a constant tension between peer culture and school.

Adolescent boys' peer talk constantly uses sexuality to establish hierarchies: 'fag', 'slag' etc. Research in secondary schools in several countries has found widespread verbal harassment of girls by boys (Everhart 1983, Lees 1986, Milligan & Thomson 1992). Yet at this age sex is still being learnt. Wood's (1984) study of boys' sex talk in a London secondary school annexe emphasizes the element of fantasy, uncertainty and boasting. The boys' pretensions can be punctured when a tough girl, or group of girls, pushes back. Wood notes the different registers of boys' sex talk, for instance the greater hesitancy in a mixed group.

In these observations the collective dimension of masculinity is clear. The peer groups, not individuals, are the bearers of gender definitions. This is presumably the explanation for a familiar observation by parents and teachers that boys who create trouble in a group by aggression, disruption and harassment—that is, an exaggerated performance of hegemonic masculinity—can be cooperative and peaceable on their own.

Taking up the offer

Masculinities and femininities are actively constructed, not simply received. Society, school and peer milieu make boys an offer of a place in the gender order; but boys determine how they take it up.

Protest masculinity is a case in point. The majority of boys learn to negotiate school discipline with only a little friction. A certain number, however, take the discipline system as a challenge, especially in peer networks which make a heavy investment in ideas of toughness and confrontation. Jack Harley, described in Chapter 8, is a clear example. His expulsion from school and disrupted learning were consequences not of a passively suffered fate but of Jack's vigorous response to his situation.

'Taking up the offer' is a key to understanding disciplinary problems in schools and boys' involvement in violence and sexual harassment. Groups of boys engage in these practices, not because they are driven to it by raging hormones, but in order to acquire or defend prestige, to mark difference and to gain pleasure. Rule-breaking becomes central to the making of masculinity when boys lack other resources for gaining these ends.

However the active construction of masculinity need not lead to conflict with the school. There are forms of masculinity much more compatible with the school's educational program and disciplinary needs. This is especially true of middle-class masculinities organized around careers, which emphasize competition through expertise rather than physical confrontation. It seems likely that the construction of masculinities which emphasize responsibility and group cohesion, rather than aggression and individuality, has helped in the educational success of youth from Chinese and Japanese ethnic backgrounds in North America (Takagi 1992, Cheng 1996). Boys who launch themselves on such trajectories are likely to have a much smoother educational passage. The schools as currently organized are a resource for them, and they are an asset for their schools.

The active responses are collective as well as individual. Thorne's (1993) documentation of the gender 'boundary work' done in elementary schools shows purposive group activity. So does the rejection by certain boys of a key part of hegemonic masculinity, heterosexual desire. For those boys who begin to think of themselves as gay, a vital step is finding a social network in which homosexual desire seems something other than the ghastly mistake that conventional gender ideology represents it to be (see Chapter 7).

The making of masculinities in schools, then, is far from the simple learning of norms suggested by 'sex-role socialization'.

It is a process with multiple pathways, shaped by class and ethnicity, producing diverse outcomes. The process involves complex encounters between growing children, in groups as well as individually, with a powerful but divided and changing institution. In some areas of school life, masculinizing practices are conspicuous, even obtrusive. In other areas they are hardly visible at all. Some masculinizing effects are intended by the school, some are unintended, and some are not wanted at all—but still occur.

Two implications are very clear. There is a need for educational thinking about this situation, and there are many possibilities for educational work. Let us now consider the shape this work might take.

EDUCATIONAL STRATEGIES IN WORK WITH BOYS

Goals

Reviewing German programs for boys, Kindler (1993) identifies three main goals: self-knowledge, developing the boys' capacity for relationships, and learning anti-sexist behaviour. Generalized a little, these can be broadly applied.

Knowledge. This is very much under-emphasized in current discussions, though 'cognitive objectives' are the traditional centre of educational discussion. In two senses, knowledge is a goal in work with boys.

First, current patterns of masculinity formation push many boys away from areas of knowledge with which they ought to be in contact. Subject English, discussed earlier, is a case in point; more broadly, languages and communication skills.

Second, it is important to acquire knowledge of gender, in one's own society and others. Learning the facts of the situation, participating in the experiences of other groups, and making a critical examination of existing culture and knowledge, are general educational goals that are quite applicable to this subject matter.

This was accepted by the Australian parliamentary enquiry into boys' education mentioned above, which proposed that gender relations be included in the 'core' subject matter of the public schools. This is now a principle in Australian gender equity policy. A movement in the same direction can be detected in the universities, where curricula in fields from literature to law now grapple with issues about gender. One must acknowledge, however, that the movement is uneven.

Good human relationships. If school education is a preparation for later life, part of its business is developing capacities for human relationships. But in contemporary Western societies, this capacity is gender-specialized. It is widely regarded as an aspect of femininity. Some elements of masculinity formation in schools—such as the cult of competitive sport—work against the development of this capacity in boys.

Some contemporary programs for boys address this issue head on, and make relationship capacities their centre. An example is the 'Personal Development Program for Boys' created by a group of teachers in Australia (Dunn et al. 1992). ('Personal Development' is a local rubric under which health, sex education, relationships and emotions are combined.) The program consists of a set of structured sessions on these topics: developing communication skills; domestic violence; conflict resolution; gender awareness; valuing girls and 'feminine' qualities; health, fitness and sexuality; life relationship goals. The program is intended to promote both gender equity and emotional support for boys, with an emphasis on being positive.

Justice. This involves somewhat more complicated issues and requires a longer discussion. Gender first came onto educational agendas as an equity issue, where change was sought to redress injustice. The usual response to equity issues by governments is to set up programs for disadvantaged groups. So far, the main educational response to gender issues has been setting up programs for girls.

Some advocates now cast educational issues about boys in that mould, defining boys as a disadvantaged group. As we have seen this is not a credible argument. On almost any measure of resources—wealth and income, cultural authority, levels of education, political influence, control of organizations—and in all parts of the world, men are the advantaged group in gender relations (United Nations Development Program 1999). It would require an unbelievable reversal, in an unbelievably short time, for boys to have lost this advantage and become a disadvantaged group.

These advantages come with certain costs. If one focusses only on the costs, an appearance of disadvantage can be produced. Men's social power, for instance, is partly exercised through institutions of violence, and men thus become the major targets of violence as well as the main perpetrators. In some situations these costs are concentrated on particular groups of men. The appalling levels of imprisonment among African-American men in the United States and Aboriginal men in Australia are notable examples. This is an issue of justice, and the educational implications will be discussed shortly.

The material advantages that men in general have, and that boys in general can expect, mean they have a broad interest in the status quo in gender relations. This interest is easily mobilized in education, as in other arenas. Kenworthy (1994) recounts a lesson in an Australian high school, based on a poem about a woman stockman (equivalent, in American terms, to a woman cowboy). The lesson worked well for a class of girls, and for a mixed class. But in an all-male class it was disrupted, under the leadership of some dominant boys who introduced a misogynist discourse and resisted opening up the gender issues. The boys in the class who could or would adopt a feminine reader position were scorned by the dominant group, in a classic display of the micro-politics of hegemony.

Boys are not, as boys, a disadvantaged group. The goal of educational work is therefore not to redress a gender disadvantage from which they suffer. We should not misread the statistics of sex differences. For instance, sufficient elementary-school boys have difficulty learning to read to produce lower average scores for boys as a common outcome of 'sex difference' studies on language skills. Literacy practitioners suggest that the restricted cultural interests associated with hegemonic masculinity—fathers pushing their boys to concentrate on sports, for instance—are a major reason (Sanderson 1995). To the extent this is true, the gender difference in reading scores is not a measure of boys' 'disadvantage', but an index of the short-term cost of maintaining a long-term privilege.

Yet the goal of justice is relevant to the education of boys, in three ways. First, some of the processes of masculinity construction explored earlier in this chapter do hamper or disrupt the education of particular groups of boys, who are disadvantaged in class or ethnic terms. For instance, the pattern of 'protest masculinity', and the high levels of conflict and drop-out connected with it, are a major problem in secondary schools serving communities in poverty. The attempt to achieve justice in education in relation to poverty must therefore address issues about masculinity.

The second way concerns the extent to which schools as institutions are just or unjust. In an important re-examination of the concept of justice, Young (1990) identifies two broad types of social relationships which are unjust: oppression, which restricts the capacity for self-expression; and domination, which restricts participation in social decision-making. Both types of relationship can be found in schools. The gender practices of boys may perpetuate them, and some boys are victims of them. Harassment of girls, homophobic abuse, the hierarchy of masculinities, bullying and racial vilification are examples. Pursuing justice in schools requires addressing the gender patterns that support these practices.

The third way concerns the quality of education. Education is a moral trade, and a good education must embody social justice. If we are not pursuing gender justice in the schools, then we are offering boys a degraded education—even though society may be offering them long-term privilege.

Forms of action
German educators have made a useful distinction between 'gender-specific' and 'gender-relevant' programs. The main form of educational work on gender throughout the industrialized

world has been gender-specific programs for girls. As issues about masculinity have been raised, the most common response has been to develop gender-specific programs for boys. The Personal Development Program for Boys outlined above is an example, and there is now considerable practical experience with such programs in the United States, Britain, Germany and Australia.

Gender-*specific* programs on masculinity are commonly small-scale and based on discussion in intimate groups. They may, however, operate on a larger scale. Chiarolli (1992) describes a whole-school program that started when the principal and staff at a Catholic boys' secondary school in Australia became concerned about sexism. They launched a range of actions addressing gender stereotypes and attitudes: library displays, a parent evening, guest speakers, student projects in the community, home economics classes for the boys, scrutiny of the division of labour among adults in the school, and a broad examination of the existing curriculum. Gilbert and Gilbert's (1998) recent survey of boys' education strategies reinforces the importance of the whole-school approach and the need for broad commitment from the staff of a school.

Gender-*relevant* programs include both boys and girls, and attempt to thematize, that is, bring to light for examination and discussion, the gender dimension in social life and education. The lesson on the 'woman stockman' discussed above is a small-scale example. A much more complex example is the sophisticated 'boys and literacy' program developed by Alloway et al. (1996), which tries a variety of ways to make gender issues explicit in classroom work on language. Contemporary work in sexuality education is also taking inclusive approaches (Epstein & Sears 1999, Laskey & Beavis 1996).

Though gender-specific programs are more familiar, some aspects of the construction of masculinity point to the need for gender-relevant programs. The symbolic gendering of knowledge, the distinction between 'boys' subjects' and 'girls' subjects' and the unbalancing of curriculum that follows, require a gender-relevant not gender-specific response— a broad re-design of curriculum, timetable, division of labour among teachers etc. The definition of masculinities in peer-group life, and the creation of hierarchies of masculinity, is a process that involves girls as well as boys. It can hardly be addressed with one of these groups in isolation from the other.

The gender-relevant logic is not the same as gender-neutrality, that is, simply attempting to avoid gender distinction. Quite the contrary: gender-relevant programs name and address gender. A much more interesting, gender-inclusive pedagogy becomes possible, as pupils have the opportunity to see the world from standpoints they normally regard as Other. Sapon-Shevin and Goodman (1992) suggest this process is critical in sex education, and call it 'learning to be the opposite sex'. Given the multiplicity of masculinities, a gender-inclusive curriculum means taking the standpoint of other masculinities as well as femininities.

Pedagogy

Educational work with boys 'must *start* with the boys' own interests, experiences and opinions', Askew and Ross (1988) argued some time ago. We cannot read off a strategy for boys by trigonometry from the needs of girls. Practitioners are unanimous about the importance of developing 'respectful ways of working with young men', as Denborough (1996) puts it, even on an issue like male violence.

Accordingly, practical accounts of gender-specific programs for boys and men typically emphasize student-centered methods. Gould (1985) recommends 'tactics of engagement' for teaching about masculinity in university courses. Reay (1990) describes an experiential program with boys in a British elementary school. Browne (1995), arguing that 'we all learn best from what we face in our own lives', develops a model for experiential programs in Australian secondary schools.

There is, however, a problem with this approach. The 'tactics of engagement' presuppose willing students. This cannot be presupposed in mass education, where classes for boys are vulnerable to the tactics of disruption—as Kenworthy (1994) found.

Reay's perceptive account of a teaching experience at upper

elementary level shows constant compromises between teacher and taught. For instance, she found herself accommodating rather than challenging peer-group hierarchies. Reay wryly concluded that at the end of the program, whatever they had learnt about gender, the boys had certainly learnt how to please the teacher.

Experiential approaches, then, need to be supplemented with methods that allow more distancing. Nilan (1995), for instance, uses script development both to bring out assumptions about masculinity and to allow students to debate them. Denborough, dealing with the very difficult issue of masculinity and violence, emphasizes getting boys to look for the counter-narrative to the conventional one—an approach that draws on the research analysis of subordinated and marginalized masculinities. Davies (1993), a post-structuralist in the classroom, has children performing astonishing feats of textual deconstruction and discursive analysis about gender. Even Davies, however, cannot prevent the boys in her groups resisting their removal from textual authority.

There is nothing against combining experiential with text-based methods, or indeed other methods. Dealing with gender across the curriculum clearly requires a mixture of teaching methods.

Whatever methods are used, work on gender with boys and men will only be successful if it opens possibilities, if it finds ways for them to move forward. The masculinity therapists are right about the damaging effect of a certain kind of feminist criticism which lumps all males together and relentlessly blames them. In teaching university courses about gender, I have repeatedly seen men students discouraged by the endless facts of sexism, experiencing feminist ideas mainly through guilt, and turning away because the alternative was to be overwhelmed. A sense of agency, of goals being achievable, is vital. The more sophisticated feminist approaches to masculinity, such as Segal's *Slow Motion* (1997), discriminate between groups of men and offer support to this process of change.

Institutional change

Reflecting on the encounter between women teachers and the heavily patriarchal culture of a Christian Brothers school, Angus (1993) acutely observes that change in the cultural handling of masculinity requires organizational change as well. Educational work on gender with boys, if it is to be more than a flash in the pan, requires institutional change in schools and systems.

Some of these changes are technical. Gender-specific classroom programs, for instance, require timetable changes in a co-educational school. Others changes are more substantive. Given the institutional definition of masculinity, the whole gender regime of a school is at issue. Grappling with the production of masculinity in the 'vortices' discussed above means replacing confrontational disciplinary systems, restructuring physical education to emphasize participation rather than competitive selection, and restructuring the gender-divided curriculum.

The curriculum issue, of course, goes well beyond an individual school. Curricula are partly controlled by system authorities, examination and testing boards, textbook publishers, employers' certification demands, and entry requirements of colleges. It is possible to move this aggregate, as feminist work in natural science and technology has shown, but it is not easy. Similarly, changing pedagogy and changing the gender division of labour among teachers requires action at system level and in teacher training institutions.

System-level change is more likely to happen if cued by changes already building up within schools. The current approach of developing school-level programs is, in that sense, justified. But it is important to move on from the school level.

A useful way of doing so is to set up systemic standards. Organizational change is more likely to happen when the people who hold organizational power have clear criteria to meet. It would be useful, and relatively cheap, to monitor school systems' performance on such issues as gender segregation in the curriculum, levels of violence and sexual harassment, the presence of men in early childhood education and women in administration, and the presence of curriculum units focussed on gender relations.

THE PROCESS OF CHANGE

In 1991 the Toronto School Board sponsored an innovative 'retreat' in which 40 high school boys and 40 high school girls, together with their teachers, worked on issues of sexism and change in masculinity. They used group discussion, drama, separate and joint meetings; then took the results back to their schools (Novogrodsky et al. 1992).

But this is not the direction in which most of the thinking about programs for boys has moved, as the international climate of opinion has become more conservative. Debates on gender in education have run into an impasse with the 'competing victims syndrome', as Cox (1995) aptly calls it. Does the discussion of masculinity and schooling have much chance of producing major change in gender relations?

The discussion has certainly raised major issues. Recent public debates have addressed three important questions: violence and harassment in schools; gender differences in academic outcomes; and the alienation of boys from schooling. The research surveyed in this chapter identifies two further issues of comparable importance: gender-divided curriculum pathways; and the organizational patterns that construct masculinities in schools.

These are longstanding issues, which do not come and go with a change in political climate. Whether they are turned into a reform program, however, depends a great deal on the interests and consciousness of the groups concerned. We must, therefore, appraise the groups and interests involved.

The boys

The broad gender privilege of men gives boys an interest in the current gender order. What might lead them to participate in educational work which must call that interest into question, and may require them to decline the offer of gender privilege?

Actual programs for boys, as Kindler (1993) reports, have

found a range of motives. They include curiosity, personal crisis, a sense of lack, a sense of justice, a desire for sharing and personal growth, and a desire for space for non-traditional conduct.

There are three underlying interests which might support these motives. First is the emotional and physical costs of patriarchy for boys and men. As Kaufman's (1993) discussion of violence emphasizes, these costs are far from trivial. Second is the interest boys and men have in personal relationships with women and girls. Boys have relationships, often close, with mothers, sisters, classmates, lovers, neighbours. They have relational interests, we might say, which cut across gender boundaries. Third are the general interests boys share with the women and girls in their lives because they are collective human interests. The shared interest in a healthy environment, for instance, can support study of the role of dominant masculinities in environmental destruction.

Parents and communities

The role of parents in relation to school programs about masculinity has yet to come into focus. There is an active discussion about the new fathering (McMahon 1999), but this is usually understood to concern the family not the school. Parents and parent groups have recently expressed public concern about boys' education, and there are indications that this is not a shallow interest. I know of schools that have been surprised by the extent of parent involvement when they announced an initiative on the subject.

Parents are easily represented as a force for conservatism in such matters. There is some basis for this view. For instance religious right mobilizations using parent representation have severely limited the capacity of US schools to deliver realistic sex education—a major problem in AIDS prevention (Sabella 1988).

Yet many parents are aware of changes in gender relations, and are deeply concerned about issues like AIDS and sexual violence. Many parents want the schools to address these issues for boys in a realistic and timely way. Parents of boys are often also parents of girls, and have an interest in a better future for their daughters. There are parent organizations which have committed themselves to deal with boys' issues in a gender equity framework (NSW Federation of Parents and Citizens Associations 1994). Parent involvement is not a synonym for gender conservatism.

Social movements
The feminist movement was the first to place gender issues on educational agendas. For a long time its main practical concern in education has been programs for girls. To some extent, therefore, feminists have been outflanked by the recent upsurge of interest in programs for boys.

A key response has been to develop comprehensive 'gender equity' policies, which are gender-relevant rather than gender-specific. Feminists face a continuing dilemma about resources. In an era of cuts to public-sector budgets, any expansion of gender programs for boys—even those intended to produce less patriarchal masculinities—is likely to compete for funds with programs for girls.

The contemporary 'men's movement' is deeply divided. There is a gender-justice current (e.g. the National Organization for Men Against Sexism), a masculinity-therapy current (e.g. the 'mythopoetic' men's retreats), a restore-patriarchy current (e.g. the Promise Keepers), and others. No unified educational program will come out of this. However, the arguments between these currents will certainly affect the balance between gender equity and boys' troubles as themes of programs for boys.

Teachers
Teachers are the workforce of educational reform. If anything large is to happen in schools, teachers must be engaged in making it happen. As Angus (1993) observes, to the extent conventional masculinity 'works' in the current educational environment, a lot of male teachers have little motive to change. Yet some men do become involved in counter-sexist work with boys. The teaching profession too contains a diversity of masculinities.

Further, teachers and administrators experience the occupational stress caused by violence and resistance among boys. Teachers have an interest in meeting challenges in their work: teaching well, reducing disruptions to learning, and achieving educational justice in the face of difficulties. There are, then, industrial and professional reasons for educators to concern themselves with issues about masculinity.

I think it virtually certain that the interplay of these groups and interests will drive an expansion of current educational work on masculinity and programs for boys. This is unlikely to grow to the scale of programs for girls, because different locations in the gender order produce a different pattern of social mobilization. But a need has been articulated and a response is developing around it. What form the expansion will take is still an open question.

It is clear that schools have a considerable capacity to make and remake gender. They are not the engine of gender revolution that liberal feminism, focussed on the task of changing attitudes and norms, once believed. Nevertheless, the school system is a weighty institution, a major employer, a key means of transmitting culture between generations. It has direct control over its own gender regimes, which have a considerable impact on the experience of children growing up; and it can set standards, pose questions, and supply knowledge, for other spheres of life.

For the most part, these capacities impact on the making of masculinities in an unreflective, inchoate way. The planned masculinizing regimes of the old boarding schools have been replaced, in mass public education, with a hodgepodge of practices impacting on the lives of boys, which are rarely thought through in gender terms. Such practices as school sport, discipline, and curriculum division, may have strong masculinizing effects—but may be at odds with each other, or in conflict with other purposes of the school. The tendency of masculinity formation, in certain situations, to undermine or completely disrupt the teaching function of the school, is particularly worrying.

A key task at present, then, is simply bringing these issues to light, asking educators to reflect on what the schools are currently doing. As we have seen, there is a good deal of research available that can help with this thinking. The research forcibly shows—in contrast to much popular thinking—that 'boys' are not a homogeneous bloc, that masculinities vary and change and that, in gender, institutions (as well as bodies) matter. All these are important conditions for educational work.

Another condition is awareness of the possibility of change. This awareness is being forced on the schools by developments in the world around them, by social movements, media attention, and policy debates that have focussed on problems of masculinity. With such challenges emerging all over the industrialized world, no contemporary education system is going to escape these issues. Addressing them thoughtfully, schools can make a real contribution to a future of more civilized, and more just, gender relations.

10

Men's health

Like other institutions in modern society, the health system has a gender regime—an internal set of gender arrangements—which marks out places for men as well as for women. The health system's gender regime over the last hundred years has included:

- a gender division of labour, assigning specific jobs to men and distinguishing them from 'women's work' such as nursing;
- gender ideologies, which contain images of masculinity, interpretations of men's bodies, beliefs about men's illnesses and forms of treatment; and
- services targeted (or tending to focus) on groups of men: such as veteran's hospitals, occupational health programs, specialties such as cardiology, sports medicine etc.

Until recently there has been no concept that would collect these issues into one basket. That we now have a concept like 'men's health' (National Men's Health Conference 1995, Sabo & Gordon 1995) is due to the critique of patriarchal medicine by the women's movement, the emergence of a debate about 'women's health', and the questioning of masculinity and male roles which the new feminism provoked.

As shown in earlier chapters, the research that resulted from this questioning demonstrates the plurality of masculinities, the importance of gender hierarchies among men, the internal complexity and often contradictory character of masculinities, the capacity for change, and the interweaving of masculinities with the structures of class and ethnicity. All these points are of importance for understanding men's health.

Centrally important is the evidence, in a wide range of settings, of the active construction of masculinity. Gender for men is not simply received from agencies of socialization or from discourses, but is very actively made, both individually and collectively, using the resources and strategies available in a given social setting. From bodybuilders in the gym to managers in the boardroom to boys in the primary school playground, a whole lot of people are working hard to produce masculinities and have them recognized by other people.

That is a crucial point for understanding gender/health issues for men. The health effects are not mechanical consequences of either the physiological or the social condition of being a man. They are the products of human practice, of things done, in relation to the gender order.

In this chapter I will show how these insights give us a better understanding of significant issues about men's health, and give guidance for attempts to promote health. It is important to be specific, both about particular health effects and particular masculinities or groups of men. It is too easy to produce sweeping statements about the 'male role' as a health hazard, statements which turn out to have more exceptions than applications.

RESEARCH EVIDENCE ON MEN'S HEALTH

In the burst of publicity about 'men's health' in the mid-1990s it was often claimed that this was a 'forgotten issue', a neglected field just now being opened up. 'The truth is at last being acknowledged', said one media headline, and that seems to have been a widespread sentiment.

In terms of research, this is by no means a new or neglected area. There has been an international discussion of health issues for men at least since the 1970s. An influential American essay of that decade was entitled 'Warning: the male sex role may be dangerous to your health' (Harrison 1978). Ten years before the recent burst of publicity, an Australian discussion of men and community health remarked that the differences between men's and women's health had been the 'subject of extensive research' already (Baum 1984).

Baum was right: there is a great deal of existing research that bears on the problems of men's health. It is another matter, however, to draw this research together and connect it with conceptual and practical problems. The discussion that follows is specifically based on the Australian health research related to men and masculinity. In 1998 I was involved, with a group of colleagues, in making a detailed survey of this research for the Australian government (the full report with citations is in Connell et al. 1999). Thus there is currently a more up-to-date and comprehensive database on men's health studies in Australia than in any other country. However, as comparable research in other countries indicates (e.g. Stillion 1995), the patterns are broadly similar across the economically advanced Western countries.

SEX DIFFERENCES IN HEALTH

The largest single body of research bearing on men's health is quantitative studies of 'sex differences', in which the state of men's health is appraised using women's health as a baseline.

In this genre of research, the same measures are applied to the men and women (or boys and girls) of a group under study. The focus of interest is the difference between group averages or rates, such as the prevalence of a disease, or the frequency of a certain behaviour or a certain cause of death. Except in studies of whole populations (e.g. censuses), whether there is a difference worth considering is generally appraised by a test of statistical significance—a procedure which, given certain assumptions, measures the probability of a given difference emerging in the research by chance alone. There is a huge volume of this kind of research in the life sciences and social sciences internationally. It is technically quite easy to do—given a measure of any human characteristic, a mixed group and a significance test.

In a sense, doing sex difference research has become automatic. 'Sex' (or 'gender', understood as the biological distinction of female from male) is now routinely one of the variables included in quantitative biomedical and social research. A large volume of descriptive research routinely reports the presence or absence of a sex difference, in exactly the way it reports differences by age, or skin colour, or country of origin. To do this does not require any specific thought about the nature of gender or the meaning of gender difference—that is typically taken for granted, or vaguely assumed to be a biological distinction (Kessler & McKenna 1978).

The most important sources of data on health-related sex differences in Australia are the surveys and compilations of the Australian Bureau of Statistics. These include the periodic National Health Surveys, regular series such as *Causes of Death*, and a variety of other series and surveys. Many other health institutions compile statistics, and as they often distinguish men and women, they too are a source of sex difference data.

'Difference' statistics from such sources are widely cited in discussions of men's health. Mathers (1996) provided a good summary of them at the first National Men's Health Conference. The differences most widely noted are:

- men's greater mortality from heart disease;
- men's shorter average life expectancy;
- men's higher rates of injury from accident, including industrial and motor vehicle injury;
- men's and boys' higher suicide rates; and
- men's higher rates of alcohol abuse.

Though there are reasons to be cautious about many sex difference results, these ones seem to be well established. They can be regarded as robust findings, of significance for health policy.

There are a great many more sex difference findings beyond these, since sex differences have been examined on a very wide range of health issues. They range from diet and weight control practices to knowledge of sexually transmitted diseases and safe sex practices, injecting drug use, emotional problems in youth, childhood dental trauma, location of skin cancers, snake bite, dog attacks—and more.

It would not be surprising if sex differences on some of these issues also proved to be robust findings. Gender is, after all, one of the major organizing structures of modern social life, involving broad divisions of labour, different social authority and control over resources, patterns of sexuality and emotional attachment, differing identities. Among the effects of gender are likely to be many differences in exposure, behaviour, interest and learning between groups of men and groups of women.

However, it is very important to recognize that finding a 'sex difference' need not imply a difference between *all* men and *all* women. In fact it usually does not. Quite small differences among a minority of the population may produce statistically significant differences in overall rates or averages. In disussions of gender (especially as results get simplified in the mass media) even small differences are liable to be misinterpreted as categorical differences between 'women' and 'men'.

It is also important to recognize that many studies searching for sex differences find none. 'No difference' is, in fact, the *usual* finding in research on psychological characteristics of women and men—contrary to popular belief, and contrary to the expectations of many of the researchers (Connell 1987, Epstein 1988). 'No difference' is also the finding in a good proportion of Australian research on health. Mathers' (1996) review of national statistics, though specifically looking for 'differentials', perforce also notes similarities between women and men—for instance in overall health expectancies and rates of hospitalization apart from pregnancy and childbirth. Specific studies have found no sex difference (or sex differences so small as to be unimportant) on issues as diverse as teenage drug use, childhood blood-lead concentration, age-related prevalence of leg ulcers, glaucoma, patterns of caring and knowledge about AIDS.

I suspect there are many more nil findings than ever get published. A finding of 'no difference' tends to be regarded as uninteresting or uninterpretable and is less likely to be written up and submitted for publication. A 'no difference' finding is perhaps less likely to be published by a research journal, and is certainly less likely to attract mass media publicity.

THE HEALTH OF SPECIFIC GROUPS OF MEN

Indigenous men

Aboriginal men, especially men in remote communities, have been the subject of considerable recent research. Some of this is biomedical research of a conventional kind, applying established research techniques and comparing Aboriginal men with norms established in European-origin populations. Some combine biomedical investigation with analysis of the economic and social circumstances and gender relations of the Aboriginal communities involved. There are also data on Aboriginal men's health from the regular statistical series, such as causes of death; and from specific cross-sectional surveys, such as the National Aboriginal and Torres Strait Islander survey carried out by the Australian Bureau of Statistics in 1994.

Taken together, these studies document an exceptionally serious range of health problems compared with the Australian population as a whole. These include reduced expectation of life, high levels of eye disease, respiratory disease, smoking, alcoholism and limited access to health services (for a useful summary see Australian Institute of Health and Welfare 1996, pp. 21–30). Given the extreme poverty of the Aboriginal population, the effects of specific indigenous cultural practices and the damaging history of race relations are difficult to disentangle from the effects of current economic inequality.

Homeless men

A small group of studies looks at another group in poverty, the homeless men of the cities. Some of this research is concerned with possible causes of homelessness, such as mental illness.

Some is concerned with the health effects of their conditions of life, such as tuberculosis. Again, exceptionally poor health is obvious in this group of men.

Specific ethnic groups

A very diverse set of studies looks at particular health issues in relation to a specific ethnic or immigrant group, for instance people of Chinese descent. Sometimes the group studied is treated almost as a biological entity; sometimes it is understood as the bearer of a particular culture, and as having a specific history of immigration and settlement. There is almost no application of modern conceptual and empirical work on 'ethnicity' and its changing construction (Bottomley 1992). There is little common ground in the health topics studied, and it is difficult to detect overall patterns in the Australian findings comparable with the US evidence of severe health problems among African-American men (Staples 1995). In all multicultural societies, however, we need to be alert to questions of ethnic difference when thinking about 'men'.

Older men

Since there is a medical specialty of gerontology, there is an international biomedical literature on older men alongside the literature on older women. Only a modest number of such studies have been done in Australia. They include work on urinary symptoms, hip fracture and bereavement. Most of the relevant studies are 'sex difference' work on older populations, for example looking at the use of general practitioner services, eye function, patterns of cancer mortality, or the problems of living alone in old age. Some indications come through, nevertheless, of generational issues in the construction of masculinity, in dealing with men who grew up in a time where acknowledging illness or emotional distress was seen as a sign of unmasculine weakness.

Boys and youth

A rather larger body of research concerns the early stages of life. There are studies of road safety issues concerning boys;

a good series of sex difference surveys on the incidence and correlates of smoking; sex difference research on young people's health beliefs and knowledge, body image and dieting, sexual practices etc. There are also studies which document traumatic experiences such as sexual abuse of boys.

Research on masculinity, popular culture and youth subcultures is highly informative about alcohol and violence. Tulloch and Tulloch (1992), in a study of young people's tolerance for violence on television, show that this tolerance is higher in the case of televised sport—a masculinized genre— than with soap operas—a feminized genre. This is an unusual demonstration of the impersonal construction of gender. Other research looks at determinants of drinking and at interpersonal violence among young men, showing its connection with the situational construction of masculinities in settings such as bars. The growing literature on masculinity and youth subcultures now includes work on non-Anglo ethnic groups which is beginning to show the role of racism and class exclusion in the production of conflict and violence.

There is also useful research about violence and intimidation in schools. This includes 'sex difference' research on bullying, and more specific examinations of boys, masculinity and school violence. There is also research on sexual harassment, which has mostly addressed girls but has many implications for understanding the gender practices of boys. It is clear that there is a considerable amount of concealed violence in schools and that in many, though not all, school contexts, intimidation and harassment are used as means of constructing gender hierarchies and defending masculine honour or prestige.

HOW SOME MASCULINIZING PRACTICES DAMAGE BODIES

Driving motor vehicles

Injury on the road is a leading cause of death for young men, and young men's road accident rates are spectacularly higher than those of other groups. Currently in New South Wales, young men drivers aged 17 to 25 are involved in four times as many serious speed-related casualties as young women (Roads and Traffic Authority of NSW 1997). A considerable number of the casualties are related to drink-driving, about which there is a frightening research literature.

When a group of young men in a car drink, drive and crash, they are not being driven to it by uncontrollable hormones, or even an uncontrollable male role. They are acting that way in order to be masculine. The dangerous driving is a resource for their making of masculinity. Here the active construction of masculinity is a key to the risk-taking behaviour, and to strategies of prevention.

This is a classic case of collective gender practice. The peer group itself, not just the individuals within it, sustains the definition of masculinity and a particular way of pursuing masculine status. Young men's peer groups, in turn, act in a context of mass media and corporate business which sustain a masculinized 'car culture' on a world scale (Walker 1998b). There is nothing peculiarly Australian about this. Here the globalization of industry and the globalization of gender have gone hand in hand.

The massive growth of the motor transport industry is a public health problem at many levels. The fact that it is strongly gendered is not always noticed, but is a key both to its cultural influence and to the pattern of death and injury it produces (Connell et al. 1997).

Drug marketing

Smoking tobacco was long seen as a distinctively masculine activity—the smoking room was a male club, the smoking jacket an article of men's dress, the smell of tobacco supposedly part of the distinctive smell of men. Advertising for tobacco products has long drawn on this connection, promoting cigars, pipes and more recently cigarettes as means of achieving masculine status. The most famous case was the 'Marlboro Man' advertising campaign, which connected cigarette smoking to a fantasy of outdoor frontier masculinity.

Most heroin deaths in Australia are of men; but the rate

of ill-health from illicit narcotics is small compared with the health problems produced by legal drugs. The mass marketing of nicotine and alcohol provides striking examples of the collective dimension of masculinity. This is seen both in the boardroom masculinity of the corporate executives who direct these toxic operations, and in the cultural imagery of he-man masculinity which is often used to sell the products.

It is not an accident that drug marketing uses highly stereotyped images of gender. Corporate profits depend on drug habits being established in youth; not many mature adults *start* drug use (whether legal or illegal). The advertising addresses anxieties that are most acute in adolescence, and often attempts to connect drug use with conspicuous displays of masculinity.

One common scenario tries to connect alcohol or nicotine with sexual freedom and success in the heterosexual dating scene. Another tries to connect drug use with elite sport. There is a gender logic to the otherwise bizarre connection of nicotine with cricket (the former 'Benson & Hedges Tests') and alcohol with football, not to mention the persistent promotion of drugs in connection with speeding cars ('motor sport').

However, tobacco has been the target of a major public health effort, which has made important gains—specifically among men, a point worth noting when sweeping claims about men's 'risk-taking' are made. Rates of smoking used to be very much higher among men than among women, but the rates have converged over the decades. The old patterns are still visible, as a kind of archaeological residue, in contemporary surveys. Young men smoke less often than their fathers' generation do (Hill et al. 1998). Unfortunately at the same time the tobacco companies have made a killing among young women.

Occupational health and safety

There is a considerable amount of information about the health problems of specific occupational groups. There are, for example, studies which document the terrible consequences of asbestos mining at Wittenoom in Western Australia, which produced fatal lung disorders among many miners; studies on the health of isolated or remote groups of workers such as coal miners, shearers and prawn trawlers; and studies of the health workforce itself. These become studies of 'men's health' to the extent that the gender division of labour in the workforce as a whole constitutes particular occupations as entirely, or mostly, for men.

For the same reason, studies of particular kinds of injuries reveal a background of men's labour. In a study of fatalities from electrical shock, all the victims were men; in a study of eye injuries in a rural area, 88 per cent were men, and most often the accidents involved hammered metal or fencing wire. A study of traumatic brain injury found this most common among young men in rural work and manual trades, very often associated with driving vehicles. Rural men's work with tractors is a particular black spot for serious injury from accidents.

The majority of serious industrial injuries are sustained by men, a fact often attributed to men acting hardy and taking risks. Before we accept the story that industrial safety is a psychological problem of men—'the blokes won't wear helmets'—we should look at why men find themselves in dangerous work situations in the first place.

Our society's gender division of labour defines as 'men's work' most labouring, most work involving heavy machinery, most transport work, most work involving weapons and dangerous tools, and most work in heavily polluted environments. These situations are also, generally speaking, working-class workplaces. The average corporate executive does not lose many fingers in drop-forges nor die of black lung. The distribution of power and the nature of work in industrial capitalism are implicated in men's health outcomes.

As Donaldson (1991) points out, working-class men have basically one asset to market—their bodily capacity to labour—and their bodies are, over time, consumed by the labour they do. In stark contrast to managers and professionals, by middle age working men's earning capacity is falling, unless they have won promotion off the shop floor. The relation between workplace and home (established in an earlier period of history) that requires a husband to be 'breadwinner' has locked in these bodily effects.

Given these conditions, working men may embrace the processes that consume their bodies, as their way of 'doing' masculinity, and claiming some self-respect in the damaging world of wage labour. Working-class culture is full of legendary examples, from the railway labourer John Henry who died defeating a steam-driven machine, and the miner who loaded 'Sixteen Tons' on the day he was born, to the 'gun' shearers of the Australian outback. And working-class life is full of all-too-real young men who disdain helmets or earmuffs, truck drivers who live on stimulants, labourers who lift too-heavy weights, machine operators who drink and work, and professional sportsmen who play hurt.

This issue is particularly clear in studies of soldiers, where the notion of an 'occupational group' merges into the very definition of masculine gender. Australian studies of the health effects of military service are not extensive, but they have begun to explore potential costs of this enactment of masculinity, in alcohol consumption, psychiatric casualties and suicide.

ATTEMPTS TO MAKE MEN'S BODIES HEALTHY

Sport

The image of sport is one of healthy bodies in vigorous action. Sport might seem our society's health-giving activity par excellence—exercise, fresh air, good fellowship. Modern sport is, the historians tell us, a product of urban capitalism, though it expresses some nostalgia for the countryside (the grassy oval, the horses, the seasonal rhythm) and even a kind of revolt against the factory, the machine, and industrial discipline (Gruneau 1999). These impulses produced mass participation in decentralized amateur and community-based sports (tennis, cricket, surfing, netball), alongside professional sports (boxing, racing) for popular entertainment, with games like football hovering between the two patterns.

With the growth of the service-based economy in the late twentieth century, professionalism has become completely dominant, and most sports have been reorganized on the same model. Sport is now mainly a branch of commercial mass entertainment, with amateur sports a recruitment zone for the real thing—bitterly competitive professional leagues supported by television advertising revenue.

Professional sport is overwhelmingly men's sport, and has become a major arena for the promotion of dominant forms of masculinity. There are several reasons to think that, far from being a health-promoting activity, sport is now a major threat to men's health.

- Most men participate in commercial sport only as consumers, with the aid of TV, snack foods and beer. The pattern is symbolized by the growing use of the American term 'fan' in Australian sport.
- The small minority who become players in elite commercial sport, under the 'win at all costs' ideology dominant there, are subject to high levels of physical stress, psychological stress, frequent injury, and pressure to enhance their performance with drugs (White et al. 1995). This is a toxic environment, reflected in high levels of physical damage, and shortened life, experienced by professional sportsmen after retirement. Certain patterns of illicit drug use, such as use of steroids, have now become common not only among professional sportsmen but also among youth who aspire to enter elite sport.
- The process of commercialization has included in the domain of 'sport' certain activities, notably car and motor-cycle racing, which have no physical benefits at all. On the contrary they glamorize practices—speeding and aggressive driving—directly implicated in road deaths and injuries among men.

AIDS prevention

Australia has an HIV epidemic of a pattern similar to that of North America and Western Europe, contrasting with the

epidemic in Central Africa, and with the newer epidemics of
Asia. In Australia the great majority of HIV infections and
deaths are among men. Most new infections are among relatively young men, though because of the long incubation
period of the virus, most AIDS cases and deaths are not among
the young.

Since Australia has an HIV epidemic on the North American/
Western European pattern, the great majority of AIDS cases
are among men who have sex with men. Accordingly, the research effort related to the epidemic principally concerns gay
men—both as the 'subjects' of research, and as researchers and
educators. The Australian response to AIDS since the mid-1980s
is noted internationally for the high level of cooperation between
government and gay communities, and for the favourable environment this created for research and for prevention education.

Gay masculinity is the main form of subordinated masculinity
in the Western gender order. The pattern of subordination
includes cultural abuse against gays (in which conservative
churches have been prominent), institutional discrimination, and
violence (mostly from young men, some of them police, attempting to establish their masculine credentials). Partly in response to
these pressures, relatively cohesive urban gay communities formed
in the later decades of the twentieth century.

In the late 1970s and 1980s the sexual networks in these
communities became pathways for the spread of HIV. They
were also the basis of the remarkable gay community response
in prevention and care. An active and sustained response included
building new institutions, undertaking a large-scale community education program to reshape sexual practices, and providing
a range of new services. All this was done in the context of
epidemic illness, bereavement and grief, and episodic struggles
with politicians, media and the medical profession (Altman
1994, Kippax et al. 1993). Though it has some limits, as we saw
in Chapter 7, it is the most impressive men's health initiative
in any field in recent decades.

The gay community response tells us something important
about men's capacities, which is obscured when we focus only
on cultural stereotypes of masculinity. Gay communities created

a range of groups concerned with psychological support, housing, home-based care, drugs, and other treatments. Though women have been part of these initiatives, men have always been prominent in them. They provide a continuing demonstration of men's capacity for *care*, and for doing the practical work of caring, which should be widely noticed.

Further, gay men's experience in collaborative work with others—including heterosexual researchers in the universities and women in health services—provide important precedents for a cooperative, rather than a separatist, approach to men's health issues.

Child care

Another area where men's caring capacities are in question is in the care of young children. There is every reason to think close relations with fathers as well as mothers is good for the health and wellbeing of children and adolescents.

Pop psychologists of the 1990s talked a great deal about boys' special 'father hunger', a concept as well supported by evidence as the idea that aliens have landed in Coonabarabran. Of course men should be involved in child care; and there are good reasons, we do not need spurious ones. Girls need fathers as much as boys do; good parenting can be done by both women and men; all children are benefited by the broad involvement of both men and women in child care. Two-gender child care diversifies children's relationships, and helps break down the belief in rigid division between masculine and feminine which is the source of some of the difficulties in growing up.

Men's level of involvement in child care can be dramatically improved by institutional changes which make such involvement economically or culturally easier. Norway, for instance, has a publicly funded parental leave scheme that, since 1993, has reserved four weeks of the leave entitlement as a 'father's quota', which can only be used by the fathers. (There is also a mother's quota, and a discretionary amount.) In 1996, about 70 per cent of the men who had this entitlement took it up. And 97 per cent of these men said they did so because they themselves wanted to (Gender Equality Ombudsman 1997). Denmark has adopted a policy of encouraging gender balance in the workforce of child-care centres, with considerable success.

In Australia the slow move in the same direction is now under threat by political and media panic over 'pedophiles'. Under the cover of child protection, this has turned into an attack on gender reform, child care outside the family, and the unmanliness of men who might have an interest in children. It is distressing to see how a rare sexual disorder has been exaggerated into a state of public fear where parents are made constantly anxious, and gay men, schoolteachers, and child-care workers are under constant threat of accusation. It is quite possible that more damage is being done by this hysteria than by the practice of pedophilia itself.

Most sexual abuse of children does not come from secret rings of 'pedophiles', nor from child-care workers or teachers. It comes from men and youths in the children's families or neighbourhoods—often from teenagers (Messerschmidt 2000). Prevention of child abuse will need to contest assumptions about men's right to sexual pleasure, as well as change the power imbalances within families that make abused children vulnerable, and the environments of poverty and violence from which many young perpetrators come.

THE 'CRADLE TO GRAVE' HEALTH DISADVANTAGE OF MEN

In a burst of Australian media publicity in the mid-1990s, it was claimed that men's health was worse than women's on all areas except sex-specific disorders. Some of the more excitable commentators spoke of a men's health 'crisis', or 'boys: a species under threat?', and claimed that 'men are losing out to women from the cradle to the grave'.

On the research evidence, these claims are very misleading. There is no general 'crisis' in men's health. As the Australian Institute of Health and Welfare (1996, p. 1) observed, 'Australia is one of the healthiest countries in the world and the health of Australians generally continues to improve', and this is true for men as well as women, measured by such indicators as life expectancy. (If there ever was an Australian men's health crisis in the twentieth century it was in the 1960s and had to do with heart disease and smoking, and perhaps the aftermath of war—see the figures in Mathers 1995.)

Nor is it true that men's health is worse than women's across the board. In some ways men as a group really are worse off—as shown in the mortality statistics, and in 'risk factors' such as being overweight, smoking, and drinking heavily. But in other respects men as a group are not worse off. In a good many research reports, men and boys have *similar* averages or rates to women and girls. And in other studies, men and boys have *better* averages or rates than women and girls.

If one trawls for health 'disadvantages' of women, as some commentators have trawled for disadvantages of men, they are not hard to find. The official statistics and broad surveys reveal some: higher rates of severe disability among women, more wide-spread minor illness, higher rates of hospitalization, higher rates of mental illness, migraine, arthritis etc. (Mathers 1996). There are also many specific studies showing apparent female 'disadvan-tage' in health issues: optic disc haemorrhage, a range of emotional disorders, prevalence of multiple sclerosis, postoperative compli-cations, insomnia, iron deficiency in adolescence, anxiety about weight, adolescent dieting etc. Some researchers suggest there is a broad pattern of lower morbidity (i.e. illness and injury) for men than women, as contrasted with the pattern of higher mortality (i.e. death rates).

These studies do not justify a counter-claim that women are health-disadvantaged. Rather, they prove that gender patterns are complex as well as powerful. The facts do not justify sweep-ing claims of men's (or women's) health disadvantage. Such claims simply feed into the 'competing victims' rhetoric, a notably unhelpful way of thinking about public policy (Cox 1995).

But this does *not* mean that 'men's health' concerns are a chimera. On the contrary, the evidence is clear that there are significant health issues that have to do with the positions of men (and women) in gender relations. We need to examine the specific circumstances and practices that produce health effects, to understand the evidence about gender.

REFLECTIONS

It is very important, then, to recognize the diversity among men in relation to health. The research evidence shows many indications of this diversity, exactly as would be expected from the social-scientific research on the plurality of masculinities and gender practices among men (Chapter 1). Part of this diversity is produced by the interplay of gender with other structures of difference (e.g. ethnicity, social class) and part by the internal complexities of the gender order.

The studies discussed above show specific health issues emerging for Aboriginal men, elderly men, boys and youth, homeless men, and men of specific immigrant groups. This is important documentation of diversity, but it is certainly not all.

The studies of sexual health show certain issues specific to gay men, and other issues specific to heterosexual men. The studies of occupational and industrial health show specific health issues in particular groups of workers and particular regions. These patterns, of course, intersect. Thus, a particular man may be gay, young, a metal worker and of Italian immigrant background; or straight, rural, elderly and Anglo; or many other combinations.

There is, then, no single pattern of 'men's health' problems; and it is extremely unlikely that any 'one size fits all' policy or education approach would be helpful.

The social-scientific research on masculinities is clear that gender practices and configurations change historically. We might therefore expect gender patterns in health to change over time. The best known example, smoking, has already been mentioned, where rates for men and for women have converged.

Smoking is not the only documented case of change. Sex differences in stroke mortality have changed over time. The male-to-female ratio in youth suicide has increased. Sex differences in health-sector employment have changed over time, with more women entering medicine, more men entering nursing etc. Gender patterns of unemployment, and its health consequences, change over time. Jain's (1993) study suggests that sex differences in overall morbidity have narrowed over time.

The fact that some patterns of difference have measurably changed should be very encouraging from the point of view of improving men's health. These studies indicate that patterns often taken to be 'natural' and therefore intractable are in fact subject to social forces and therefore may be open to conscious social intervention. 'Men's health' as an issue is basically a public health problem (Schofield et al. 2000) and is, potentially, amenable to all the techniques of public health intervention.

The new field of 'men's health' can be the vehicle for back-lash politics. But it can also be an important opportunity for men to grasp the significance of the perspectives opened up by feminism. This opportunity is certainly open in current discussions of men's health, with its emphasis on diversity and on the construction of masculinities. The more the field can be developed within a broad gender perspective, with an emphasis on the interactive and historical character of masculinities, the less chance there is of it degenerating into separatism-for-men and competition with women's health programs.

PART 5

CHANGING
MASCULINITIES

11

The politics of change
in masculinity

In 1970 my wife and I, temporarily in the United States, were among a hundred thousand people who marched on Washington—in our case by Volkswagen—to protest against President Nixon's invasion of Cambodia, and the subsequent killing of students during a protest at Kent State University.

The action was one of those dramas of confrontation that Americans do so well. A chanting avant garde of students, mostly men, tried to storm the line of buses parked in a defensive ring around the White House. Through clouds of tear gas, they were turned back by rows of scowling police, all men. Meanwhile tens of thousands of other protestors massed in the wide parklands and crowded into the streets of downtown Washington in support.

In 1994 I went to another demonstration against violence, this time in Sydney. It was organized by the Australian group Men Against Sexual Assault (MASA), to protest against men's acts of violence against women. We marched through the streets from near Central Station and held a rally with speeches and music in the main park of the city. About 70 people came. There was no tear gas and there were no arrests, though there were a few police.

One event is in the history books, the other is not. But this is not the only difference. Looking back, we can now see the 1970 demonstration, for all its radicalism, as a patriarchal event. The confrontation was a display of masculinity on both sides, a declaration of toughness, which sidelined women physically and morally, even though women made up a large proportion of the protestors. This pattern in the anti-war movement was a key reason why the women's liberation movement was emerging at that time.

The 1994 protest was tiny because there was no social movement backing it. The Kent State protest had a specific target, a perpetrator of great visibility, living right there in the building facing us. The MASA protest had as target the same group that was making the protest: 'men'. Though the moral point of the protest was equally clear, both being actions against violence, the political situation was much muddier. And the demand being made on the demonstrators themselves was more complex. For MASA was criticizing the very masculinity that produced 'the demonstration' as a confrontational genre of political action.

The issues at stake in this critique of masculinity seem to me far more important than is suggested by media jokes about Sensitive New Age Guys, or Wild Men beating on drums and pretending to be bears. For men to gain a deeper understanding of themselves, especially at the level of emotions, is a key to the transformation of personal relationships, sexuality and domestic life. Men's gender practices raise large questions of social justice, given the scale of economic inequality, domestic violence, and institutional barriers to women's equality.

Further, masculinities are deeply implicated in organized violence, such as the civil wars in central Africa, former Jugoslavia, and East Timor; and in technologies and production systems that threaten environmental destruction and nuclear war. The path of the HIV/AIDS epidemic is closely connected to recent social changes in men's sexualities.

The list could go on, but this is enough to establish the point. In thinking about change in masculinities, we are dealing with issues of importance for global society as well as for personal life.

THE HISTORICAL MOMENT

For much of this century there has been a gradually increasing awareness of the possibility of change in gender. This consciousness erupted in the women's liberation, gay liberation, and men's liberation movements in the years around 1970.

To people energized by these movements, it seemed that millennia of patriarchy and oppression could now end. The technological conditions for the equality of the sexes now existed, and the crucial change of consciousness had arrived. Feminist women began to invent a new language for a post-patriarchal world and a new politics based on 'consciousness-raising' and 'sisterhood'.

For the brothers in men's liberation, many of whom had a background in the anti-war movement, this sense of a great historical drama unfolding gave resonance to otherwise modest reform proposals and vague rhetorics of change. A genre of books criticizing 'the male role' emerged in the 1970s (popular examples were Fasteau 1975 and Nichols 1975). Most of the critics believed that masculinity was in crisis, and that the crisis itself would drive change forward. The end would be a world where masculinity as we know it would be annihilated, replaced by some kind of androgyny.

Decades later, this apocalyptic thinking has become rare and even seems naive. We are all so much more sophisticated now! Yet those innocent pioneers did us a tremendous favour. The shift in thinking about gender achieved by the liberation movements of the 1970s is irreversible.

Historicity is now the presupposition, not the heresy. Even the conservatives who have moved onto this terrain, such as evangelical Christians in the 'Promise Keepers', engage in historical thinking about masculinity. They accept the fact of social transformations in gender however much they deplore them or try to reverse them.

This historical consciousness is the distinctive feature of

current masculinity politics, and the horizon of contemporary thought on masculinity. Without this consciousness it would be impossible to imagine the popularity of commentators on masculinity such as Robert Bly in the United States, or Walter Hollstein in Germany.

How should we understand the political possibilities this historical consciousness opens up—and how can we act on these possibilities? In thinking these questions through, we can draw on the new generation of social research on masculinities to analyze political processes and formulate purposes.

MEN'S INTERESTS

In the attempt to set up a 'men's liberation' movement in the 1970s, it was assumed that feminism was good for men, because men too suffered from rigid sex roles. As women broke out of their sex role, men would be enabled to break out of theirs, and would have fuller, better, and healthier lives as a result.

The failure of any large number to sign on as the men's auxiliary to feminism, in the years since, suggests a flaw in this analysis. Men's dominant position in the gender order has a material pay-off, and the discussions of masculinity have constantly under-estimated how big this is. In the rich capitalist countries, including Australia, men's average incomes are approximately double the average incomes of women. Men have seven times the political access of women worldwide (measured by representation in parliaments: Inter-Parliamentary Union 1999). Men have even greater control of corporate wealth (looking at top management in major corporations). It is men who control the ultimate argument of power, the means of violence, in the form of weapons and armed forces.

This pay-off for men as a group, the patriarchal dividend, is not withering away. The gender segregation of the workforce in the rich countries has declined little in recent years. Men's percentage of representatives in parliaments worldwide was 88.9 per cent in 1991 and is 87.2 per cent in 1999. As corporations have gone multinational—under the aegis of corporate hegemonic masculinity—they have increasingly escaped the main political structures through which women have gained some leverage (e.g. through anti-discrimination laws), because these structures are located at the level of the individual nation-state. The new international garment manufacturing and microprocessor assembly industries, for instance, are arenas of rampant sexism. Violence against women has not measurably declined.

Yet not all men are corporate executives or mass killers. Though men in general gain the patriarchal dividend, specific groups of men gain very little of it. For instance, working-class youth, economically dispossessed by structural unemployment, may gain no economic advantage at all over the women in their communities.

Other groups of men pay part of the price, alongside women, for the maintenance of an unequal gender order. Gay men are systematically made targets of prejudice and violence. Effeminate and wimpish men are constantly put down. Black men, in the United States (as in South Africa) suffer massively higher levels of lethal violence than white men; and Aboriginal men endure massively higher rates of imprisonment than other Australians. The new 'men's health' movement has shown that health costs of conventional masculinities (e.g. in road trauma, alcohol abuse, poor diet) are quite widespread, as seen in Chapter 10.

There are, then, divisions of interest among men on gender issues. Further, many interests are relational rather than egotistic. That is, they are constituted in the social relations one shares with other people. Most men have relational interests that they share with particular women. For instance, as parents needing child-care provision and good health services for children. Or as workers, needing improved conditions and security. Aboriginal men share with Aboriginal women an interest in ending racism. Gay men share with lesbians an interest in fighting sex-based discrimination.

In most men's lives there are dense networks of relationships with women: with mothers, wives, partners, sisters, daughters, aunts, grandmothers, friends, workmates, neighbours. Very few men have a life-world that is blocked off from women, that is genuinely a 'separate sphere'.

Each of these relationships can be the basis for men's relational interest in reform. For instance, I have an interest in my daughter's being free of sexual harassment at school, in her having access to any kind of training and all occupations, in her growing up a confident and autonomous person. I have an interest in my mother's having the best possible health care, in my sisters' and my nieces' having adequate jobs, job security and equal pay, and being free of the threat of intimidation or rape.

Men's interest in gender hierarchy, defined by the patriarchal dividend, is real and large. But it is internally divided, and it is cross-cut by relational interests shared with women. Which of these interests is actually pursued by particular men is a matter of politics—politics in the quite familiar sense of organizing in the pursuit of programs.

Men who try to develop a politics in support of feminism, whether gay or straight, are not in for an easy ride. They are likely to be met with derision from many other men, and from some women—it is almost a journalistic cliché that women despise Sensitive New Age Guys. They will not necessarily get warm support from feminist women, some of whom are deeply distrustful of all men, most of whom are wary of men's power, and all of whom make a political commitment to solidarity with women. Since change in gender requires reconstructing personal relations as well as public life, there are many opportunities for personal hurt, mistaken judgments, and anger.

I do not think men seeking progressive reforms of masculinity can expect to be comfortable, while we live in a world marked by gendered violence and inequality. Masculinity therapy, of the kind promoted by the pop psychologists who are currently the best-selling authors about men and masculinity, offers personal comfort as a substitute for social change. But this is not the only use for emotional support. As shown by Rowan (1987) and Kupers (1993), therapeutic methods and emotional exploration can be used to support men, as feminist therapy supports women, in the stresses of a project of social change.

PURPOSES

Given the difficulties of reforming gendered ways of life, what might motivate men to press on into the flames? We need some conception of where the politics should be headed, a vision of the world we are trying to produce. Other forces certainly are making choices, which impact on our children in a barrage of advertising masquerading as sport, militarism masquerading as entertainment, and commercial sex masquerading as personal freedom.

The goal defined by sex-role reformers in the 1970s was the abolition of masculinity (and femininity) by a movement towards androgyny, the blending of two existing sex roles. This grasped the fact that we have to change personal life. But the idea of androgyny underestimated the complexity of masculinities and femininities, put too much emphasis on attitudes and not enough on material inequalities and issues of power.

We might better think of the goal as recomposing the elements of gender; making the full range of gender symbolism and practice available to all people.

Though this may sound exotic when formulated as a strategy, bits of it are quite familiar in practice. In schools, for instance, it is quite a common goal to expand the options for girls, by trying to make science and technology courses more available to them; and expand the options for boys, by encouraging an interest in literature, in emotional relationships, and even in being able to cook and sew.

It has been argued that the most effective form of sex education with teenagers is 'learning to be the opposite sex', that is, trying to get girls and boys to think through heterosexual relationships from the point of view of the other party. (Most school sex education is forbidden to go beyond heterosexual thoughts.) As I mentioned in Chapter 9, educators such as Davies (1993) show that children can readily learn to move among different gender positions in their culture.

The bodily dimension of gender is often thought to be the absolute limit of change. When I am interviewed on radio about changing masculinity, interviewers often seem to think that bodily difference (either in sport or in reproduction) is a knock-out question. But if we understand gender as being about the way bodies are drawn into a historical process, then we can recognize contradictions in existing embodiments and can see enormous possibilities of *re-embodiment* for men. There are different ways of using, feeling and showing male bodies.

But re-arranging elements is not enough. As Chapkis (1987) argues, playing with the elements of gender can be benign only if we unpack the 'package deal' that, for women, links beauty and status, and for men links desirability and power. We can re-arrange difference only if we contest dominance. So a re-composing strategy requires a project of social justice.

Gender relations involve different spheres of practice, so there is an unavoidable complexity in gender politics. I have argued in Chapter 2 that gender involves four major structures: the relations of power, the relations of production, patterns of emotional connection, and systems of symbolism. In each we can define directions for a politics of gender justice.

Power relations

Pursuing justice in power relations means contesting men's predominance in the state, professions and management, and ending violence against women.

Some groups of men have specifically focussed on the issue of men's violence towards women. Generally maintaining a relationship (sometimes tense) with women's groups mobilizing around domestic violence or rape, such groups have worked with violent men to try to reduce the chance of further violence, and have launched wider educational campaigns. The most extensive has been the White Ribbon campaign in Canada, which arose from commemorations of the 1989 massacre of women at the University of Montreal. In this case, mass media and mainstream politicians as well as community groups have been brought into a campaign to end violence against women, with considerable impact at a national level (Kaufman 1999).

Production relations

Pursuing justice in economic relations means equalizing incomes, sharing the burden of household work and equalizing access to education and training. A key vehicle for such politics is workers' organizations.

While male-controlled unions have often been antagonistic to women, even in totally masculinized industries some unions have taken progressive action. In the 1970s the Builders Labourers' Federation in New South Wales sponsored the entry of women workers to exclusively male building sites. In this case, the women clerks in the union office had challenged the sexism of a left-wing male leadership and persuaded them to change their policy (Burgmann & Burgmann 1998). In a Canadian example, in electrical manufacturing in Westinghouse plants, it was pressure from below that led to the integration of women into formerly all-male shops. Stan Gray, the activist who tells the story, notes that this was only the beginning of the process. A sprawling struggle, in the context of recession and layoffs, nevertheless moved on to campaigns against workplace sexism; some of the men came to see sexism as divisive and against their own interests as workers (Gray 1987).

Emotional relations

Pursuing justice in this sphere means ending homophobia, reconstructing heterosexual relations on the basis of reciprocity not hierarchy, and disconnecting masculinity from pressures towards violence.

The peace movement is perhaps the longest-established forum where significant numbers of men have been engaged in a critique of an important part of hegemonic masculinity, its openness towards violence. Quaker traditions, the Gandhian legacy, the non-violent Civil Rights movement in the United States, and the anti-war tradition in Australian unionism are all parts of this heritage. Though the peace movement has not generally defined masculinity as its target (that connection being made by feminist groups in actions such as the Greenham Common encampment in Britain), it has provided a forum for political action that in fact contests hegemonic masculinity as embodied in militarism.

Symbolism

Pursuing justice in this sphere means separating the symbolism of difference from the symbolism of dominance; and making cultural resources as fully available to the least advantaged groups as they are to the most.

Gay men's movements, contesting the stereotypes and cultural abuse of homosexual men, are the best examples of groups of men engaged in this kind of struggle. The work of writers such as Patrick White, opening up the complexities and dilemmas of gendered experience, are implicitly part of a cultural struggle over gender. Intellectuals more broadly are involved here; and magazines such as *Achilles Heel* (Britain), *Changing Men* (USA) and *XY* (Australia) are important in formulating different gender meanings for men, and images of different ways of living.

Along these lines we can define an agenda for a progressive politics of masculinity, and we can find many examples of worthwhile practice. That still leaves open the question of the overall form this politics should take.

A MEN'S MOVEMENT?

It is commonly assumed that a progressive politics of masculinity must take the form of a social movement. The usual model is feminism; many writers imply a close parallel between the women's movement and a men's movement. The gay movement provides the most important example of a social movement of men around issues of gender and sexuality. More remotely, the labour movement and civil rights movements serve as models.

I think there are serious problems with these parallels. The movements just listed are mobilizations of oppressed or exploited groups to end their subordination. They seek the unity of the group and assert the dignity of a previously stigmatized identity.

'Men' as a group, and heterosexual men in particular, are not oppressed or disadvantaged. As I have noted, men in general gain a patriarchal dividend. Hegemonic masculinity is not a stigmatized identity. Quite the opposite: the culture already honours it. Seeking the unity of 'men' can only mean emphasizing the experiences and interests men have that separate them from women, rather than the interests they share with women that might lead towards social justice.

This is not an abstract theoretical point. It has happened in practice in the history of some anti-sexist men's groups, such as the American group MOVE, studied by Lichterman (1989). Initially involved both in anti-violence work with batterers and in raising public issues about masculinity, this group gradually moved towards a therapeutic ideology, developed a concern with being 'positive' about men, and moved away from public stands and issues about the structure of power. What happened in this specific case also happened much more broadly in the transition from 'men's liberation' in the early 1970s to masculinity therapy in the 1980s.

The most conspicuous recent examples of mass mobilization of men around masculinity issues are the American evangelical Christian 'Promise Keepers' and the African-American 'Million Man March' of 1995 (Messner 1997). Both followed the model of a social movement and both have been vehicles for promoting patriarchal understandings of masculinity. The idea of a husband as the responsible 'head of the family' has proved attractive in mobilizing middle-class men (and has proved attractive to many women, too, where the alternative is abandonment or violence). The definition, and the movement, are carefully policed against homosexuality (gay men, but not their gayness, are welcome in the 'Promise Keepers'—they are seen as potential converts).

To fight for justice in gender relations often means, paradoxically, doing the opposite of the things that would create a 'men's movement'. That is, tackling issues that inevitably divide men rather than unite them: issues like homophobia, affirmative action for women, equal pay, sexual harassment and violence.

This is not to doubt the importance of solidarity among the men involved with these issues. Indeed, I would emphasize this point strongly. Experience has shown that work on these issues is stressful, often painful, and difficult to sustain without support. This points to the importance, for men engaged in such struggles, of networks such as the National Organization for Men Against Sexism in the United States.

Rather than a grand 'men's movement', we should be thinking of a variety of struggles in diverse sites, linked through networking rather than mass mobilization or formal organization. Men are likely to be detached from the defence of patriarchy in small numbers at a time, in a great variety of circumstances. So the likely political pattern is one of unevenness between situations, with differently configured issues and possibilities of action.

The cases of the White Ribbon movement, the union movement and the peace movement illustrate these points. In all three cases, what has occurred is not a social movement of men focussed on masculinity, but some kind of alliance politics. Here the project of social justice depends on the overlapping of interests or commitments between different groups. The overlapping may be temporary, but can be long-term (a perfectly familiar situation in politics). Existing power resources can be used for new ends. We do not have to start from scratch all the time.

It is often assumed that alliance means compromise and therefore containment. The familiar militant gesture of insisting on revolutionary purity is not unknown in men's counter-sexist politics. The chances of actually changing the world this way are slight.

Pluralism in alliance-making is necessary, but containment is not a necessary result. Given that patriarchy is a historical structure, not a timeless dichotomy of men abusing women, it will be ended by a historical process. The strategic problem is to generate pressures that will in the long run transform the structure. Any initiative that sets up pressure in that direction is worth having. Segal (1997), in the best feminist appraisal of issues about masculinity, is cool about the pace of change; her book is called *Slow Motion*. But she is in no doubt about the possibilities of change, through hard work in familiar institutions such as workplaces, unions and political parties.

In the long run, as Keynes remarked, we are all dead; and while we are still alive, we want to see something more than a rise in the probability of social justice in the distant future. So as well as long-term educational strategies, we also need what British feminists called 'prefigurative politics'—at least samples of paradise, at least little bits of justice, here and now.

Again, this is familiar in several arenas of practice. Progressive education hoped to prefigure the good society in democratic schools. Industrial democracy hoped to prefigure a democratically controlled economy in each workplace. Some households influenced by feminism—including the 'fair families' described by Risman (1998) in the United States, and similar attempts in other countries—have tried to prefigure a society in which gender equality and sexual tolerance are routine, bedrocks of civilization.

However the prefigurative politics of gender and sexuality are not necessarily rock-like. They may, on the contrary, be scandalous, hilarious or disturbing: the Mardi Gras parade in Sydney; AIDS prevention programs run by prostitutes and former prostitutes; the pleasures and dangers of queer culture; integrated sports in schools. Prefiguration may also be placid: fathers taking toddlers and babies in push-chairs for an outing. Hype about 'the new father' to the contrary, it is still not common for men to take on a major share of the care of young children (McMahon 1999). When that has become so common we hardly notice it, we will really have got somewhere.

12

Arms and the man: The question of peace

Arma virumque cano, Troiae qui primus ab oris
Italiam fato profugus Lavinaque venit
Litora . . .

(I sing of arms and the man who came first from the shores
of Troy, exiled by fate, to Italy and its Lavinian coast . . .)

Virgil, *Aeneid*, Book I

WHY WAR?

Nearly 70 years ago, the League of Nations' permanent committee on literature and the arts—an ancestor of UNESCO—published a small book by two well-known intellectuals on a topic of current interest. The authors were called Einstein and Freud, the topic was violence, and the book was called *Why War?*.

Freud, whose long answer to Einstein's question provided the main text of the book, argued that violence grew from deep in the human psyche, and that there could be no end to aggression. But this did not mean there could be no end to war. There were means of opposing war, both direct and indirect. The psychological impulses to aggression could be directed into other channels. Indeed, Freud suggested, opposition to war was built into the very fabric of human civilization: 'we are bound to rebel against it [war]; we simply cannot any longer put up with it'. As human culture developed, Freud thought, there was growing control over instinctual impulses.

That was published in 1933—ironically the same year that the National Socialists came to power and began to turn the cultural and technical resources of Germany towards an even more horrifying war than Einstein and Freud had seen. In turn, that war came to an end with the nuclear massacres at Hiroshima and Nagasaki. It seemed as if history itself had refuted Freud. The development of civilization, far from favouring pacifism, was producing new and more horrifying techniques of destruction.

Doubtless Freud's specific argument was wrong. But Freud and Einstein were not wrong to pose the problem of the sources of violence, nor to use the intellectual tools at their disposal to explore it, and to help in the prevention of violence. In this chapter I want to take up their project again, with tools provided by modern gender and masculinity research.

THE PROBLEM OF MEN AND VIOLENCE

It is not hard to show that there is some connection between gender and violence. This is obvious in the institutions which are dedicated to the techniques of violence, state agencies of force. The twenty million members of the world's armed forces today are overwhelmingly men. In many countries all soldiers, military sailors and aviators are men. Even in those countries which admit women to the military, women are a small minority, and commanders are almost exclusively men. Men also dominate other branches of enforcement, both in the public sector as police officers and prison guards, and in the private sector as security agents. Further, the targets of enforcement are mainly men. For instance, in 1999 no less than 94 per cent of the prisoners in Australian gaols were men; in the United States in 1996, 89 per cent of prison inmates were men.

In private life too, men are more likely to be armed and

violent. In the United States, careful research by the criminologists Smith and Smith (1994) established that private gun
ownership runs four times as high among men as among
women, even after a campaign by the gun industry to persuade
women to buy guns. In the same country, official statistics for
1996 show men accounting for 90 per cent of those arrested
for aggravated assault and 90 per cent of those arrested for
murder and manslaughter (US Bureau of the Census 1998). In
Australia in 1992–93 men were 90 per cent of those charged
with homicide (Australian Institute of Criminology 1995).
These figures are not exceptional.

There is a debate about the gender balance of violence
within households, and it is clear that many women are capable
of violence (e.g. in punishing children). The weight of evidence, however, indicates that major domestic violence is
overwhelmingly by husbands towards wives, in wealthy countries at least (Dobash et al. 1992). Rape is overwhelmingly by
men on women. Criminal rape shades into sexual intercourse
under pressure. The national survey of sexual behaviour in the
United States by Laumann et al. (1994) finds women six times
as likely as men to have had an experience of forced sex, almost
always being forced by a man.

Further, men predominate in warlike conduct in other
spheres of life. Body-contact sports, such as boxing and football, involve ritualized combat and often physical injury. These
sports are almost exclusively practised by men. Dangerous
driving is increasingly recognized as a form of violence. It is
mainly done by men. Young men die on the roads at a rate
four times that of young women, and kill on the roads at an
even higher ratio. Older men, as corporate executives, make
the decisions that result in injury or death from the actions
of their businesses—industrial injuries to their workers, pollution injury to neighbours and environmental destruction. Case
studies of such decisions (e.g. Messerschmidt's [1997] study
of the *Challenger* spacecraft explosion) show their connection
to a masculinized management style emphasizing toughness,
risk-taking, and ruthlessness about profit.

So men predominate across the spectrum of violence.

A strategy for peace must concern itself with this fact, the reasons for it, and its implications for work to reduce violence.

There is a widespread belief that it is natural for men to be violent. Males are inherently more aggressive than women, the argument goes. 'Boys will be boys' and cannot be trained otherwise; rape and combat—however regrettable—are part of the unchanging order of nature. There is often an appeal to biology, with testosterone in particular, the so-called 'male hormone', as a catch-all explanation for men's aggression.

Careful examination of the evidence shows that this biological essentialism is not credible. Testosterone levels for instance, far from being a clearcut *source* of dominance and aggression in society, are as likely to be the *consequence* of social relations (Kemper 1990). Cross-cultural studies of masculinities (e.g. Cornwall & Lindisfarne 1994) reveal a diversity that is impossible to reconcile with a biologically fixed master pattern of masculinity.

When we speak statistically of 'men' having higher rates of violence than women, we must not slide to the inference that therefore *all* men are violent. Almost all soldiers are men, but most men are not soldiers. Though most killers are men, most men never kill or even commit assault. Though an appalling number of men do rape, most men do not. It is a fact of great importance, both theoretically and practically, that there are many non-violent men in the world. This too needs explanation, and must be considered in a strategy for peace.

Further, when we note that most soldiers, sports professionals, or executives are men, we are not just talking about individuals. We are speaking of masculinized institutions. The organizational culture of armies, for instance, is heavily gendered. Social research inside armed forces in Germany (Seifert 1993), the United States (Barrett 1996) and Australia (Agostino 1998) reveals an energetic effort to produce a narrowly defined hegemonic masculinity.

Similarly, organized sport does not just reflect, but actively produces, particular versions of masculinity (Messner & Sabo 1994). Boys' schools too may display a vehement gender regime designed to produce a combative, dominating masculinity (Morrell 1994).

So it is in social masculinities rather than biological differences that we must seek the main causes of gendered violence, and the main answers to it.

IMPLICATIONS OF MASCULINITY RESEARCH

In Chapter 1 of this book I outlined the main conclusions of recent research on masculinities. Let us now consider implications of these findings for the problem of violence and peace.

Multiple masculinities

Different cultures and different periods of history construct gender differently. In multicultural societies there are likely to be multiple definitions of masculinity. Equally important, more than one kind of masculinity can be found within a given culture, even within a single institution such as a school or workplace.

Implications. In any cultural setting, violent and aggressive masculinity will rarely be the only form of masculinity present. There is, then, usually some alternative for anti-violence programs to build on—a point strongly made by Denborough (1996) in his work with boys and male youth.

It is important that education and other anti-violence programs should recognize diversity in gender patterns, such as ethnic diversity. They must also recognize the tensions that develop around social difference; racism, of course, is a well-recognized source of violence. On the positive side, the research which documents multiple masculinities may itself be an asset. Peace education programs need concrete examples of more peaceable ways of living and acting.

Hierarchy and hegemony

Different masculinities exist in definite relations with each other, often relations of hierarchy and exclusion. There is generally a hegemonic form of masculinity, the centre of the system of gendered power. The hegemonic form need not be the most common form of masculinity.

Implications. The hierarchy of masculinities is itself a source of violence, since force is used in defining and maintaining the hierarchy. Bashings and murders of gay men reveal this, even in the language used by perpetrators; while the fear of being at the bottom of the hierarchy, being defined as a poofter or a sissy, is a familiar way of training boys and men to participate in combat and violent sports.

Large numbers of men and boys have a divided, tense, or oppositional relationship to hegemonic masculinity. This is an important fact of life though it is often concealed by the enormous attention focussed (e.g. in the media) on hegemonic masculinity. Clearcut alternatives, however, are often culturally discredited or despised. Men who practise them are likely to be abused as wimps, cowards, fags etc. The most powerful groups of men usually have few personal incentives for gender change. At the same time, however, the very hierarchy of masculinities may give other groups strong motives for change.

Collective masculinities

Masculinities are sustained and enacted not only by individuals, but also by groups, institutions, and cultural forms like mass media. Multiple masculinities may be produced and sustained by the same institution.

Implications. Violent masculinities are usually collectively defined and/or institutionally supported, whether in informal peer groups (youth 'gangs'), formal armies, or groups somewhere in between (such as the murderous 'militias' in East Timor). Most violence is not a matter of individual pathology.

Therefore the institutionalization of masculinity is a major problem for peace strategy. Building a culture of peace means changing the organizational culture of police forces, the military, the media etc. In practice, this means that corporations, workplaces, voluntary organizations, and the state are all important sites of action in producing or popularizing less violent forms of masculinity. The reshaping of institutions is as necessary as the reform of individual life.

Bodies as arenas

Men's bodies do not fix patterns of masculinity, but they are still very important in the construction and expression of masculinities. This constantly involves bodily experience, bodily pleasures, and the vulnerabilities of bodies.

Implications. Violence is, of course, a relationship between bodies; it is power exercised directly on the body. The bodily capacity to commit violence becomes, for many boys and young men, part of their sense of masculinity, and a willingness to put their bodies on the line in violence remains as a test of hegemonic masculinity.

If people's experience of masculinity to such a large extent involves their bodies, then bodies must be an important site of action for peace. It is a mistake if anti-violence work and peace education is all 'in the head'. Health, sport and sexuality are issues which must be addressed in changing masculinity. Part of the task is finding nonviolent forms of embodiment for men, and making these as satisfying as violent forms currently seem to be.

Active construction.

Masculinities do not exist prior to social interaction, but come into existence as people act. Masculinities are actively produced, using the resources available in a given milieu.

Implications. The process of constructing masculinity, rather than the end state, is often the source of violence. We often see men involved in violence in order to prove their masculinity, or to defend their masculine honour, or to challenge others. We might pre-empt some of this violence by removing the occasions for these challenges or proofs.

This also means that no pattern of masculine violence is fixed, beyond all hope of social reform. This is ground for optimism. Unfortunately it also means that no reform is final. Gender reforms can be overthrown and more violent patterns of masculinity re-introduced. This seems to be the goal of some current neo-fascist groups, and it will be dangerous if this agenda gets wider support.

Internal complexity and contradiction

Masculinities are not homogeneous but are likely to be internally divided. Men's lives often embody tensions between contradictory desires or practices.

Implications. Any pattern of masculinity has potential for change. Certainly some are less likely to change than others—especially where a certain pattern of masculinity is strongly buttressed by the surrounding institutions and culture—but in principle no pattern of masculinity is entirely proof against change.

It is also important to recognize that any given group of men is likely to have complex and conflicting interests. We cannot speak of 'men' as a single bloc with exactly the same interests. Some have interests (e.g. in their relations with women and children) which will support change towards more peaceable gender patterns.

Dynamics

Masculinities are created in specific historical circumstances. They are liable to be contested, reconstructed or displaced. The forces producing change include contradictions within gender relations, as well as the interplay of gender with other social forces.

Implications. Masculinities are always changing. Though many people deny this in principle, everyone is aware in practice that gender relations change, and the lives of men change too. This creates motives for learning, since boys and men have a need to understand what is happening to them.

However, as any agenda for change is likely to be against some groups' interests, controversy and conflict are to be expected. No reforms or changes in this area of life are likely to be smooth and trouble-free.

These conclusions can be put to work in practical ways, in programs to reduce violence and build peace. Anti-violence programs addressed to men have now accumulated a certain amount of experience. Much of it concerns violence against women, particularly domestic violence and rape, and some concerns violence against gay men and lesbians. However, broad crime-prevention measures are still usually gender-unaware.

GLOBAL PATTERNS

The new research on masculinity has mostly operated at the local level and has had a distinctly ethnographic flavour. This has been helpful in developing a more sophisticated account of masculinities. But as I argued in Chapter 3, it has also resulted in a weakness: a tendency to ignore gender relations and masculinity formation on the large scale, especially at the level of world society.

This is a major problem for understanding violence, as it has meant little attention being paid to the connection of gender with the most important source of violence in modern history—imperialism. We must now think about the issue of masculinity and violence on a global scale.

The history of globalization outlined in Chapters 3 and 4 involved sustained and massive violence. The economic and political expansion of European states from the fifteenth century on; the creation of colonial empires based on the North Atlantic metropole; the creation of neo-colonial systems of economic, political and cultural dependency—all these stages involved force. Indeed they involved obvious force in the shape of expeditions of conquest, armies of occupation, and post-colonial wars.

But what of the latest stage, the contemporary system of global markets dominated by the trilateral powers of the 'North'? This surely involves some demilitarization, with the end of the cold war and the fading of the last remnants of colonial rule.

As suggested in Chapter 2, the hegemonic form of masculinity in the current world gender order is the masculinity associated with those who control its dominant institutions:

the business executives who operate in global markets, and the political executives who interact with them.

Transnational business masculinity does not require bodily force, since the wealth on which it rests is accumulated by impersonal, institutional means. But corporations increasingly use mass-media images of the bodies of elite sportsmen as a marketing tool (we have noted the phenomenal growth of corporate 'sponsorship' of sport), and they have powerful effects on real bodies through their marketing and financial strategies. It is the indirect, mediated effects that most concern the problem of violence.

Neo-liberalism in the metropole does not indulge in the warrior cults, the enthusiasm for 'blood and iron', that earlier masculinities did. But as the NATO air assault on Jugoslavia beginning in March 1999 showed—and the continuing Anglo-American bombing of Iraq continues to show—the neo-liberal leadership represented by Blair, Clinton and Schröder values a mediated, technological violence as a means towards its ends.

At the receiving end of this violence, and of the display of metropolitan financial power through the restructuring agendas of the International Monetary Fund and World Bank, we see another pattern of the relation between masculinities and violence. Many have been surprised by the emergence of ethnic conflict as a major factor in 'successor states' in former communist regions, or in the post-colonial world. Given the importance of patriarchy in state legitimation, it is relatively easy to ground a new state on patriarchal local powers. Ethnicity is constituted in large measure through gender relations. The notion of extended 'kinship' is central to the rhetoric of ethnicity—'our kith and kin', in the old language of British racism.

Gender relations thus provide a vehicle for new claims to authority for male leaders, and define boundaries of the group to which loyalty is demanded. The state becomes the basis for constructing collective identities, which may be vehemently enforced through schooling, policing and mass media. This is likely to generate conflicting claims for territory, and anyway the process is resisted by excluded or stigmatized minorities. New patterns of ethno-nationalism and violence are thus produced, duly misinterpreted by the Western media as a recurrence of primitive 'tribalism'.

The interweaving of masculinity dynamics with other social forces is very clear in one of the main contemporary threats to peace, the international arms trade. The gender meaning of weapons is familiar and has deep historical roots. Fernbach (1981) speaks of the 'masculine specialization in violence' that can be traced from the first armies in the first urban societies. Still the gender meaning must be constantly regenerated and reproduced. A study by Gibson (1994) shows one way this is accomplished. Gibson traces the emergence of a hypermasculine cult of weaponry in 'paramilitary culture' in the United States, the cult of the 'new war' developed in the period since the US defeat in Vietnam.

What is worked out culturally in gun cults and violent 'action movies' is also an economic reality in the form of the arms trade. Arms trading, of course, is a broad category, ranging from the government-to-government sales of high-technology weapons systems, to the private circulation of small arms in countries whose governments officially permit arms sales or cannot prevent them. The largest part of the arms trade is the legal equipping of military and paramilitary forces. This is no small industry, though it has shrunk a little with the end of the cold war. Legal exports of conventional weapons from the United States in 1997 totalled $11 billion, with Russia, France and Britain exporting another $9 billion worth between them.

Because of the social forms in which armaments are embedded, the arms trade is a vector of the globalization of gender, much as the international state is. Indeed, the two overlap, since the arms trade is connected to the globally linked military and intelligence apparatuses of the major powers. The social forms of military masculinity are exported to post-colonial states by military aid and advice programs (the mechanism by which the United States became involved in the Vietnamese war in the 1960s, with US advisers constantly urging greater aggressiveness on officers of the Saigon regime), and by the training of officers in the military schools of the metropole.

A striking feature of twentieth century political history is the attempt to overcome the anarchy of the system of sovereign states through international institutions. These agencies are gendered and have gender effects. For the most part their gender regimes replicate those of the territorial states that gave rise to them. Not only is a patriarchal gender order produced internationally through military aid, the largest single component of international aid. 'Peacekeeping' also tends to be a patriarchal process, carried out by bands of armed men who have been duly trained as fighters in their home countries. It is not surprising that 'peacekeeping' interventions often call out the very processes they are supposed to be directed against.

There are, nevertheless, reform agendas concerned with masculinity (see Chapter 11), and anti-violence movements which take account of these issues. There is, for instance, practical work as well as research concerned with homophobic violence by men (Tomsen 1998), and with men's violence against women (Hearn 1998a).

Very recently, this approach has addressed international institutions also. The Culture of Peace program at UNESCO is a case in point, which has challenged the international institutions of the United Nations to question their own patriarchal and hierarchical cultures as part of the process of preventing war.

As this international perspective and institutional understanding connects with the grassroots spread of masculinity reform agendas—for instance in men's health, where issues of violence are also emerging—we will have the basis for a new practice of peacemaking. The possibilities are already visible.

PEACE STRATEGIES AND MASCULINITIES

There are many causes of violence, including dispossession, poverty, greed, nationalism, racism and other forms of inequality, bigotry and desire. Gender dynamics are by no means the whole story. Yet given the concentration of weapons and the practices of violence among men, gender patterns appear to be strategic. Masculinities are the forms in which many dynamics of violence take shape.

Evidently, then, strategy for peace must include a strategy of change in masculinities. This is the new dimension in peace work which studies of men suggest: contesting the hegemony of masculinities which emphasize violence, confrontation and domination, replacing them with patterns of masculinity more open to negotiation, cooperation and equality.

The relationship of masculinity to violence is more complex than appears at first sight, so there is not just one pattern of change required. Institutionalized violence (e.g. by armies) requires more than one kind of masculinity. The masculinity of the general is different from the masculinity of the front-line soldier, and armies acknowledge this by training them separately. The differing masculinities that are hegemonic in different cultures may lead to qualitatively different patterns of violence, as Kersten (1993) argues in a comparison of Japan with Germany and Australia.

Some violent patterns of masculinity develop in response to violence, they do not simply cause it. An important example is the 'protest masculinity' that emerges in contexts of poverty and ethnic oppression (for instance, under apartheid in South Africa: Xaba 1997). On the other hand, some patterns of masculinity are not personally violent, but their ascendancy creates conditions for violence, such as inequality and dispossession. The case of transnational business masculinity has already been mentioned.

A gender-informed strategy for peace must, therefore, be sophisticated about patterns of masculinity. It must also be designed to operate across a broad front, broader than most agendas of sex-role reform would suggest. The arenas for action to reduce masculine violence include:

• *development*—schooling, child rearing and adult–child relationships in families, classrooms, play groups etc (including the issues commonly thought of as 'sex-role modelling');

- *personal life*—marital relations and sexuality, family relationships, friendship (including the role of sexual and domestic violence in constructions of masculinity);
- *community life*—peer groups, neighbourhood life, leisure including sports (and youth subcultures as bearers of violent masculinities);
- *cultural institutions*—higher education, science and technology, mass media, the arts and popular entertainment (including exemplary masculinities in broadcast sports);
- *workplaces*—occupational cultures, industrial relations, corporations, unions and bureaucracies; the state and its enforcement apparatuses (armies, police etc.); and
- *markets*—the labour market and the effects of unemployment; capital and commodity markets both international and local; management practices and ideologies.

What principles might link action across this very broad spectrum? I do not think we should follow the model of gender reform that demands men adopt a new character and instantly become 'the new man'. Such hero-making agendas deny what we already know about the multiplicity and the internal complexity of masculinities.

Rather, strategy for peace needs to be embedded in a practicable strategy of change in gender relations. The goal should be to develop gender practices for men which shift gender relations in a democratic direction. Democratic gender relations are those that move towards equality, nonviolence, and mutual respect between people of different genders, sexualities, ethnicities and generations.

A peace strategy concerned with masculinities, then, does not demand a complete rupture with patterns of conduct men are now familiar with. Some of the qualities in 'traditional' definitions of masculinity (e.g. courage, steadfastness, ambition) are certainly needed in the cause of peace. Active models of engagement are needed for boys and men, especially when peace is understood not just as the absence of violence but as a positive form of life.

The task is not to abolish gender but to reshape it; to

disconnect (for instance) courage from violence, steadfastness from prejudice, ambition from exploitation. In the course of that reshaping, diversity will grow. Making boys and men aware of the diversity of masculinities that already exist in the world, beyond the narrow models they are commonly offered, is an important task for education.

Though the hierarchy of masculinities is part of the problem in gender relations, the fact that there are different masculinities is in itself an asset. At the lowest level, it establishes that masculinity is not a single fixed pattern. More positively, multiple masculinities represent complexity of interests and purposes, which open possibilities for change. Finally the plurality of gender prefigures the creativity of a democratic social order.

For men, the democratic remaking of gender practices requires persistent engagement with women, not the separatism-for-men which is strong in current masculinity politics. The 'gender-relevant' programs discussed in Chapter 9 are examples in the realm of education. Educational and social action must be inclusive in another sense too, responding to the differing cultural meanings of gender and the different socio-economic circumstances in which students live. A program apt for suburban middle-class students may be very inappropriate for ethnically diverse inner-city children in poverty, or rural children living in villages.

No one with experience of struggles for peace, or of attempts at gender reform, will imagine these are easy tasks. Recognizing the interplay of masculinities with strategies for peace is not a magic key. In some ways, indeed, it makes familiar strategies seem more complex and difficult.

But it also, I believe, opens ways of moving past obstacles which both peace movements and the movement for gender democracy have encountered. If the research on masculinities presented in this book does no more than that, it will have been worthwhile.

Acknowledgments and sources

Chapters 5, 6 and 8 draw on a life-history study of Australian men, whose methods are described on pp. 89–92 of my book *Masculinities*. All names of men interviewed have been changed. Norm Radican and Pip Martin did most of the interviews, the field work being done in 1985 to 1987 in Sydney and other parts of the state of New South Wales. The project was funded by the Australian Research Grants Committee, with supplementary grants from Macquarie University. My thanks to the men who were interviewed, both for their time and for their willingness to tackle difficult issues.

Chapter 7 was co-written with Mark Davis and Gary Dowsett. This chapter draws from a study on class and men who have sex with men, conducted in two Australian cities in 1989 to 1990. Again all names have been changed. The project was funded by the Commonwealth AIDS Research Grants Committee. Eleven of the 21 men had been respondents to our 1986–87 mass survey, the Social Aspects of Prevention of AIDS project, having then volunteered for follow-up interviews. The others were contacted by networking and snowballing in the course of field work. The authors gratefully acknowledge the contribution of all respondents; and also the help of L. Watson,

D. Baxter, K. Davis, M. O'Brien and Y. Roberts and the original Social Aspects of the Prevention of AIDS team (Macquarie University, New South Wales).

Part of Chapter 10 draws on a study of research needs in men's health, co-written with Toni Schofield, Lin Walker, Julian Wood, Di Butland, John Fisher and John Bowyer. This project was funded by the Commonwealth Department of Health. Another part draws on a project on masculinity issues in road safety education, conducted jointly with Lin Walker, Julian Wood, Di Butland and John Fisher. This project was funded by the Roads and Traffic Authority of New South Wales. Another part draws on an address to the Second National Conference on Men's Health; I am grateful to Allan Huggins for the invitation that led to this paper.

Part of Chapter 2 comes from an address to a conference in Bielefeld; I am grateful to Christof Armbruster and Ulla Müller for this invitation and for putting me in touch with German work in the field. Chapter 4 comes from an address to a conference in Santiago; I am grateful to Teresa Valdés for the invitation, and for introducing me to a rich body of Latin American work on gender. Chapter 11 originated as an address to a conference in München sponsored by the Hans Böckler Foundation of the German union movement; I am grateful to Heinz Kindler and Gudrun Linne for the invitation and to participants for information on union-based education and youth work in Germany. Chapter 12 comes from a UNESCO-sponsored conference in Oslo; I am grateful to Ingeborg Breines for the invitation, and for putting me in touch with the world of international peacemaking. Some friends and colleagues have given support, ideas, hospitality and advice that have sustained years of work on these questions. My profound thanks go to Gary Dowsett, Heinz Kindler, Mike Messner, Robert Morrell, Ulla Müller, Toni Schofield, Lynne Segal, Barrie Thorne and Lin Walker.

The final production of this manuscript was assisted by Kath Selkirk, Marion Lupton and Chelvi Singaram, to all of whom I am very grateful. The decision to create the book was influenced by a three-month appointment as Marie-Jahoda

ACKNOWLEDGMENTS AND SOURCES • 229

Professor of Gender Studies at the Ruhr-University Bochum during 1999; my particular thanks to Ilse Lenz and Paula-Irene Villa, as well as the other people who gave invitations to share in European discussions.

Pam Benton, who inspired and shared the political project from the start, died in 1997. It is hard for me to imagine this book appearing without her. I have dedicated it to Kylie Benton-Connell, our daughter.

Most of these chapters first appeared as papers in journals or edited volumes. All have been re-written for this book, some extensively, in an attempt both to bring the argument up to date and to bring out the connections between a wide range of topics. The papers describing field work have been the least altered.

Original versions were published in these places: Chapter 2, 'Neue Richtungen für Geschlechtertheorie, Männlichkeitsforschung und Geschlechterpolitik', in L. Christof Armbruster, Ursula Müller & Marlene Stein-Hilbers (eds), *Neue Horizonte? Socialwissenschaftliche Forschung über Geschlechter und Geschlechtverhältnisse*, Opladen, Leske & Budrich, 1995, pp. 61–83; Chapter 3, 'Masculinities and globalization', *Men and Masculinities*, 1998, vol. 1, no. 1, pp. 3–23; Chapter 4, 'El imperialismo y el cuerpo de los hombres', in Teresa Valdés and José Olavarría, ed., *Masculinidades y equidad de género en América Latina*, Santiago, FLACSO-Chile, 1998, pp. 76–89; Chapter 5, 'An iron man: the body and some contradictions of hegemonic masculinity', in M. Messner & D. Sabo (eds), *Sport, Men and the Gender Order*, Champaign, Human Kinetics Books, 1990, pp. 83–95; Chapter 7, 'A bastard of a life: homosexual desire and practice among men in working-class milieux', *Australian and New Zealand Journal of Sociology*, 1993, vol. 29, no. 1, pp. 112–35; Chapter 8, 'Cool guys, swots and wimps: the interplay of masculinity and education', *Oxford Review of Education*, 1989, vol. 15, no. 3, pp. 291–303; Chapter 9, 'Teaching the boys: new research on masculinity and gender strategies for schools', *Teachers College Record*, 1996, vol. 98, no. 2, pp. 206–235; Chapter 10, parts draw on a keynote address to the Second National Men's Health Conference, Fremantle, Western Australia, 1997, and other parts draw on R.W. Connell,

T. Schofield, L. Walker, J. Wood, D.L. Butland, J. Fisher & J. Bowyer, *Men's Health: A Research Agenda and Background Report*, Department of Health and Aged Care, Canberra, 1999; Chapter 11, 'Politics of changing men', *Socialist Review*, 1995, vol. 25, no. 1, pp. 135–59; Chapter 12, 'Arms and the man: using the new research on masculinity to understand violence and promote peace in the contemporary world', paper for UNESCO expert group meeting on Male Roles and Masculinities in the Perspective of a Culture of Peace, Oslo, 1997. My thanks to the original publishers for permission to reproduce.

References

Agenda 1998, 'The new men?', Special issue, ed. R. Morrell, no. 37.

Agostino, K. 1998, 'The making of warriors: men, identity and military culture', *Journal of Interdisciplinary Gender Studies* vol. 3 no. 2, pp. 58–75

Alloway, N., Davies, B., Gilbert, P. & King, D. 1996, *Boys and Literacy: Meeting the Challenge*, Department of Employment Education, Training and Youth Affairs, Canberra

Altman, D. 1994, *Power and Community: Organizational and Cultural Responses to AIDS*, Taylor & Francis, London

——1996, 'Rupture or continuity? The internationalization of gay identities', *Social Text* 48, vol. 14, no. 3, pp. 77–94

Angus, L. 1993, 'Women in a male domain: Gender and organizational culture in a Christian Brothers college' in *Education, Inequality and Social Identity*, ed. L. Angus, Falmer, London

Askew, S. & Ross, C. 1988, *Boys Don't Cry*, Open University Press, Philadelphia

Austin, D.E., Clark, V.B. & Fitchett, G.W. 1971, *Reading Rights for Boys: Sex Role in Language Experience*, Appleton-Century-Crofts, New York

Australian Institute of Criminology 1995, *Homicides in Australia 1992–93*, AIC, Canberra

Australian Institute of Health and Welfare 1996, *Australia's Health 1996*, AIHW, Canberra

Australian Schools Commission 1975, *Girls, School and Society*, Australian Government Publishing Service, Canberra

Barbalet, J.M. 1998, *Emotion, Social Theory and Social Structure: A Macrosociological Approach*, Cambridge University Press, Cambridge

Barrett, F.J. 1996, 'The organizational construction of hegemonic masculinity: The case of the US Navy', *Gender, Work and Organization* vol. 3, no. 3, pp. 129–42

Baum, F. 1984, unpublished, 'Men and Community Health', Southern Community Health Services Research Unit

BauSteineMänner (ed.) 1996, *Kritische Männerforschung*, Argument, Berlin

Biddulph, S. 1995, *Manhood: An Action Plan for Changing Men's Lives*, Finch, Sydney

Bishop, R. & Robinson, L.S. 1998, *Night Market: Sexual Cultures and the Thai Economic Miracle*, Routledge, New York

Bitterli, U. 1989, *Cultures in Conflict: Encounters between European and non-European Cultures, 1492–1800*, Stanford University Press, Stanford

Bly, R. 1990, *Iron John: A Book about Men*, Addison-Wesley, Reading

Board of Studies NSW 1998, 'Statistics—School Certificate 1998' updated at 22.12.1998 *http://www.boardofstudies.nsw.edu.au/docs_stats/sc98_y10.. html*

——1999, '1998 Higher School Certificate Examination Statistics', NSW Board of Studies, Sydney

Bolin, A. 1988, *In Search of Eve: Transsexual Rites of Passage*, Bergin & Garvey, Westport

Bottomley, G. 1992, *From Another Place—Migration and the Politics of Culture*, Cambridge University Press, Melbourne

Breines, I., Connell, R. & Eide, I. (eds) 2000, *Male Roles and Masculinities: A Culture of Peace Perspective*, UNESCO, Paris

Browne, R. 1995, 'Working with boys and masculinities' in *Boys and Schools: Addressing the Real Issues—Behaviour, Values and Relationships*, eds R. Browne & R. Fletcher, Finch, Sydney

Bryson, L. & Winter, I. 1999, *Social Change, Suburban Lives: An Australian Newtown 1960s to 1990s*, Allen & Unwin, Sydney

Buchbinder, H., Burstyn, V., Forbes, D. & Steedman, M. 1987, *Who's on Top? The Politics of Heterosexuality*, Garamond, Toronto

Bulbeck, C. 1988, *One World Women's Movement*, Pluto, London

——1992, *Australian Women in Papua New Guinea: Colonial Passages 1920–1960*, Cambridge University Press, Cambridge

Burgmann, M. & Burgmann, V. 1998, *Green Bans, Red Union: Environmental Activism and the New South Wales Builders' Labourers Federation*, University of NSW Press, Sydney

Butler, J. 1990, *Gender Trouble: Feminism and the Subversion of Identity*, Routledge, New York

Cain, P.J. & Hopkins, A.G. 1993, *British Imperialism: Innovation and Expansion, 1688–1914*, Longman, New York

Carrier, J. 1992, 'Miguel: Sexual life history of a gay Mexican American' in *Gay Culture in America: Essays from the Field*, ed. G. Herdt, Beacon Press, Boston

Chapkis, W. 1987, *Beauty Secrets*, South End Press, Boston

Cheng, C. 1996, '"We choose not to compete": The "merit" discourse in the selection process, and Asian and Asian American men and their masculinity' in *Masculinities in Organizations*, ed. C. Cheng, Sage, Thousand Oaks

Chiarolli, M. 1992, 'Gender issues and the education of boys', *Catholic Ethos* vol. 7, pp. 2–3

Chodorow, N. 1994, *Femininities, Masculinities, Sexualities: Freud and Beyond*, University Press of Kentucky, Lexington

Clatterbaugh, K. 1998, 'What is problematic about masculinities?', *Men and Masculinities* vol. 1, no. 1, pp. 24–45

Cockburn, C. 1983, *Brothers: Male Dominance and Technological Change*, Pluto, London

Cohen, J. 1991, 'NOMAS: Challenging male supremacy', *Changing Men* Winter/Spring, pp. 45–6

Connell, R.W. 1983, 'Men's bodies' in *Which Way is Up?*, Allen & Unwin, Sydney

——1987, *Gender and Power*, Polity, Cambridge

——1990, 'The state, gender and sexual politics: Theory and appraisal', *Theory and Society* vol. 19, pp. 507–44

——1994, 'Psychoanalysis on masculinity' in *Theorizing Masculinities*, eds H. Broad & M. Kaufman, Sage, Thousand Oaks

——1995, *Masculinities*, Polity, Cambridge

——2000, 'Bodies, intellectuals and world society' in *Reframing the Body*, eds N. Watson & S. Cunningham-Burley, Macmillan, London

Connell, R.W., Butland, D., Fisher, J. and Walker, L. 1997, *Gender, Road Safety Education, and Boys: An Examination of Research Literature and Current Educational Approaches*, Roads and Traffic Authority of NSW, Sydney

Connell, R.W., Dowsett, G.W., Rodden, P., Davis, M.D., Watson, L. & Baxter, D. 1991, 'Social class, gay men, and AIDS prevention', *Australian Journal of Public Health* vol. 15, no. 3, pp. 178–89

Connell, R.W. & Irving, T.H. 1992, *Class Structure in Australian History* 2nd edn, Longman Cheshire, Melbourne

Connell, R.W., Schofield, T., Walker, L., Wood, J. Butland, D., Fisher, J. & Bowyer, J. 1999, *Men's Health: A Research Agenda and Background Report*, Commonwealth Department of Health and Aged Care, Canberra

Cornwall, A. & Lindisfarne, N. (eds) 1994, *Dislocating Masculinity: Comparative Ethnographies*, Routledge, London

Couch, M. 1991, 'Production and reproduction of masculinity in a mining community', Paper presented at the Conference on Research on Masculinity and Men in Gender Relations, Sydney

Cox, E. 1995, 'Boys and girls and the costs of gendered behaviour', *Proceedings of the Promoting Gender Equity Conference*, Ministerial Council for Education, Employment, Training and Youth Affairs, Canberra

Craig, S. (ed.) 1992, *Men, Masculinity and the Media*, Sage, Newbury Park, CA

Davies, B. 1993, *Shards of Glass: Children Reading and Writing Beyond Gendered Identities*, Allen & Unwin, Sydney

Dawson, G. 1991, 'The blond Bedouin: Lawrence of Arabia, imperial adventure and the imagining of English-British masculinity' in *Manful Assertions: Masculinities in Britain since 1800*, eds M. Roper, J. Tosh, Routledge, London

Denborough, D. 1996, 'Step by step: developing respectful ways of working with young men to reduce violence' in *Men's Ways of Being*, eds C. McLean, M. Carey & C. White, Westview Press, Boulder

Dinnerstein, D. 1976, *The Mermaid and the Minotaur: Sexual Arrangements and Human Malaise*, Harper & Row, New York

Dobash, R.P., Dobash, E.R. & Wilson, M. 1992, 'The myth of sexual symmetry in marital violence', *Social Problems* vol. 39, pp. 71–91

Donaldson, M. 1991, *Time of our Lives: Labour and Love in the Working Class*, Allen & Unwin, Sydney

——1998, 'Growing up very rich: The masculinity of the hegemonic', *Journal of Interdisciplinary Gender Studies* vol. 3, no. 2, pp. 95–112

Dowsett, G.W. 1990, 'Reaching men who have sex with men in Australia. An overview of AIDS education: community intervention and community strategies', *Australian Journal of Social Issues* vol. 25, no. 3, pp. 186–98

——1996, *Practicing Desire: Homosexual Sex in the Era of AIDS*, Stanford University Press, Stanford

Dowsett, G.W. & Davis, M.D. 1992, *Transgression and Intervention: Homosexually Active Men and Beats*, National Centre for HIV Social Research (Macquarie University Unit), Sydney

Drägestein, B. and Grote, C. 1997/98, 'Halbe Hemden—Gauze Kerle: Jungenarbeit als Gewaltprävention', *Landesstelle Jungendschutz Niedersachsen, Hannover*

Draper, J. 1993, 'We're back with Gobbo: The re-establishment of gender relations following a school merger' in *Gender and Ethnicity in Schools: Ethnographic Accounts*, eds P. Woods & M. Hammersley, Routledge/Open University, London

Dunn, J. et al. 1992, *Personal Development Program for Boys*, ACT Government, Canberra

Dwyer, P., Wilson, B. & Woock, R. 1984, *Confronting School and Work*, Allen & Unwin, Sydney

Dyson, A.H. 1994, 'The Ninjas, the X-men, and the ladies: Playing with power and identity in an urban primary school', *Teachers College Record* vol. 96, pp. 219–39

Easthope, A. 1986, *What a Man's Gotta Do: The Masculine Myth in Popular Culture*, Paladin, London

Embling, J. 1986, *Fragmented Lives: A Darker Side of Australian Life*, Penguin, Ringwood

Enloe, C. 1990, *Bananas, Beaches and Bases: Making Feminist Sense of International Politics*, University of California Press, Berkeley

Epstein, C.F. 1988, *Deceptive Distinctions: Sex, Gender and the Social Order*, Yale University Press, New Haven

Epstein, D. & Sears, J.T. (eds) 1999, *A Dangerous Knowing: Sexuality, Pedagogy and Popular Culture*, Cassell, London

Everhart, R.B. 1983, *Reading, Writing and Resistance: Adolescence and Labor in a Junior High School*, Routledge & Kegan Paul, Boston

Farrell, W. 1993, *The Myth of Male Power: Why Men Are the Disposable Sex*, Simon & Schuster, New York

Fasteau, M.F. 1975, *The Male Machine*, McGraw Hill, New York

Fausto-Sterling, A. 1992, *Myths of Gender: Biological Theories about Women and Men* 2nd edn, Basic Books, New York

Featherstone, M. 1995, *Undoing Culture: Globalization, Postmodernism and Identity*, Sage, London

Ferguson, A. 1994, 'Boys will be boys: defiant acts and the social construction of black masculinity', Draft PhD dissertation, University of California, Berkeley

Fernbach, D. 1981, *The Spiral Path: A Gay Contribution to Human Survival*, Gay Men's Press, London

Foley, D.E. 1990, *Learning Capitalist Culture: Deep in the Heart of Tejas*, University of Pennsylvania Press, Philadelphia

Frank, B. 1993, 'Straight/strait jackets for masculinities: Educating for "real men"', *Atlantis* vol. 18, pp. 47–59

Freud, S. & Einstein, A. 1933, *Why War?*, International Institute of Intellectual Cooperation, Paris, Republished in S. Freud *Complete Psychological Works*, vol. 22, Hogarth Press, London, 1964.

Frowner, G. & Rowniak, S. 1989, 'The health outreach team: Taking AIDS education and health care to the streets', *AIDS Education and Prevention* vol. 1, no. 2, pp. 105–18

Fuentes, A. & Ehrenreich, B. 1983, *Women in the Global Factory*, South End, Boston

Garvey, T. 1994, 'Streaming as a masculinizing practice in the 1950s and 1960s', Paper presented to the Annual Conference of the Australian and New Zealand History of Education Society, Perth

Gee, J.P., Hull, G. & Lankshear, C. 1996, *The New Work Order: Behind the Language of the New Capitalism*, Allen & Unwin, Sydney

Gender Equality Ombudsman 1997, 'The father's quota', Information sheet on parental leave entitlements, Oslo

Gerschick, T.J. & Miller, A.S. 1994, 'Gender identities at the crossroads of masculinity and physical disability', *Masculinities* vol. 2, no. 1, pp. 34–55

Gibson, J.W. 1994, *Warrior Dreams: Paramilitary Culture in post-Vietnam America*, Hill & Wang, New York

Gilbert, R. & Gilbert, P. 1998, *Masculinity Goes to School*, Allen & Unwin, Sydney

Godenzi, A. 2000, 'Determinants of culture: men and the economic power' in *Male Roles and Masculinities: A Culture of Peace Perspective*, eds I. Breines, R.W. Connell & I. Eide, UNESCO, Paris

Gould, M. 1985, 'Teaching about men and masculinity', *Teaching Sociology* vol. 12, pp. 285–98

Grant, C.A. & Skeeter, C.E. 1986, *After the School Bell Rings*, Falmer, Philadelphia

Gray, S. 1987, 'Sharing the shop floor' in *Beyond Patriarchy: Essays by Men on Pleasure, Power, and Change*, ed. M. Kaufman, Oxford University Press, Toronto

Greenberg, D.F. 1988, *The Construction of Homosexuality*, University of Chicago Press, Chicago

Gruneau, R. 1999, *Class, Sports, and Social Development* 2nd edn, Human Kinetics, Champaign

Gruneau, R. & Whitson, D. 1993, *Hockey Night in Canada: Sport, Identity and Cultural Politics*, Garamond Press, Toronto

Hacker, H.M. 1957, 'The new burdens of masculinity', *Marriage and Family Living* vol. 19, p. 229

Hagemann-White, C. & Rerrich, M.S. (eds) 1988, *FrauenMännerBilder*, AJZ-Verlag, Bielefeld

Hansot, E. & Tyack, D. 1988, 'Gender in public schools: Thinking institutionally', *Signs* vol. 13, pp. 741–60

Harding, S. & Hintikka, M. (eds) 1983, *Discovering Reality*, Reidel, Dordrecht

Hargreaves, D.H. 1967, *Social Relations in a Secondary School*, Routledge & Kegan Paul, London

Harrison, J. 1978, 'Warning: The male sex role may be dangerous to your health', *Journal of Social Issues* vol. 34, no. 1, pp. 65–86

Hearn, J. 1992, *Men in the Public Eye: The Construction and Deconstruction of Public Men and Public Patriarchies*, Routledge, London

—— 1996, 'Is masculinity dead? A critique of the concept of masculinity/ masculinities' in *Understanding Masculinities*, ed. M. Mac an Ghaill, Open University Press, Buckhingham

—— 1998a, *The Violences of Men: How Men Talk About and How Agencies Respond to Men's Violence to Women*, Sage, London

—— 1998b, 'Theorizing men and men's theorizing: Varieties of discursive practices in men's theorizing of men', *Theory and Society* vol. 27, no. 6, pp. 781–816

Henriksson, B. 1995, *Risk Factor Love: Homosexuality, Sexual Interaction and HIV Prevention*, Goteborgs Universitet, Goteborg

Herdt, G.H. 1981, *Guardians of the Flutes: Idioms of Masculinity*, McGraw-Hill, New York

—— (ed.) 1984, *Ritualized Homosexuality in Melanesia*, University of California Press, Berkeley

Herek, G. & Berrill, K. 1992, *Hate Crimes: Confronting Violence Against Lesbians and Gay Men*, Sage, Newbury Park

Heward, C. 1988, *Making a Man of Him: Parents and their Sons' Education at an English Public School 1929–50*, Routledge, London

Hill, D.J., White, V.M. et al. 1998, 'Smoking behaviours of Australian adults in 1995: Trends and concerns', *Medical Journal of Australia* vol. 16, no. 5, pp. 209–13

Hinsch, B. 1990, *Passions of the Cut Sleeve: The Male Homosexual Tradition in China*, University of California Press, Berkeley

Hirst, P. & Thompson, G. 1996, *Globalization in Question: The International Economy and the Possibilities of Governance*, Polity, Cambridge

Hochschild, A. 1983, *The Managed Heart: Commercialization of Human Feeling*, University of California Press, Berkeley

Holland, D.C. & Eisenhart, M.A. 1990, *Educated in Romance: Women, Achievement, and College Culture*, University of Chicago Press, Chicago

Hollstein, W. 1992, *Machen Sie Platz, mein Herr! Teilen statt Herrschen*, Rowohlt, Hamburg

Holland, A. 1983, *The Managed Heart: Commercialization of Human Feeling*, University of California Press, Berkely

Hollway, W. 1984, 'Gender difference and the production of subjectivity' in *Changing the Subject*, eds J. Henriques, W. Hollway, C. Urwin, C. Venn, V. Walkerdine, Methuen, London

—— 1994, 'Separation, integration and difference: Contradictions in a gender regime' in *Power/Gender: Social Relations in Theory and Practice*, eds H.L. Radtke & H. Stam, Sage, London

Holter, Ø.G. 1989, *Menn*, Aschehoug, Oslo

—— 1995, 'Family theory reconsidered' in *Labour of Love: Beyond the*

Self-Evidence of Everyday Life, eds T. Borchgrevink & Ø.G. Holter, Avebury, Aldershot

——1996, 'Authoritarianism and masculinity', *IASOM Newsletter* vol. 3, no. 1, pp. 18–35

——1997, 'Gender, patriarchy and capitalism: A social forms analysis' Dr philos. dissertation, Faculty of Social Science, University of Oslo

Hondagneu-Sotelo, P. & Messner, M.A. 1994, 'Gender displays and men's power: The '"new man" and the Mexican immigrant man', in *Theorizing Masculinities*, eds H. Brod & M. Kaufman, Sage, Thousand Oaks

Humphreys, L. 1970, *Tearoom Trade: A Study of Homosexual Encounters in Public Places*, Duckworth, London

Hunt, P. 1980, *Gender and Class Conciousness*, Macmillan, London

Hunter, C.StJ. & Harman, D. 1979, *Adult Illiteracy in the United States*, McGraw Hill, New York

Inter-Parliamentary Union 1999, 'Women in National Parliaments: Situation as of 5 December 1999', IPU webpage *http://www.ipu.org/wmn-e/world.htm*

Ito, Kimio, 1993, *Otokorashisa-no-yukue*, Shinyo-sha, Tokyo

Jain, S.K. 1993, 'Morbidity and multi-morbidity in Australia: Evidence from National Health Surveys', *Journal of the Australian Population Association* vol. 10, no. 1, pp. 31–52

Jeffords, S. 1989, *The Remasculinization of America: Gender and the Vietnam War*, Indiana University Press, Bloomington

Johnson, L. (ed.) 1968, *Free U*, Free University, Sydney

Jolly, M. 1997, 'From point Venus to Bali Ha'i: Eroticism and exoticism in representations of the Pacific' in *Sites of Desire, Economies of Pleasure: Sexualities in Asia and the Pacific*, eds L. Manderson & M. Jolly, University of Chicago Press, Chicago

Jordan, E. 1995, 'Fighting boys and fantasy play: The construction of masculinity in the early years of school', *Gender and Education* vol. 7, pp. 69–86

Kandiyoti, D. 1994, 'The paradoxes of masculinity: Some thoughts on segregated societies' in *Dislocating Masculinity: Comparative Ethnographies*, eds A. Cornwall & N. Lindisfarne, Routledge, London

Kaufman, M. 1993, *Cracking the Armour: Power, Pain and the Lives of Men*, Viking, Toronto

——1997, 'Working with men and boys to challenge sexism and end men's violence', Paper presented at UNESCO meeting on Male Roles and Masculinities in the Perspective of a Culture of Peace, Oslo

——(ed.) 1999, 'Men and violence', *International Association for Studies of Men Newsletter* vol. 6, special issue

Keen, S. 1991, *Fire in the Belly: On Being a Man*, Bantam, New York

Kemper, T.D. 1990, *Social Structure and Testosterone*, Rutgers University Press, New Brunswick

Kenworthy, C. 1994, '"We want to resist your resistant readings": Masculinity and discourse in the English classroom', *Interpretations* vol. 27, pp. 74–95

Kersten, J. 1993, 'Crime and masculinities in Australia, Germany and Japan', *International Sociology* vol. 8, no. 4, pp. 461–78

Kessler, S., Ashenden, D.J., Connell, R.W. & Dowsett, G.W. 1985, 'Gender relations in secondary schooling', *Sociology of Education* vol. 58, no. 1, pp. 34–48

Kessler, S.J. & McKenna, W. 1978, *Gender: An Ethnomethodological Approach* Wiley, New York

Kimmel, M.S. 1987, 'Rethinking "masculinity": New directions in research' in *Changing Men: New Directions in Research on Men and Masculinity*, ed. M.S. Kimmel, Sage, Newbury Park

——1996, *Manhood in America: A Cultural History*, Free Press, New York

Kimmel, M.S. & Mosmiller, T.E. (eds) 1992, *Against the Tide: Profeminist Men in the United States, 1776–1990, a Documentary History*, Beacon, Boston

Kindler, H. 1993, *Maske(r)ade: Jungen- und Männerarbeit für die Praxis*, Schwäbisch Gmünd und Tübingen, Neuling

King, R. 1978, *All Things Bright and Beautiful? A Sociological Study of Infants' Classrooms*, Wiley, Chichester

Kinmonth, E.H. 1981, *The Self-made Man in Meiji Japanese Thought: From Samurai to Salary Man*, University of California Press, Berkeley

Kinsey, A.C., Pomeroy, W.B. & Martin, C.E. 1948, *Sexual Behaviour in the Human Male*, Saunders, Philadelphia

Kipling, R. [1901] 1987, *Kim*, Penguin, London

Kippax, S., Connell, R.W., Dowsett, G.W. & Crawford, J. 1993, *Sustaining Safe Sex: Gay Communities Respond to AIDS*, Falmer, London

Klein, A.M. 1993, *Little Big Men: Bodybuilding Subculture and Gender Construction*, State University of New York Press, Albany

Krafft-Ebing, R. von [1886] 1965, *Psychopathia Sexualis* 12th edn, Paperback Library, New York

Kupers, T.A. 1993, *Revisioning Men's Lives: Gender, Intimacy, and Power*, Guilford Press, New York

Lankshear, C. 1987, *Literacy, Schooling and Revolution*, Falmer Press, New York

Las Casas, B. de 1971, *History of the Indies*, trans. A. Collard., Harper & Row, New York

Laskey, L. & Beavis, C. (eds) 1996, *Schooling and Sexualities: Teaching for a Positive Sexuality*, Deakin Centre for Education and Change, Geelong

Laumann, E.O., Gagnon, J.H., Michael, R.T. & Michaels, S. 1994, *The Social Organization of Sexuality: Sexual Practices in the United States*, University of Chicago Press, Chicago

Leahy, T. 1992, 'Positively experienced man/boy sex: the discourse of seduction and the social construction of masculinity', *Australian and New Zealand Journal of Sociology* vol. 28, no. 1, pp. 71–88

Lees, S. 1986, *Losing Out: Sexuality and Adolescent Girls*, Hutchinson, London

Lewes, K. 1988, *The Psychoanalytic Theory of Male Homosexuality*, Simon & Schuster, New York

Lichterman, P. 1989, 'Making a politics of masculinity', *Comparative Social Research* vol. 11, pp. 185–208

Lingard, B. & Douglas, P. 1999, *Men Engaging Feminisms: Pro-feminism, Backlashes and Schooling*, Open University Press, Buckingham

Mac an Ghaill, M. 1994, *The Making of Men: Masculinities, Sexualities and Schooling*, Open University Press, Buckingham

MacDonald, R.H. 1994, *The Language of Empire: Myths and Metaphors of Popular Imperialism, 1880–1918*, Manchester University Press, Manchester

Marcus, S. 1966, *The Other Victorians: A Study of Sexuality and Pornography in Mid-nineteenth-century England*, Corgi Books, London

Marcuse, H. 1955, *Eros and Civilization*, Beacon Press, Boston

Martino, W. 1994, 'Masculinity and learning: Exploring boys' underachievement and under-representation in subject English', *Interpretations* vol. 27, pp. 22–57

Mathers, C. 1994, *Health Differentials among Adult Australians aged 25–64 Years*, Australian Government Publishing Service, Canberra

——1995, 'Health differentials between Australian males and females: a statistical profile', *National Men's Health Conference 10–11 August 1995*, Australian Government Publishing Service, Canberra

——1996, *Health Differentials among Young Australian Adults*, Australian Government Publishing Service, Canberra

McElhinny, B. 1994, 'An economy of affect: Objectivity, masculinity and the gendering of police work' in *Dislocating Masculinity: Comparative Ethnographies*, eds A. Cornwall & N. Lindisfarne, Routledge, London

McKay, J. & Huber, D. 1992, 'Anchoring media images of technology and sport', *Women's Studies International Forum* vol. 15, no. 2, pp. 205–18

McMahon, A. 1999, *Taking Care of Men: Sexual Politics in the Public Mind*, Cambridge University Press, Cambridge

Mealyea, R. 1993, 'Reproducing vocationalism in secondary schools: Marginalization in practical workshops' in *Education, Inequality and Social Identity*, ed. L. Angas, Falmer, London

Messerschmidt, J.W. 1993, *Masculinities and Crime: Critique and Recon-ceptualization of Theory*, Rowman & Littlefield, Lanham
——1997, *Crime as Structured Action: Gender, Race, Class, and Crime in the Making*, Sage, Thousand Oaks
——2000, *Nine Lives: Adolescent Masculinities, the Body, and Violence*, Westview, Boulder
Messner, M.A. 1990, 'Boyhood, organized sports, and the construction of masculinities', *Journal of Contemporary Ethnography* vol. 18, no. 4, pp. 416–44
——1992, *Power at Play: Sports and the Problem of Masculinity*, Beacon, Boston
——1997, *The Politics of Masculinities: Men in Movements*, Sage, Thousand Oaks
Messner, M.A. & Sabo, D.F. 1994, *Sex, Violence and Power in Sports: Rethinking Masculinity*, Crossing Press, Freedom, CA
Metz-Göckel, S. & Müller, U. 1985, *Der Mann: Die Brigitte-Studie*, Beltz, Hamburg
Mies, M. 1986, *Patriarchy and Accumulation on a World Scale: Women in the International Division of Labour*, Zed, London
Milligan, S. & Thomson, K. 1992, *Listening to Girls*, Ashenden & Associates, Australia
Moodie, T.D. with Ndatshe, V. 1994, *Going for Gold: Men, Mines, and Migration*, Witwatersrand University Press, Johannesburg
Morrell, R. 1993–4, 'Masculinity and the white boys' boarding schools of Natal, 1880–1930', *Perspectives in Education* vol. 15, pp. 27–52
——1994, 'Boys, gangs, and the making of masculinity in the white secondary schools of Natal, 1880–1930', *Masculinities* vol. 2, no. 2, pp. 56–82
——(ed.) 1996, *Political Economy and Identities in KwaZulu-Natal: Historical and Social Perspectives*, Indicator Press, Durban
——1998, 'Of boys and men: masculinity and gender in Southern African studies', *Journal of Southern African Studies* vol. 24, no. 4, pp. 605–30
Nakamura, A. 1994, *Watashi-no Danseigaku*, Kindaibugei-sha, Tokyo
National Men's Health Conference: 10–11 August 1995, Australian Government Publishing Service, Canberra
New South Wales Federation of Parents and Citizens Associations 1994, *Submission to Parliamentary Enquiry on Boys' Education*, Federation of Parents and Citizens Associations, Sydney
Nichols, J. 1975, *Men's Liberation: A New Definition of Masculinity*, Penguin, New York
Nielsen, H.B. & Rudberg, M. 1994, *Psychological Gender and Modernity*, Scandinavian University Press, Oslo
Nilan, P. 1995, 'Making up men', *Gender and Education* vol. 7, pp. 175–87

Novikova, I. 2000, 'Soviet and post-Soviet masculinities: After men's wars in women's memories' in *Male Roles and Masculinities: A Culture of Peace Perspective*, eds I. Breines, R.W. Connell & I. Eide, UNESCO, Paris

Novogrodsky, M., Kaufman, M., Holland, D. & Wells, M. 1992, 'Retreat for the future: An anti-sexist workshop for high schoolers', *Our Schools/Ourselves* vol. 3, no. 4, pp. 67–87

O'Connor, J.S., Orloff, A.S., & Shaver, S. 1999, *States, Markets, Families*, Cambridge University Press, Cambridge

O'Doherty, S. (chair) 1994, *Challenges and Opportunities: A Discussion Paper. Report on the Inquiry into Boys' Education*, NSW Government Advisory Committee on Education, Training and Tourism, Sydney

Patton, C. 1990, *Inventing AIDS*, Routledge, New York

Pearson, K. 1982, 'Conflict, stereotypes and masculinity in Australian and New Zealand Surfing', *Australian and New Zealand Journal of Sociology*, vol. 18, no. 2, pp. 117–35

Pease, B. 1997, *Men and Sexual Politics: Towards a Profeminist Practice*, Dulwich Centre Publications, Adelaide

Petersen, A. 1998, *Unmasking the Masculine: 'Men' and 'Identity' in a Sceptical Age*, Sage, London

Phillips, J. 1987, *A Man's Country? The Image of the Pakeha Male: A History*, Penguin, Auckland

Pleck, J.H. & Sawyer, J. (eds) 1974, *Men and Masculinity*, Prentice Hall, Englewood Cliffs

Plummer, K. 1983, *Documents of Life: An Introduction to the Problems and Literature of a Humanistic Method*, Allen & Unwin, London

Poynting, S., Noble, G. and Tabar, P. 1998, '"If anybody called me a wog, they wouldn't be speaking to me alone": Protest Masculinity and Lebanese Youth in Western Sydney', *Journal of Interdisciplinary Gender Studies* vol. 3, no. 2, pp. 76–94

Prendergast, S. 1996, 'Boys, bodies and pedagogy: Constructing emotions in school', Paper delivered at Gender, Body and Love Seminar, Centre for Women's Research, University of Oslo

Reay, D. 1990, 'Working with boys', *Gender and Education* vol. 2, pp. 269–82

Reich, W. 1972, *Sex-Pol: Essays 1929–1934*, ed. L. Baxandall, Vintage, New York

Rich, A. 1979, *On Lies, Secrets and Silence*, Norton, New York

Risman, B.J. 1998, *Gender Vertigo: American Families in Transition*, Yale University Press, New Haven

Roads and Traffic Authority of NSW 1997, 'Project Outline for Research and Development into Gender Issues in Communicating Road Safety Messages to Boys', Tender background document, RTA, Sydney

Robins, D. & Cohen, P. 1978, *Knuckle Sandwich: Growing Up in the Working-class City*, Penguin, Harmondsworth

Roper, M. 1994, *Masculinity and the British Organization Man Since 1945*, Oxford University Press, Oxford

Rowan, J. 1987, *The Horned God: Feminism and Men as Wounding and Healing*, Routledge & Kegan Paul, London

Rowe, D. & McKay, J. 1998, 'Sport: Still a man's game' *Journal of Interdisciplinary Gender Studies* vol. 3, no. 2, pp. 113–28

Rubin, L.B. 1976, *Worlds of Pain: Life in the Working-class Family*, Basic Books, New York

Sabella, W. 1988, 'Introducing AIDS education in Connecticut schools', *New England Journal of Public Policy* vol. 4, pp. 335–41

Sabo, D. & Gordon, D.F. (eds) 1995, *Men's Health and Illness: Gender, Power, and the Body*, Thousand Oaks, Sage

Sanderson, G. 1995, 'Being "cool" and a reader' in *Boys in Schools: Addressing the Real Issues–Behaviour, Values and Relationships*, eds R. Browne & R. Fletcher, Finch, Sydney

Sapon-Shevin, M. & Goodman, J. 1992, 'Learning to be the opposite sex: Sexuality education and sexual scripting in early adolescence' in *Sexuality and the Curriculum*, ed. J.T. Sears, Teachers College Press, New York

Sartre, J-P. [1943] 1958, *Being and Nothingness: An Essay on Phenomenological Ontology*, Methuen, London

Schofield, T., Connell, R.W., Walker, L., Wood, J. & Butland, D. 2000, 'Understanding men's health: A gender relations approach to masculinity, health and illness', *Journal of American College Health*, in press

Schwalbe, M. 1996, *Unlocking the Iron Cage: The Men's Movement, Gender Politics, and the American Culture*, Oxford University Press, New York

Segal, L. 1987, *Is the Future Female?*, Virago, London

——1997, *Slow Motion: Changing Masculinities, Changing Men*, rev. edn, Virago, London

Seidler, V.J. 1989, *Rediscovering Masculinity: Reason, Language and Sexuality*, Routledge, London

——(ed.) 1991, *Achilles Heel Reader: Men, Sexual Politics and Socialism*, Routledge, London

Seifert, R. 1993, *Individualisierungsprozesse. Geschlechterverhältnisse und die soziale Konstruktion des Soldaten*, Socialwissenschaftliches Institut der Bundeswehr, München

Sennett, R. & Cobb, J. 1972, *The Hidden Injuries of Class*, Vintage Books, New York

Sewell, T. 1997, *Black Masculinities and Schooling: How Black Boys Survive Modern Schooling*, Trentham Books, Stoke on Trent

Sexton, P. 1969, *The Feminized Male: Classrooms, White Collars, and the Decline of Manliness*, Random House, New York

Shakespeare, T. 1998, *The Disability Reader: Social Science Perspectives*, Cassell, London

Shire, C. 1994, 'Men don't go to the moon: Language, space and masculinities in Zimbabwe' in *Dislocating Masculinity: Comparative Ethnographies*, eds A. Cornwall & N. Lindisfarne, Routledge, London

Simpson, A. 1993, *Xuxa: The Mega-marketing of Gender, Race and Modernity*, Temple University Press, Philadelphia

Sinha, M. 1995, *Colonial Masculinity: The Manly Englishman and the Effeminate Bengali in the Late Nineteenth Century*, Manchester University Press, Manchester

Skelton, A. 1993, 'On becoming a male physical education teacher: The informal culture of students and the construction of hegemonic masculinity', *Gender and Education* vol. 5, pp. 289–303

Sleeter, C.E. & Grant, C.A. 1991, 'Race, class, gender and disability in current textbooks' in *The Politics of the Textbook*, eds M.W. Apple & L.K. Christian-Smith, Routledge, New York

Smith, T.W. & Smith, R.J. 1994, 'Changes in firearm ownership among women, 1980–1994', Paper presented to the American Society of Criminology, Miami

Staples, R. 1995, 'Health among Afro-American males', in *Men's Health and Illness*, eds D. Sabo & D.F. Gordon, Thousand Oaks, Sage

Stillion, J.M. 1995, 'Premature death among males: extending the bottom line of men's health' in *Men's Health and Illness*, eds D. Sabo & D.F. Gordon, Thousand Oaks, Sage

Takagi, D.Y. 1992, *The Retreat from Race: Asian-American Admissions and Racial Politics*, Rutgers University Press, New Brunswick

Taylor, D. 1985, 'Women: An analysis' in *Women: A World Report*, Methuen, London

Theberge, N. 1991, 'Reflections on the body in the sociology of sport', *Quest* vol. 43, pp. 123–34

Thompson, E.P. 1968, *The Making of the English Working Class*, 2nd edn, Penguin, Harmondsworth

Thorne, B. 1993, *Gender Play: Girls and Boys in School*, Rutgers University Press, New Brunswick

Tillner, G. 1997, 'Masculinity and xenophobia', Paper presented at UNESCO meeting on Male Roles and Masculinities in the Perspective of a Culture of Peace, Oslo

Tomsen, S. 1997, 'A top night: Social protest, masculinity and the culture of drinking violence', *British Journal of Criminology* vol. 37, no. 1, pp. 90–103

——1998, '"He had to be a poofter or something": Violence, male honour and heterosexual panic', *Journal of Interdisciplinary Gender Studies* vol. 3, no. 2, pp. 44–57

Tosh, J. 1991, 'Domesticity and manliness in the Victorian middle class: The family of Edward White Benson' in *Manful Assertions: Masculinities in Britain since 1800*, eds M. Roper & J. Tosh, Routledge, London

Trudell, B.N. 1993, *Doing Sex Education: Gender Politics and Schooling*, Routledge, New York

Tulloch, J. & Tulloch, M. 1992, 'Tolerating violence: children's responses to television', *Australian Journal of Communication* vol. 19, no. 1, pp. 9–21

Turner, B.S. 1984, *The Body and Society*, Blackwell, Oxford

United Nations Development Program 1999, *Human Development Report 1999*, Oxford University Press, New York

United States Bureau of the Census 1998, *Statistical Abstract of the United States: 1998*, 118th edn, Washington, DC

Walby, S. 1990, *Theorizing Patriarchy*, Blackwell, Oxford

Walker, J.C. 1988, *Louts and Legends: Male Youth Culture in an Inner-city School*, Allen & Unwin, Sydney

Walker, L. 1998a, 'Chivalrous masculinity among juvenile offenders in western Sydney: A new perspective on young working-class men and crime', *Current Issues in Criminal Justice* vol. 9, no. 3, pp. 279–93

——1998b, 'Under the bonnet: Car culture, technological dominance and young men of the working class', *Journal of Interdisciplinary Gender Studies* vol. 3, no. 2, pp. 23–43

Wallerstein, I. 1974, *The Modern World-system: Capitalist Agriculture and the Origins of the European World-economy in the Sixteenth Century*, Academic Press, New York

Warren, S. 1997, 'Who do these boys think they are? An investigation into the construction of masculinities in a primary classroom', *International Journal of Inclusive Education* vol. 1, no. 2, pp. 207–22

Welch, A. 1996, *Australian Education: Reform or Crisis?*, Allen & Unwin, Sydney

White, D. 1993, *A Summary of Suspensions in Four High Schools in the Hoxton Park Cluster*, self-published, Sydney

White, P.G., Young, K. & McTeer, W.G. 1995, 'Sport, masculinity, and the injured body' in *Men's Health and Illness*, eds D. Sabo & D.F. Gordon, Thousand Oaks, Sage

Whitson, D. 1990, 'Sport in the social construction of masculinity' in *Sport, Men, and the Gender Order: Critical Feminist Perspectives*, eds M.A. Messner & D.F. Sabo, Human Kinetics Books, Champaign

Whyte, W.F. 1943, 'A slum sex code', *American Journal of Sociology* vol. 49, pp. 24–32

Widersprüche 1995, Special issue: Männlichkeiten vol. 56/57

Williams, C. 1988, *Blue, White and Pink Collar Workers in Australia*, Allen & Unwin, Sydney

Williams, W.L. 1986, *The Spirit and the Flesh: Sexual Diversity in American Indian Culture*, Beacon, Boston

Willis, P. 1977, *Learning to Labour*, Saxon House, Farnborough

Wilson, E. 1985, *Adorned in Dreams: Fashion and Modernity*, University of California Press, Berkeley

Winter, M.F. & Robert, E.R. 1980, 'Male dominance, late capitalism, and the growth of instrumental reason', *Berkeley Journal of Sociology* vol. 24/25, pp. 249–80

Wood, J. 1984, 'Groping towards sexism: Boys' sex talk' in *Gender and Generation*, eds A. McRobbie & M. Nava, Macmillan, London

Wotherspoon, G. 1991, *City of the Plain: History of a Gay Sub-culture*, Hale & Iremonger, Sydney

Xaba, T. 1997, 'Masculinity in a transitional society: The rise and fall of the "young lions"' Paper presented at the conference Masculinities in Southern Africa, University of Natal, Durban

Yates, L. 1993, *The Education of Girls: Policy, Research and the Question of Gender*, Australian Council for Educational Research, Hawthorn

Young, I.M. 1990, *Justice and the Politics of Difference*, Princeton University Press, Princeton

Zulehner, P.M. & Volz, R. 1998, *Männer im Aufbruch: Wie Deutschlands Männer sich selbst und wie Frauen sie sehen*, Schwabenverlag, Ostfildern

Index

258 · THE MEN AND THE BOYS

Index by Geraldine Suter